George Greenlief Evans

Illustrated History of the United States Mint

With a complete description of American coinage, from the earliest period to the

present time. The process of melting, refining, assaying, and coining gold and silver

fully described

George Greenlief Evans

Illustrated History of the United States Mint
With a complete description of American coinage, from the earliest period to the present
time. The process of melting, refining, assaying, and coining gold and silver fully described

ISBN/EAN: 9783337097622

Printed in Europe, USA, Canada, Australia, Japan

Cover: Foto ©ninafisch / pixelio.de

More available books at **www.hansebooks.com**

GEORGE WASHINGTON.

ILLUSTRATED HISTORY

OF THE

UNITED STATES MINT

WITH A COMPLETE DESCRIPTION OF

AMERICAN COINAGE,

From the earliest period to the present time. The
Process of Melting, Refining, Assaying, and
Coining Gold and Silver fully described:

WITH BIOGRAPHICAL SKETCHES OF

Thomas Jefferson, Alexander Hamilton, Robert Morris, Benjamin Rush,
John Jay Knox, James P. Kimball, Daniel M. Fox, and the Mint
Officers from its foundation to the present time.

TO WHICH ARE ADDED

A GLOSSARY OF MINT TERMS

AND THE

LATEST OFFICIAL TABLES

OF THE

Annual Products of Gold and Silver in the different
States, and Foreign Countries, with Monetary
Statistics of all Nations.

————— ◆ —————

ILLUSTRATED with PHOTOTYPES, STEEL PLATE PORTRAITS and WOOD ENGRAVINGS,
with NUMEROUS PLATES of Photographic Reproductions of RARE AMERICAN
COINS, and Price List of their numismatic value.

————— ◆ —————

New Revised Edition, Edited by the Publisher.

————— ◆ —————

PHILADELPHIA:
GEORGE G. EVANS, PUBLISHER.
1888.

INDEX.

PAGE

INDEX TO ILLUSTRATIONS.

INTRODUCTION.

MONEY OF THE PAST AND PRESENT.

The need of a circulating medium of exchange has been acknowledged since the earliest ages of man. In the primeval days, bartering was the foundation of commercial intercourse between the various races; but this gave way in time, as exchanges increased. In the different ages many commodities have been made to serve as money,—tin was used in ancient Syracuse and Britain; iron, in Sparta; cattle, in Rome and Germany; platinum, in Russia; lead, in Burmah; nails, in Scotland; silk, in China; cubes of pressed tea, in Tartary; salt, in Abyssinia; slaves, amongst the Anglo Saxons; tobacco, in the earliest settlements of Virginia; codfish, in New Foundland; bullets and wampum, in Massachusetts; logwood, in Campeachy; sugar, in the West Indies; and soap, in Mexico. Money of leather and wood was in circulation in the early days of Rome; and the natives of Siam, Bengal, and some parts of Africa used the brilliantly-colored cowry shell to represent value, and some travelers allege that it is still in use in the remote portions of the last-named country. But the moneys of all civilized nations have been, for the greater part, made of gold, silver, copper, and bronze. Shekels of silver are mentioned in the Bible as having existed in the days of Abraham, but the metals are believed to have been in bars, from which proportionate weights were chipped to suit convenience. The necessity for some convenient medium having an intrinsic value of its own led to coinage, but the exact date of its introduction is a question history has not yet determined. It is supposed the Lydians stamped metal to be used as money twelve hundred years before Christ, but the oldest coins extant were made 800 B. C., though it is alleged that the Chinese circulated a square bronze coin as early as 1120 B. C. All of these coins were rude and shapeless, and generally engraved with representations of animals, deities, nymphs, and the like; but the Greeks issued coins, about 300 B. C., which were fine specimens of workmanship, and which are not even surpassed in boldness and beauty of design by the products of the coiners of these modern times. Even while these coins were in circulation spits and skewers were accepted by the Greeks in exchange for products, just as wooden and metal coins were cir-

culated simultaneously in Rome, 700 B. C., and leather and
metal coins in France, as late as 1360 A. D.   The earliest coins
bearing portraits are believed to have been issued about 480
B. C., and these were profiles.   In the third century, coins
stamped with Gothic front faces were issued, and after that date
a profusion of coins were brought into the world, as every self-
governing city issued money of its own.   The earliest money
of America was coined of brass, in 1612, and the earliest colonial coins were stamped in Massachusetts, forty years later.

Ancient and extensive as the use of money has been in all its
numerous forms and varied materials, it merely represented a
property value which had been created by manual labor and preserved by the organic action of society.   In a primitive state,
herds of cattle and crops of grain were almost the only forms of
wealth; the natural tendency and disposition of men to accumu-
late riches led them to fix a special value upon the metals, as a
durable and always available kind of property.   When their value
in this way was generally recognized, the taxes and other revenues,
created by kings and other potentates, was collected in part or
wholly in that form of money.   The government, to facilitate
public business, stamped the various pieces of metal with their
weight and quality, as they were received at the Treasury; and
according to these stamps and marks, the same pieces were paid
out of the Treasury, and circulated among the people at an authorized and fixed value.   The next step was to reduce current
prices of metal to a uniform size, shape, and quality, value and
denomination, and make them, by special enactment, a legal
tender for the payment of all taxes or public dues.

Thus, a legalized currency of coined money was created, and
the exchangeable value of the various metals used for that purpose fully established, to the great convenience of the world at
large.

ANCIENT COINING.

The die for the obverse of the piece to be struck having been
engraved, so as to properly present the religious or national
symbol used for a device and whatever else was to be impressed
upon the coin, was fixed immovably in an anvil or pedestal, face
upwards.   The lumps or balls of metal to be coined, having
been made of a fixed and uniform weight and nearly of an
oblate sphere in form, were grasped in a peculiarly constructed
pair of tongs and laid upon the upturned die.   A second oper-
ative then placed a punch squarely upon the ball of metal;
heavy blows from a large hammer forced the punch down until
the metal beneath it had been forced into every part of the die,
and a good impress secured.   In the meantime the punch

would be imbedded in the lump of metal, and on being withdrawn the reverse of the coin would show a rough depression corresponding to the shape given the end of the punch, thereby making an uneven surface and disfiguring the piece; punch marks gradually developed into forms, and these forms combined with figures wrought into artistic design, until, by degrees, the punch itself became a die, making the reverse of each piece upon which it was used equal in every respect to the obverse of which it was the opposite. This perfection of the reverse was, however, secured at the expense of the effectiveness of the punch for its original purpose.

The striking of coin between two dies, which were required to accurately oppose each other, was an operation requiring great dexterity, and the results were not at all certain. The artisans at this stage of the work, hit upon the expedient of using both the obverse and reverse die in a ring of such a size and depth, as to be a guide to each of them. The balls or disks of metal being struck inside the ring, between the dies, were forced to assume an even thickness, and a circular form corresponding with the inside of the ring. After the ring had been used in this way for some time, it was engraved upon the inside, and the coins produced were not only circular in shape, but stamped upon their edges. Thus was produced the perfect coin, and through the introduction of machinery has secured uniformity in the result and saved an immense amount of labor in striking vast sums of money; the artistic beauty of some of the antique specimens has not been surpassed in modern times.

PORTRAITURE UPON COINS.

It is said that no human head was ever stamped upon coins until after the death of Alexander the Great; he being regarded as somewhat of a divinity, his effigy was impressed upon money, like that of other gods.

The knowledge of coins and medals, through the inscriptions and devices thereon, is, to an extent, a history of the world from that date in which metals were applied to such uses. Events engraven upon these, remain hidden in tombs or buried in the bosom of the earth, deposited there in ages long past, by careful and miserly hands, only awaiting the research of the patient investigator to tell the story of their origin. Numismatic treasures are scanned as evidence of facts to substantiate statements upon papyrus or stone, and dates are often supplied to define the border line between asserted tradition and positive history. Gibbon remarks: "If there were no other record of Hadrian, his career would be found written upon the coins of his reign."

The rudeness or perfection of coins and medals **furnish testi-**
mony of the character and culture of the periods of their production. This is equally true of that rarest specimen of antiquity,
the Syracusan silver medal—the oldest known to collectors—and
the latest triumph of the graver's art in gold, the Metis medal.

It is not generally known that the rarest portraits of famous
heroes are found upon coins and medals. The historian, es-
pecially the historic artist, is indebted to this source alone for
the portraits of Alexander, Ptolemy, Cleopatra, Mark Antony,
Cæsar, and many other celebrities. Perhaps the valuation of
a rare coin or medal may be estimated by reference to one piece
in **the** Philadelphia Mint. **It is an** Egyptian coin as large **as
a** half-eagle, and has on **the** obverse the head of the wife **of**
Ptolemy—Arsinoe—the only portrait of her yet discovered.

INCIDENTS OF HISTORY

Are not alone recorded; **and as** an example of a very different
nature may be cited the medals commemorating the destruction
of Jerusalem, and the whole series marking that episode, es-
pecially those classed "**Judæa** capta." They tell **sadly of a
people's** humiliation: **the tied** or chained captive; **the mocking
goddess of** victory, **all made more real by reason of the introduction, on the reverse of each piece, of a Jewess** weeping
bitterly, and though she sits under a palm-tree, the national
lament of another captivity is forcibly recalled.

An interesting specimen of the series above mentioned was
recently found **in the south of France** called, "Judæa Na-
villas," valuable particularly because it strengthens Josephus's
assertion which had **provoked some** comment, viz.: the fact of
the escape of a large **number of Jews from** the Romans, by
means of ships, at Joppa.

Coins and medals mark the introduction of laws; **for**
example, an old Porcian coin gives the date of the "law **of**
appeal," under which, **two** centuries and a half later, Paul
appealed to Cæsar. Another relic dates the introduction of
the ballot-box; **and a fact** interesting to the agriculturist is
established by **an** old silver coin of Ptolemy, upon which a
man is represented cutting millet (a variety of Indian corn)
with a scythe. Religions have been promulgated by coins.
Islamism says upon a gold coin, "No God but God. Mo-
hammed is the Prophet and God's chosen apostle."

Persian coins, in mystic characters, symbolize the dreadful
sacrifices of the Fire-Worshippers. **Henry VIII**, with characteristic egotism, upon a medal announces in Hebrew, Greek,
and Latin: "Henry Eighth, King of England, France, and

Ireland; Defender of the Faith, and in the land of England and Ireland, under Christ, the Supreme Head of the Church."

COSTUMES ON COINS.

We also find stamped upon coins and medals the costumes of all ages, from the golden net confining the soft tresses of the "sorceress of the Nile," and the gemmed robe of Queen Irene, to the broidered stomacher of Queen Anne, and the stately ruff of Elizabeth of England.

In this connection may be mentioned the " bonnet piece " of Scotland, a coin of the reign of James VI., which is extremely rare, one of them having been sold for £41. The coin received its name from a representation of the king upon it, with a curiously plaited hat or bonnet which this monarch wore, a fashion that gave occasion for the ballad, " Blue Bonnets over the Border."

HERALDIC EMBLEMS

Are faithfully preserved through this medium; in truth, medalic honors may be claimed as the very foundation of heraldic art. We discover medals perpetuating revolutions, sieges, plots, and murders, etc. We prefer directing attention to the fact that coins and medals are not only the land-marks of history, but a favorite medium of the poetry of all nations. Epics are thus preserved by the graver's art in exceedingly small space. Poets turn with confidence to old coins for symbol as well as fact.

One of the most graceful historical allusions is conveyed in the great seal of Queen Anne, after the union of Scotland with England. A rose and a thistle are growing on one stem, while, from above, the crown of England sheds effulgence upon the tender young plant.

HUMOR PICTURED ON MEDALS.

The medal of George I., on the reverse, boastfully presents " the horse of Brunswick" flying over the northwest of Europe, symbolizing the Hanoverian succession. The overthrow of the " Invincible Armada " was the occasion of a Dutch medal, showing the Hollanders richer in faith than in art culture, for the obverse of this medal presents the church upon a rock, in mid-ocean, while the reverse suggests the thought that the luckless Spanish mariner was driving against the walls of the actual building.

ARCHITECTURE INDEBTED TO COINS.

Architecture is largely indebted to coins, medals, and seals for accuracy and data. We learn from the medal of Septimus

Severus the faultless beauty of the triumphal arch erected to celebrate his victory over Arabs and Parthians. This medal was produced two centuries before the Christian era, and is a marvel of art, for its perspective is wrought in bas-relief—an achievement which was not again attained before the execution of the celebrated Bronze Gates by Ghiberti, for the Baptistery at Florence, A. D. 1425. This exhumed arch was excavated long after its form and structure were familiar to men of letters through the medals.

LANGUAGE UPON COINS AND MEDALS.

The effect of coin on language is direct, and many words may be found whose origin was a coin, such as Daric, a pure gold coin; Talent, mental ability; Sterling, genuine, pure; while Guinea represents the aristocratic element, and, though out of circulation long ago, "no one who pretends to gentility in England would think of subscribing to any charity or fashionable object by contributing the vulgar *pound*. An extra shilling added to the *pound* makes the *guinea*, and lifts the subscriber at once into the aristocratic world."

Copper is much preferred to gold for medals. Its firm, unchanging surface accepts and retains finer lines than have yet been produced upon gold and silver, and it offers no temptation to be thrown into the crucible.*

In the preparation of this work, I am much indebted to several gentlemen connected with the United States Mint; also, to Messrs. R. Coulton Davis, Ph.G., and E. Locke Mason, who are acknowledged authority on the subject of numismatics.

If it shall be found useful to the public, and especially to visitors of the Mint, it will be a source of satisfaction, and more than repay the labor bestowed in its preparation.

G. G. E.

Philadelphia, March 1, 1888.

---

* Collectors estimate the loss to numismatography as very great by reason of the temptation the gold possesses for hoarding, and they are possibly the only class of people who have any apology to offer for the miser. Yet the world is debtor to this despised habit for some of its most invaluable specimens of art, and important corroborative history of the old world.

THE UNITED STATES MINT.

THE subject of a National Mint for the United States was first introduced by Robert Morris,* the patriot and financier of the revolution; as head of the Finance Department, Mr. Morris was instructed by Congress to prepare a report on the foreign coins, then in circulation in the United States. On the 15th of January, 1782, he laid before Congress an exposition of the whole subject. Accompanying this report was a plan for American coinage. But it was mainly through his efforts, in connection with Thomas Jefferson and Alexander Hamilton, that a mint was established in the early history of the Union of the States. On the 15th of April, 1790, Congress instructed the Secretary of the Treasury, Alexander Hamilton, to prepare and report a proper plan for the establishment of a National Mint, and Mr. Hamilton presented his report at the next session. An act was framed establishing the mint, which finally passed both Houses and received President Washington's approval April 2, 1792.†

NOTES ON THE EARLY HISTORY OF THE MINT.

FROM ROBERT MORRIS'S DIARY.

1781. July 16th. Wrote to Mr. Dudley at Boston inviting him hither in consequence of the Continental Agent Mr. Bradford's Letter respecting him referred to me by Congress.

July 17th. Wrote Mr. Bradford respecting Mr. Dudley.

Nov. 10th. Ordered some money on application of Mr. Dudley to pay his expences.

Nov. 12th. Sent for Mr Dudley to consult him respecting the quantity of Alloy Silver will bear without being discoloured, he says he can put 6 drops into an ounce. Desired him to assay some Spanish Dollars and French Crowns, in order to know the quantity of pure Silver in each.

Nov. 16th. Mr. Dudley assayed a number of Crowns and dollars for our information respecting the Mint.

1782. Jan. 2d. Mr. Benjamin Dudley applied for money to pay his Board which I directed to be paid by Mr. Swanwick, this gentleman is detained at the public expence as a person absolutely necessary in the Mint, which I hope soon to see established. My propositions on that subject are to be submitted to Congress so soon as I can get the proper assays made on Silver coins &c.

---

* Robert Morris was born in England, and came to America when he was thirteen years old, (Sparks' life of Governeur Morris.)

† During the Confederation the different States had the unquestioned right to coin money, but only according to the standard of fineness, weight, and value, prescribed by the central government.

Jan. 7th. Mr. Dudley applies about getting his wife **from England. I** promised him every assistance in my power.*

Jan. 18th. I went to Mr. Gouvr Morris's Lodging to examine the plan we had agreed on, and which we had drawn up respecting the Establishment of a Mint, we made some alterations and amendments to my satisfaction and from a belief that this is a necessary and salutary **measure. I have** ordered it copied to be sent into Congress.

Jan. 26th. **Mr. Dudley** applied for money to pay his Lodgings &c. I ordered Mr. **Swanwick to** supply him with fifty dollars, informed him that the Plan **of a Mint is before** Congress, **and** when passed, that he shall be directly **employed, if not** agreed to by **Congress**, I shall compensate him for his time &c.

Feb. 26th. Mr. **Benjamin Dudley** brought me the rough drafts or plan for the rooms of a Mint &c. **I desired** him **to** go to Mr. Whitehead Humphreys to consult him about **Screws**, Smithwork &c. that will be wanted for the Mint, and to bring me a list thereof with an estimate of the Cost.

Feb 28th. Mr. Dudley informs me that a Mr. Wheeler, a Smith in the Country, can make the **Screws, Rollers &c.** for the Mint. Mr. Dudley proposes the **Dutch Church, that which is** now unoccupied, **as** a place suitable for the Mint, I sent him to view it, & he returns satisfied **that** it will answer, wherefore I must enquire about it.

March 22d. Mr. Dudley and Mr. Wheeler came and brought **with them some** Models of the Screws and Rollers necessary for the Mint. I found Mr. Wheeler entertained some doubts respecting **one** of these Machines which Mr. Dudley insists will answer the purposes and says he will be **responsible for it.** I agreed with Mr. Wheeler that he should perform **the work; and, as neither** he or I could judge of the value that ought to be paid for it, he is to perform the same agreeable **to** Mr. Dudley's directions, and when finished, we are to have it valued **by** some Honest Man, judges of such work, he mentioned Philip Syng, Edwd. Duffield, **William** Rush and———all **of whom I believe are** good judges and very honest men, therefore I readily agreed to this proposition. And **I desired Mr.** Dudley to consult Mr. Rittenhouse and Francis Hopkinson Esquire, as to the **Machine or** Wheel in dispute, **and let me have their opinion.**

March 23d. Mr. Dudley called **to inform** me that **Mr.** Rittenhouse & Mr. Hopkinson agree to his plan **of the Machine &c.**

April 12th. Mr. Dudley wants **a horse to go up to** Mr. Wheelers &c.

---

* The following, from the Morris Papers, serve to illustrate this subject:

"1.—Robt. Morris to Richard Yates.

" Philad'a, Jan. 23, 1792.

"Sir,

"At the request of a very honest Man who seems much distressed for the welfare of "his wife, now in London, I beg to trouble you with the enclosed Letter, praying that "you will forward it, and if in consequence thereof Mrs. Dudley should come to New "York, I beg of you to procure Liberty for her to come to her Husband at this place. "The money for her Passage and reasonable expenses in New York, which must be "reasonable as possible, she may draw upon her Husband, Mr. Benjamin Dudley, and "I engage that the Draft shall be paid. I shall thank you for your attention to this "poor Lady when she arrives, and remain Sir,

"**your** most obedient and
"humble servant
"Robert Morris."

"2.—Robt. Morris to the Commissary General of Prisoners.

" Philad'a, Jan. 23, 1782.

"Sir,

"I send herewith an open letter for Mr. Richard Yates containing one for Mrs. Dud-"ley in London, from her Husband now here. I wish these may be safely delivered to "Mr. Yates, and therefore pray you to send them into New York, by some person that "will not only promise, but perform the delivery of them. I am Sir,

"your most obedient and
"humble servant
"Robert Morris."

May 20th. Mr. Dudley wrote me a Letter this day and wanted money. I directed Mr. Swanwick to supply him, and then disired him to view the Mason's Lodge to see if it would Answer for a Mint, which he thinks it will, I desired him to go up to Mr. Wheelers to see how he goes on with the Rollers &c.

June 17th. Mr. Dudley applied for money to pay his Bill. I directed Mr. Swanwick to supply him.

June 18th. Issued a warrant in favor of B. Dudley £7.11.6.

July 15th. Mr. B. Dudley applied for money, he is very uneasy for want of employment, and the Mint in which he is to be employed and for which I have engaged him, goes on so slowly that I am also uneasy at having this gentleman on pay and no work for him. He offered to go and assist Mr. Byers to establish the Brass Cannon Foundry at Springfield. I advised to make that proposal to Genl. Lincoln and inform me the result to-morrow.*

July 16th. Mr. B. Dudley to whom I gave an order on Mr. Swanwick for fifty dollars, and desired him to seek after Mr. Wheeler to know whether the Rollers &c. are ready for him to go to work on rolling the copper for the Mint.

August 22d. Mr. Saml. Wheeler who made the Rollers for the Mint, applies for money. I had a good deal of conversation with this ingenious gentleman.

August 26th. Mr. Dudley called and pressed very much to be set at work.

Sept 3d. Mr. B. Dudley applied for a passage for his Friend Mr. Sprague, pr. the Washington to France & for Mrs. Dudley back. Mr. Wheeler applied for money which I promised in a short time.

Sept. 4th. Mr. Wheeler for money. I desired him to leave his claim with Mr. McCall Secretary in this office, and I will enable the discharge of his notes in the Bank when due.

Novr. 8th. Mr. Dudley applies for the amount of his Bill for Lodgings and Diet &c. and I directed Mr. Swanwick to pay him, but am very uneasy that the Mint is not going on.

Dec. 23d. Mr. Dudley and Mr. Wilcox brought the subsistance paper, and I desired Mr. Dudley to deliver 4000 sheets to Hall and Sellers.†

---

* This letter will illustrate this subject:

ROBERT MORRIS TO THE REV. WILLIAM GORDON, D. D.

[From the Morris Papers.]

"SIR,   "PHILAD'A 25th July, 1782.

"In consequence of your Letter of the nineteenth of June, I sent for Mr. Dudley, "told him the information you had so kindly given to me, and assured him of my desire "to make him easy and happy. The business in which he is intended to be employed, "is like many other important matters, retarded by the tediousness of the States in "supplying the Continental Treasury.

"The Hon'ble Secretary at War has commenced a correspondence with General Gates "at my request, which I think, will produce what he wishes. Be assured that I take "particular pleasure in promoting the interest and happiness of worthy men, and that "I am with great esteem Sir,

"your most obedient
"and humble Servant,
"ROBERT MORRIS."

† This letter will illustrate this matter:

ROBERT MORRIS TO BENJAMIN DUDLEY.

[From the Morris Papers.]

"SIR,   "OFFICE OF FINANCE, 29 Novr., 1782.

"You will herewith receive the Form for making a particular kind of Paper—You "are to proceed to the Paper Mill of Mr. Mark Wilcox, in Ash Town Chester County, "who has the Stuff prepared, and there to superintend the making of sundry reams of "Paper upon this Form—in doing of which you are to be particularly careful not to "leave it in the power of any person or persons to make any paper upon this Form "without your immediate Inspection.

"You are to attend the Workmen constantly whilst they are at work, and when you "retire from the Mill upon any occasion, you are to take the Form with you. You are "to count the Paper as it is made sheet by sheet and when you have finished the whole, "you are to bring it to me together with the Form. I am Sir,

"Your most obedient servant,
"ROBERT MORRIS."

Decr. 26th. Mr. Hall the printer brought 100 Sheets of the subsistence notes this day, and desired that more paper might be sent to his Printing Office, accordingly I sent for Mr. Dudley and desired him to deliver the same from time to time, until the whole shall amount to 4000 Sheets.

1783. April 2d. I sent for Mr. Dudley who delivered me a piece of Silver Coin, being the first that has been struck as an American Coin.

April 16th. Sent for Mr. Dudley and urged him to produce the Coins to lay before Congress to establish a Mint.

April 17th. Sent for Mr. Dudley to urge the preparing of Coins &c for Establishing a Mint.

April 22d. Mr. Dudley sent in several Pieces of Money as patterns of the intended American Coins.

May 6th. Sent for Mr. Dudley and desired him to go down to Mr. Mark Wilcox's, to see 15,000 Sheets of paper made fit to print my Notes on.

May 7th. This day delivered Mr. Dudley the paper Mold for making paper, mark'd United States, and dispatched him to Mr. Wilcok's, but was obliged to advance him 20 dollars.

May 27th. I sent for Mr. Dudley to know if he has compleated the paper at Mr. Wilcock's paper mill for the Certificates intended for the pay of the Army. He says it is made, but not yet sufficiently dry for the printers use. I desired him to repair down to the Mill and bring it up as soon as possible.

May 28th. Mr. Whitehead Humphreys to offer his lot and buildings for erecting a Mint.

July 5th. Mr. Benjn. Dudley gave notice that he has received back from Messrs. Hall and Sellers the Printers, three thousand sheets of the last paper made by Mr. Wilcocks. I desired him to bring it to this office. He also informs of a Minting Press being in New York for sale, and urges me to purchase it for the use of the American Mint.

July 7th. Mr. Dudley respecting the Minting Press, but I had not time to see him.

August 19th. I sent for Mr. Benjamin Dudley, and informed him of my doubts about the establishment of a Mint, and desired him to think of some employment in private service, in which I am willing to assist him all in my power. I told him to make out an account for the services he had performed for the public, and submit at the Treasury office for inspection and settlement.

August 30th. Mr. Dudley brought the dies for Coining in the American Mint.

Sept. 3d. Mr. Dudley applies for money for his expenses which I agree to supply, but urge his going into private business.

Sept. 4th. Mr. Dudley for money, which is granted. Directed him to make three models for constructing Dry———

Nov. 21st. Mr. Dudley applies for money He says he was at half a guinea a week and his expenses borne when he left Boston to come about the Mint, and he thinks the public ought to make that good to him. I desired him to write me and I will state his claims to Congress.

Nov. 26th. Mr. Dudley for money, which was granted.

Dec. 17th. Mr. Dudley with his account for final settlement. I referred him to Mr. Milligan.

1784. Jan. 5th. Mr. Dudley applies for a Certificate of the Time which he was detained in the public service. I granted him one accordingly.

Jan. 7th. Mr. Dudley after the settlement of his account, which I compleated by signing a warraut.

Congreſs of the United States:

AT THE THIRD SESSION,

Begun and held at the City of Philadelphia, on Monday the ſixth of December, one thou-ſand ſeven hundred and ninety.

RESOLVED *by the* SENATE *and* HOUSE *of* REPRESENTATIVES *of the United States of America in Congreſs aſſembled,* That a mint ſhall be eſtabliſhed under ſuch regulations as ſhall be directed by law.

Reſolved, That the Preſident of the United States be, and he is hereby authorized to cauſe to be engaged, ſuch principal artiſts as ſhall be neceſſary to carry the preceeding reſolution into effect, and to ſtipulate the terms and conditions of their ſervice, and alſo to cauſe to be procured ſuch apparatus as ſhall be requiſite for the ſame purpoſe.

FREDERICK AUGUSTUS MUHLENBERG,
Speaker of the Houſe of Repreſentatives.

JOHN ADAMS, *Vice-Preſident of the United States, and Preſident of the Senate.*

APPROVED, March the third, 1791.

GEORGE WASHINGTON, *Preſident of the United States.*

DEPOSITED among the ROLLS in the OFFICE of the SECRETARY of STATE.

Th: Jefferson *Secretary of State.*

The following is a copy of an old pay roll, framed and hanging upon the wall of the Cabinet.

NAMES AND SALARIES OF THE OFFICERS, CLERKS, AND WORKMEN EMPLOYED AT THE MINT THE 10th OCTOBER, 1795.

Henry Wm. DeSaussure, Director.......................... @ 2,000 Drs. per Ann.
Nicholas Way, Treasurer................................... 1,200   "   "
Henry Voigt, Chief Coiner................................ 1,500   "   "
Albion Cox, Assayer....................................... 1,500   "   "
Robert Scott, Engraver.................................... 1,200   "   "
David Ott, Melter and Refiner pro tem............ 1,200   "   "
Nathaniel Thomas, Clerk to the Treasurer............ 700   "   "
Isaac Hough, ditto to Director and Assayer............ 500   "   "
Lodewyk Sharp, ditto to Chief Coiner.................. 500   "   "
John S. Gardiner, Assistant Engraver.................. 936   "   "
Adam Eckfeldt, Die Forger and Turner............... 500   "   "

Workmen Employed in Chief Coiner's Department.

	Wages per day. Doll.	Cts.
John Schreiner, Chief Pressman..	1	80
John Cope, Chief Adjuster........	1	60
William Hayley, Roller..	1	40
Nicholas Sinderling, Annealer......................	1	40
John Ward, Miller...........................	1	20
Joseph Germon, Drawer...	1	20
Lewis Laurenger, Brusher...	1	20
Henry Voigt, Junr, Adjuster..		88
Sarah Waldrake, ditto...		50
Rachael Summers, ditto..		50
Lewis Bitting, ditto..	1	20
Lawrence Ford, ditto..	1	20
Christopher Baum, Pressman..	1	
John Keyser, ditto..	1	
Frederick Bauck, ditto...	1	
Barney Miers, Cleaner..	1	
Martin Summers, Doorkeeper...	1	
Adam Seyfert, Hostler..	1	
John Bay, Boy...		66

Workmen Employed at the Furnace of the Mint.

	Doll.	Cts.
Peter LaChase, Melter...	1	60
George Myers, ditto...	1	50
Eberhart Klumback, ditto...	1	40
Patrick Ryan, Filer...	1	25
Valentine Flegler, Labourer...	1	25
Andrew Brunet, ditto..	1	
William Ryan, ditto...	1	

Endorsed in **two** places, "Names and Salaries of the Officers, Clerks and Workmen employed in the Mint the 10th Oct. 1795."

THE PHILADELPHIA MINT.

THE popular estimation in which the Mint is held in the United States, is, for obvious reasons, more distinctively marked than that entertained for other public institutions. Its position, in a financial point of view, is so important, its use so apparent, and its integrity of management so generally conceded, that it enjoys a pre-eminence and dignity beyond that accorded to general governmental departments. Party muta-

THE FIRST MINT IN THE UNITED STATES, ERECTED IN 1792.

tions usually effect changes in its directorship, with but slight interference, however, with the other officials, as those of attainments, skill, and long experience in the professional branches, required to intelligently perform the various duties assigned, are few in all countries. Those occupying positions are chosen for their proficiency in the various departments, their characters being always above question. The confidence reposed in the officials of the United States Mint has never been violated, as, for nearly a century of its operations, no shadow of suspicion has marred the fair name of any identified with its history.

The need of a mint in the Colonies was keenly felt to be a serious grievance against England for years before the Revolution, and as soon as practicable after the establishment of Independence, the *United States Mint* was authorized by an Act of Congress—April 2, 1792,

A lot of ground was purchased on Seventh Street near Arch, and appropriations were made for erecting the requisite buildings. An old still-house, which stood on the lot, had first to be removed. In an account book of that time we find an entry on the 31st of July, 1792, of the sale of some old materials of the still-house for seven shillings and sixpence, which " Mr. Rittenhouse directed *should be laid out for punch in laying the foundation stone.*" *

The first building erected in the United States for public use, under the authority of the Federal Government, was a structure for the United States Mint. This was a plain brick edifice, on the east side of Seventh street, near Arch. the corner-stone of which was laid by David Rittenhouse, Director of the Mint, on July 31, 1792. In the following October operations of coining commenced. It was occupied for about forty years. On the 19th of May, 1829, an Act was passed by Congress locating the United States Mint on its present site.

The first coinage of the United States, was silver half-dimes in October, 1792, of which Washington makes mention in his address to Congress, on November 6, 1792, as follows : " There has been a small beginning in the coinage of half-dimes; the want of small coins in circulation, calling the first attention to them." The first metal purchased for coinage was six pounds of old copper at one shilling and three pence per pound, which was coined and delivered to the Treasurer, in 1793. The first deposit of silver bullion was made on July 18, 1794, by the Bank of Maryland. It consisted of " coins of France," amounting to $80,715.73½. The first returns of silver coins to the Treasurer, was made on October 15, 1794. The first deposit of gold bullion for coinage, was made by Moses Brown, merchant, of Boston, on February 12, 1795; it was of gold ingots, worth $2,276.72, which was paid for in silver coins.

The first return of gold coinage, was on July 31, 1795, and consisted of 744 half eagles. The first delivery of eagles was in September 22, same year, and consisted of four hundred pieces.

*The building is still standing (March, 1888) Nos. 37 and 39 North Seventh street, and is occupied for various purposes.

Previous to the coinage of silver dollars, at the Philadelphia Mint, in 1794, the following amusing incidents occurred in Congress, while the emblems and devices proposed for the reverse field of that coin were being discussed.

A member of the House from the South bitterly opposed the choice of the eagle, on the ground of its being the "king of birds," and hence neither proper nor suitable to represent a nation whose institutions and interests were wholly inimical to monarchical forms of government. Judge Thatcher playfully, in reply, suggested that perhaps a goose might suit the gentleman, as it was a rather humble and republican bird, and would also be serviceable in other respects, as the goslings would answer to place upon the dimes. This answer created considerable merriment, and the irate Southerner, conceiving the humorous rejoinder as an insult, sent a challenge to the Judge, who promptly declined it. The bearer, rather astonished, asked, "Will you be branded as a coward?" "Certainly, if he pleases," replied Thatcher; "I always was one and he knew it, or he would never have risked a challenge." The affair occasioned much mirth, and, in due time, former existing cordial relations were restored between the parties; the irritable Southerner concluding there was nothing to be gained in fighting with one who fired nothing but jokes.

EXTRACT FROM THE RULES AND REGULATIONS ADOPTED FOR THE MINT, JANUARY 1, 1825.

The operations of the Mint throughout the year, are to commence at 5 o'clock in the morning, under the superintendence of an officer, and continue until 4 o'clock in the afternoon, except on Saturdays, when the business of the day will close at 2 o'clock, unless on special occasions it may be otherwise directed by an officer. Extra work will be paid for in proportion, on a statement being made of it through the proper officer, at the end of each month. A strict account is to be kept by one of the officers, as they may agree of the absentees from duty, if the absence be voluntary, the full wages for the time will be deducted, if it arise from sickness a deduction will be made at the discretion of the proper officer. A statement of these deductions will be rendered at the end of the month, and the several accounts made out accordingly.

The allowance under the name of *drink money* is hereafter to be discontinued, and in place of it *three dollars extra wages* per month will be allowed for the three summer months to those workmen who continue in the Mint through that season. No workman can be permitted to bring spirituous liquors into the Mint. Any workman who shall be found intoxicated within the Mint must be reported to the Director, in order that he may be discharged. No profane or indecent language can be tolerated in the Mint. Smoking within the Mint is inadmissible. The practice is of dangerous tendency; experience proves that this indulgence in public institutions, ends at last in disaster. Visitors may be admitted by permission of an officer, to see the various operations of the Mint on all working days except Saturdays and rainy days; they are to be attended by an officer, or some person designated by him. The new coins must not be given in exchange for others to accommodate visitors, without the consent of the Chief Coiner. Christmas day and the Fourth of July, and no other days, are established holidays at the Mint. The pressmen will carefully lock the several coining presses when the work for the day is finished, and leave the keys in such places as the Chief Coiner shall designate. When light is necessary to be carried from one part of the Mint to the other, the watchman will use a dark lanthorn but not an open candle. He will keep in a proper **arm** chest securely locked, **a** musket and bayonet, two pistols and a sword. **The arms are** to be kept in **perfect** order and to be inspected by an officer **once a month,** when the **arms are to** be discharged and charged anew.

The watchman **of** the Mint must attend from **6 o'**clock in the evening **to** 5 o'clock in the morning, and until relieved **by the** permission of an officer, or until **the** arrival of the door-keeper. He **will** ring the yard bell precisely every hour by the Mint clock, from **10** o'clock until relieved by the door-keeper, or an officer, or the workmen **on** working days, and will send the watch dog through the yard immediately after ringing the bell. He will particularly examine the departments of the engine and all the rooms where fire has been on the preceding day, conformably **to** his secret instructions. For this purpose he will have keys of access **to** such rooms as he cannot examine without entering them.

If an attempt be made on the Mint he will act conformably to his secret instructions on that subject. In **case** of fire occurring in or near the Mint, he will ring the Alarm **Bell if one has** been provided, or sound the alarm with his rattle, and thus **as soon as** possible bring some one **to** him **who can** be dispatched to **call** an officer, and in other particulars **will follow his** secret instructions. The secret instructions given him **from time to time** he must be careful not to disclose. The delicate trust **reposed in all** persons employed in the Mint, presupposes that their char**acter** is free from all suspicion, but the director feels it his duty neverthe**less, in** order that none may plead ignorance on the subject, to warn them **of the danger of** violating so high a trust. Such a crime as the embezzle**ment of** any **of** the coins struck at the Mint, or of any of the metals **brought** to the Mint for coinage, would be punished under the laws of **Pennsylvania,** by a fine and penitentiary imprisonment at hard labor. **The** punishment annexed **to** this crime by the laws of the United States, enacted for the special protection of deposits made at the Mint, is DEATH. The 19th Section **of** the Act of Congress, establishing the Mint, passed April 12, 1792, is in the following words: Section 19, *and* be it further enacted, That if any of the gold or silver coins, which shall be struck or coined at the said Mint, shall be debased or made worse as to the proportion of fine gold or fine silver, therein contained, or shall be of less weight or value than the same ought to be, pursuant to the directions of this act, through the default or with the connivance of any of the officers or per**sons** who shall be employed at said Mint, for the purpose of profit or gain, **or** otherwise, with a fraudulent intent, and if any of the said officers or **persons** shall embezzle any of the metal which shall at any time be com**mitted to their** charge, **for the purpose of** being coined, or any of the coins **which shall be** struck or **coined at** the said Mint, every such officer or **person** who shall commit any **or** either of the said offences, shall **be deemed** guilty of Felony, and shall suffer death. Printed copies of the **Rules** here recited are to be kept in convenient places for the inspection of **the** workmen, but as all may not be capable of reading them, it shall be the duty of the proper officer of the several departments, or such person as he may appoint, to read them **in** the hearing of the workmen, at least **once a year,** and especially to **read** them, to every person newly employed **in the Mint.**

SAMUEL MOORE,
Director.

Up to 1836 the work at the Mint was done entirely by hand or horse power. In that year steam was introduced. At different periods during the years 1797, 1798, 1799, 1802, and 1803, the operations of the Mint were suspended on account of the prevalence of yellow fever.

"BOND OF INDEMNITY OR AGREEMENT of Operatives to return to the service of the Mint." Dated August, 1799.

" We, the subscribers, do hereby promise and engage to return to the service of the Mint as soon as the same shall be again opened, after the prevailing fever is over, on the penalty of twenty pounds."

"As witness our hands this 31st day of August, 1799.

"GEORGE WATT'N,	GEORGE MYERS,
JOHN COPE,	CHARLES BENJ. K——,
LEWIS BITTING,	GEORGE BAILY,
GEO. BOEMING,	JOHN MANN,
JAMES ANDERSON,	(In German) JOHANNES ——,
JOHN SCHREINER,	SAML. THOMPSON,
JOHN BIRNBAUM,	MARTIN SUMMERS."

The above are the signatures of the parties agreeing, written on old hand-made unruled foolscap paper.

This is part of the Mint records, which has been framed for convenience and protection. It hangs in the Cabinet.

THE MINT ESTABLISHED.

The Mint was established by Act of Congress the second of April, 1792, and a few half-dimes were issued towards the close of that year. The general operations of the institution commenced in 1793. The coinage effected from the commencement of the establishment to the end of the year 1800 may be stated in round numbers at $2,534,000; the coinage of the decade ending 1810 amounted to $6,971,000, and within the ten years ending with 1820—$9,328,000. The amount within the ten years ending with 1830 is stated at $18,000,000, and the whole coinage from the commencement of the institution at $37,000,000. On the second of March, 1829, provisions were made by Congress for extending the Mint establishment, the supply of bullion for coinage having increased beyond the capacity of the existing accommodations. The Mint edifice, erected under this provision, stands on a lot purchased for the object at the northwest corner of Chestnut and Juniper streets, fronting 150 feet on Chestnut street and extending 204 feet to Penn Square, (the central and formerly the largest public square in the city). The corner-stone of the new edifice was laid on the fourth of July, 1829; the building is of marble and of the Grecian style of architecture, the roof being covered with copper. It presents on Chestnut street and Penn Square a front of 123 feet, each front being ornamented with a portico of 60 feet, containing six Ionic columns. In the centre of the structure there was formerly a court-yard (now built up) extending 85 by 84 feet, surrounded by a piazza to each story, affording an easy access to all parts of the edifice. Present officers of the Mint: Hon. Daniel M. Fox, Superintendent; William S. Steel, Coiner; Jacob B. Eckfeldt, Assayer; Patterson Du Bois, Assistant Assayer, James C. Booth, Melter and Refiner; N. B. Boyd, Assistant Melter and Refiner; Charles E. Barber, Engraver; George T. Morgan and William H. Key, Assistant Engravers; M. H. Cobb, Cashier; George W. Brown, Doorkeeper.

On July 4, 1829, Samuel Moore, then Director, laid the corner stone of the present building, located at the northwest corner of Chestnut and Juniper streets. It is of white marble, and of the Grecian style of architecture, and was finished, and commenced operations, in 1833. Subsequent to that date necessary changes in the interior arrangements, to accommodate the increase in business, have been introduced at various times, and it was made more secure as a depository for the great amount of bullion contained within its vaults, by having been rendered fire-proof in 1856.

COPY OF THE PAPER LAID IN THE CORNER STONE OF THE MINT, JULY 4, 1829.

This corner stone of the Mint of the United States of America, laid on the 4th day of July, 1829, being the fifty-third anniversary of our independence, in the presence of the Officers thereof, Members of Congress of the adjacent districts, architect, and artificers employed in the building, and a number of citizens of Philadelphia, in the which with this instrument are deposited specimens of the Coins of our Country struck in the present year. The Mint of the United States commenced operations in the year A. D., 1793, increasing constantly in utility, until its locality and convenience required extension and enlargement, which was ordered by the passage of a bill appropriating $120,000 for the erection of new and convenient buildings, to accommodate its operations, vesting the disbursement in the judgment and taste of the Director and President of the United States. In pursuance of the above bill, passed during the Presidency of John Quincy Adams, arrangements were made and designs adopted: William Strickland appointed architect; John Struthers, marble mason; Daniel Groves, bricklayer; Robert O'Neil, master carpenter, and in the first year of the Presidency of Andrew Jackson, this corner stone was placed in southeast corner of the edifice.

The names of the officers of the Mint of the United States at this time, are as follows:

Doctor SAMUEL MOORE, Director,
ADAM ECKFELDT, Coiner,
JOSEPH CLOUD, Melter and Refiner,
JOSEPH RICHARDSON, Assayer,
Doctor JAMES RUSH, Treasurer,
WM. KNEASS, Engraver,
GEORGE EHRENZELDER, Clerk.

MINT OF THE UNITED STATES,
Philadelphia, March 20, 1838.

To HON. LEVI WOODBURY,
Secretary of the Treasury.

Sir:—I had the honor to receive your letter asking my attention to a resolution of the House of Representatives of the United States, passed March 5, 1838, as follows:

EXTRACT FROM RESOLUTION OF CONGRESS RELATING TO MINT.

"*Resolved*, That the Secretary of the Treasury report to this House the cost of erecting the principal Mint and its branches, including buildings, fixtures, and apparatus; the salaries and expenses of the different officers; the amount expended in the purchase of bullion; the loss arising from wastage, and all other expenses; and the average length of time it requires to coin at the principal Mint all the bullion with which it can be furnished; and further, what amount of coin has been struck at the several branch mints, since their organization."

MINT OF THE UNITED STATES, PHILADELPHIA.

The cost of the edifice, machinery, and fixtures, was...	$173,390
Ground, enclosure, paving, etc............................	35,840
Total cost of buildings, etc...........................	$209,230

This amount does not include expenditures made under special appropriations for the years 1836 and 1837, for milling and coining by steam power; and for extensive improvements in the assaying, melting, and parting rooms, and machine shops, amounting to $28,270.

It may be proper to mention that the Mint building is on the best street in the city, is of large dimensions, with the whole exterior of marble, and two Ionic porticos; and that the machinery and apparatus are of the best construction. The cost must therefore be considered as very moderate. The new Mint lately erected by the British India Government at Calcutta, cost 24 lacs of rupees, or about $1,138,000.

The Director receives per annum	$3,500
Treasurer	2,000
Chief Coiner	2,000
Assayer	2,000
Melter and Refiner	2,000
Engraver	2,000
Second Engraver	1,500
Assistant Assayer	1,300
Treasurer's Clerk	1,200
Bookkeeper	1,000
Clerk of the weighing room	1,200
Director's Clerk	700
Total for salaries	**$20,400**

No expenses are allowed, beyond the above sums, to any officer, assistant, or clerk, for the performance of his duties.

As all the gold and silver brought to the Mint is purchased at the nett Mint price, there is no expense, properly so called, incurred on this account.

R. M. PATTERSON,
Director of the Mint.

Previous to the passage of the law by the Federal government for regulating the coins of the United States, much perplexity arose from the use of no less than four different currencies or rates, at which one species of coin was recoined, in the different parts of the Union. Thus, in New Hampshire, Massachusetts, Maine, Rhode Island, Connecticut, Vermont, Virginia and Kentucky, the dollar was recoined at six shillings; in New York and North Carolina at eight shillings; in New Jersey, Pennsylvania and Maryland at seven shillings and six pence; in Georgia and South Carolina at four shillings and eight pence. The subject had engaged the attention of the Congress of the old confederation, and the present system of the coins is formed upon the principles laid down in their resolution of 1786, by which the denominations of money of account were required to be dollars (the dollar being the unit), dismes or tenths, cents or hundredths, and mills or thousandths of a dollar. Nothing can be more simple or convenient than this decimal subdivision. The terms are proper because they express the proportions which they are intended to designate. The dollar was wisely chosen, as it corresponded with the Spanish coin, with which we had been long familiar.

VISITING THE MINT.

The Mint, on Chestnut street near Broad, is open to the public daily, excepting Sundays and holidays, from 9 to 12 A. M. Visitors are met by the courteous ushers, who attend them through the various departments. It is estimated that over forty thousand persons have visited the institution in the course of a single year. Owing to the immense amount of the precious metals which is always in course of transition, and the watchful care necessary to a correct transaction of business, the public are necessarily excluded from some of the departments. These, however, are of but little interest to the many and are described under their proper heads. The system adopted in the Mint is so precise and the weighing so accurate, that the abstraction of the smallest particle of metal would lead to almost immediate detection.

On entering the rotunda, the offices of the Treasurer and Cashier are to the right and left. Farther in, in the hall, to the rear, on the right, is the room of the Treasurer's clerks; a part of this was formerly used by the Adams Express Company, who transport to and from the Mint millions of dollars worth of metal, coin, etc.

THE DEPOSIT OR WEIGHING-ROOM.

On the left is the Deposit or Weighing-room, where all the gold and silver for coining is received and first weighed. The largest weight used in this room is five hundred ounces, the

SCALES.

smallest, is the thousandth part of an ounce. The scales are wonderfully delicate, and are examined and adjusted on alternate days. On the right of this room is one of the twelve

vaults in the building.   Of solid masonry, several of them are
iron-lined, with double doors of the same metal and most complicated and burglar-proof locks.

It is estimated that about fifteen hundred million dollars
worth of gold has been received and weighed in this room;
probably nine-tenths of this amount was from California, since
its discovery there in the year 1848.   Previous to that time
the supplies of gold came principally from Virginia, North
Carolina, and Georgia.   During the past ten years considerable
quantities have been received from Nova Scotia, but most of

AUTOMATIC WEIGHING SCALES.

the gold that reaches the Mint, at the present time, comes
from California, Montana, Colorado, Idaho, Nevada. Arizona,
Oregon, Dakota, Virginia, South Carolina, and New Mexico.

Formerly the silver used by the Mint came principally from
Mexico and South America, but since the discovery of the
immense veins of that metal in the territories of the United
States the supply is furnished from the great West.

The copper used comes principally from the mines of Lake
Superior, the finest from Minnesota.   The nickel is chiefly from
Lancaster County, Pa.

THE DEPOSIT MELTING ROOM.

After the metal has been carefully weighed in the presence of the depositor and the proper officials, it is locked in iron boxes and taken to the melting room, where it is opened by two men, each provided with a key to one of the separate locks. There are four furnaces in this room, and the first process of melting takes place here. The gold and silver, being mixed with borax and other fluxing material, is placed in pots, melted and placed in iron moulds, and when cooled is again taken to the deposit room in bars, where it is reweighed, and a small piece cut from each lot by the Assayer. From this the fineness of the whole is ascertained, the value calculated, and the depositor paid. The metal in its rough state is then transferred to the Melter and Refiner.

OFFICE OF THE MELTER AND REFINER.

Adjoining the Deposit Melting Room are the Melter and Refiner and assistants. This is the general business office of the head of this department, and is also used for weighing the necessary quantities of the metals used in alloying coin.

THE PROCESS OF ASSAY.

The two essential things regarding every piece of metal offered in payment of any dues were, first, the weight or quantity, next, the fineness or purity of the same. The process of weighing even the baser metals used in coining must be conducted by the careful use of accurate scales, with precise notes of the results. In precious metals, gold, silver, and their high grade alloys, a very small variation in the fineness makes a great difference in the value. Nothing is more essential than the accurate determination of the weight of the sample and of the metal obtained from it. It requires keen sight and most delicate adjustment in the hand which manipulates the Lilliputian scales of an Assayer's table. The smallest weight used in the Mint is found in the Assay Room; it is the thirteen-hundredth part of a grain, and can scarcely be seen with the naked eye, unless on a white ground. The Assay Department is strictly a technical and scientific branch of the service. It has been practically under one regime, for the last fifty years. There have been but three Chief Assayers in that time, the only removals being by death, the only appointments by promotion. Its workmen are all picked men, selected from other parts of the Mint for special fitness and good character

THE ASSAYING ROOMS.

These are on the second floor, in the southwest corner of the building. In one of these are fires, stills, and other appliances used in the delicate and complicated process of assay, by which the specific standard of the fineness and purity of the various metals are established and declared.

ASSAYING GOLD.

The gold is melted down and stirred, by which a complete mixture is effected, so that an assay piece may be taken from any part of the bar after it is cast. The piece taken for this purpose is rolled out for the convenience of cutting. It is then taken to an assay balance (sensible to the ten-thousandth of a half gramme or less), and from it is weighed a half gramme, which is the normal assay weight for gold, being about 7.7 grains troy. This weight is stamped 1000; and all the lesser weights (afterwards brought into requisition) are decimal divisions of this weight, down to one ten-thousandth part.

Silver is next weighed out for the quartation (alloying), and as the assay piece, if standard, should contain 900-thousandths of gold, there must be three times this weight, or 2700-thousandths of silver; and this is the quantity used. The lead used for the cupellation is kept prepared in thin sheets, cut in square pieces, which should each weigh about ten times as much as the gold under assay. The lead is now rolled into the form of a hollow cone; and into this are introduced the assay gold and the quartation silver, when the lead is closed around them and pressed into a ball. The furnace having been properly heated, and the cupels placed in it and brought to the same temperature, the leaden ball, with its contents, is put into a cupel (a small cup made of burned bones, capable of absorbing base metals), the furnace closed, and the operation allowed to proceed, until all agitation is ceased to be observed in the melted metal, and its surface has become bright. This is an indication that the whole of the base metals have been converted into oxides, and absorbed by the cupel.

The cupellation being thus finished, the metal is allowed to cool slowly, and the disc or button which it forms is taken from the cupel. The button is then flattened by a hammer; is annealed by bringing it to a red heat; is laminated by passing it between the rollers; is again annealed; and is rolled loosely into a spiral or coil called a *cornet*. It is now ready for the process of quartation. This was formerly effected in a glass matrass, and that mode is still used occasionally, when there are few assays. But a great improvement, first introduced into this country by the Assayer in 1867, was the—"platinum apparatus," invented in England. It consists of a platinum vessel in which to boil the nitric acid, which is to dissolve out the silver, and a small tray containing a set of platinum thimbles with fine slits in the bottom. In these the silver is taken out, by successive supplies of nitric acid, without any decanting as in the case of glass vessels. The cornets are also annealed in the thimbles; in fact there is no shifting from the coiling to the final weighing, which determines the fineness of the original sample by proportionate weights in thousandths. In this process extra care has to be taken in adding the proportions of silver, as the "shaking" of any one cornet, might damage the others.

ASSAYING SILVER.

The process of assaying silver differs from that of gold. To obtain the assay sample, a little of the metals is dipped from the pot and poured quickly into water, producing a granulation, from portions of which that needed for assay is taken. In the case of silver alloyed with copper there is separation, to a greater or less degree, between the two metals in the act of solidification. Thus an ingot or bar, cooled in a mould, or any single piece cut from either, though really 900-thousandths fine on the average, will show such variations, according to the place of cutting, as might exceed the limits allowed by law. But the sudden chill produced by throwing the liquid metal into water, yields a granulation of entirely homogeneous mixture that the same fineness results, whether by assaying a single granule, or part of one, or a number.

From this sample the weight of 1115 thousandths is taken; this is dissolved in a glass bottle with nitric acid. The standard solution of salt is introduced and chloride of silver is the result, which contains of the metallic silver 1000 parts; this is repeated until the addition of the salt water shows but a faint trace of chloride below the upper surface of the liquid. For instance: if three measures of the decimal solution have been used with effect, the result will show that the 1115 parts of the piece contained 1003 of pure silver; and thus the proportion of pure silver in the whole alloyed metal is ascertained. Extensive knowledge and experience are required in such matters as making the bone-ash cupels, fine proof gold and silver, testing acids, and other special examinations and operations. The Assayer must, himself, be familiar with all the operations of minting, as critical questions are naturally carried to him.

The rendering of decisions upon counterfeit or suspicious coins has long been a specialty in this department. Once a year the President appoints a scientific commission to examine the coins of the preceding year. There has never yet been a Philadelphia coin found outside of the tolerance of fineness.

THE SEPARATING ROOM.

This department occupies the largest part of the west side of the building, on the second floor. Here the gold and silver used by the Mint in the manufacture of coin and fine bars are separated from each other, or whatever other metals may be mixed with them, and purified. It goes to this room after having been once melted and assayed. In separating and purifying gold, it is always necessary to add to it a certain quantity of pure silver. The whole is then immersed in nitric acid, which dissolves the silver into a liquid which looks like pure water. The acid does not dissolve the gold, but leaves it pure. The silver solution is then drawn off, leaving the gold at the bottom of the tub. It is then gathered up into pans and washed.

The silver in the condition in which it is received from the hands of the depositor, and generally filled with foreign impurities, is melted and then granulated, after which the whole mass is dissolved with nitric acid. The acid dissolves the base metals as well as the silver. The liquid metals are then run into tubs prepared for it, and precipitated, or rendered into a partially hard state, by being mixed with common salt water. After being precipitated it is called " chloride," and resembles very closely new slacked lime. By putting spelter or zinc on the precipitated chloride, it becomes metallic silver, and only needs washing and melting to make the purest virgin metal. The base metals remain in a liquid state, and being of little value are generally thrown away. The process of refining silver is of two kinds; that of melting it with saltpetre, etc., which was known some thousands of years since, and the modern process of dissolving it in nitric acid, like the method of extracting it from gold in the above described operation.

After the separating process has been completed, the gold or silver is conveyed to the Drying Cellar, where it is put under pressure of some eighty tons, and all the water pressed out. It is then dried with heat, and afterwards conveyed in large cakes to the furnaces.

THE MELTING ROOMS.

are on the first floor, in the west side of the building. Here all the metal used in coining is alloyed, melted and poured into narrow moulds. These castings are called ingots; they are about twelve inches long, a half-inch thick, and vary from one to two a half-inches in breadth, according to the coin for which they are used, one end being wedge-shaped to allow its being

CASTING INGOTS.

passed through the rollers. The value of gold ingots is from $600 to $1,400; those of silver, about $60. The fine gold and silver bars used in the arts and for commercial purposes, are also cast in this department.

INGOTS.

These are stamped with their weight and value in the deposit room. The floors that cover the melting rooms are made of iron in honey-comb pattern, divided into small sections, so that they can be readily taken up to save the dust; their roughness acting as a scraper, preventing any metallic particles from clinging to the soles of the shoes of those who pass through the department, the sweepings of which, and including the entire building, averages $23,000 per annum, for the last five years.

The copper and nickel melting rooms, wherein all the base metals used are melted and mixed, is on the same side and adjoining to the gold and silver department. Up to the year 1856, the base coin of the United States was exclusively copper. In this year the coinage of what was called the nickel cents was commenced. These pieces, although called nickel, were composed of one-eighth nickel; the balance was copper.

The composition of the five and three cent pieces is one-fourth nickel; the balance copper. The bronze pieces were changed in 1859, and are a mixture of copper, zinc and tin, about equal parts of each of the two last; the former contributing about 95 per cent. There are seven furnaces in this room, each capable of melting five hundred pounds of metal per day. When the metal is heated and sufficiently mixed, it is poured into iron moulds, and when cool, and the rough ends clipped off, is ready to be conveyed to the rolling room.

THE ROLLING ROOM.

From the melting rooms through the corridor we reach the rolling room. The upright engine, on the right, of one hundred and sixty horse power, supplies the motive force to the rolling machines, four in number. Those on the left, are massive and substantial in their frame-work, with rollers of steel, polished by service in reducing the ingots to planchets for coining. The first process or rolling is termed breaking down; after that it requires to be passed through the machine until it is reduced to the required thinness—ten times if gold, eight if silver, being annealed in the intervals to prevent breaking. The rollers are adjustable and the space between them can be increased or diminished at pleasure, by the operator. About two hundred ingots are run through per hour on each pair of rollers.

The pressure applied is so intense that half a day's rolling heats, not only the strips and rollers, but even the huge iron stanchions, weighing several tons, so hot that you can hardly hold your hand on them.

When the rolling is completed the strip is about six feet long, or six times as long as the ingot.

It is impossible to roll perfectly true. At times there will be a lump of hard gold, which will not be quite so much compressed as the rest. If the planchets were cut from this place, it would be heavier and more valuable than one cut from a thinner portion of the strip. It is, therefore, necessary to " draw " the strips, after being softened by annealing.

ROLLING MACHINE.

ANNEALING FURNACES.

These are in the same room, to the right facing the rollers. The gold and strips are placed in copper canisters, and then placed in the furnaces and heated to a red heat; silver strips being laid loosely in the furnace. When they become soft and pliable, they are taken out and allowed to cool slowly.

THE DRAWING BENCHES.

These machines resemble long tables, with a bench on either side, at one end of which is an iron box secured to the table. In this are fastened two perpendicular steel cylinders, firmly supported in a bed, to prevent their bending or turning around, and presenting but a small portion of their circumference to the strip. These are exactly at the same distance apart that the thickness of the strip is required to be. One end of the

strip is somewhat thinner than the rest, to allow it to pass
easily between the cylinders. When through, this end is put
between the jaws of a powerful pair of tongs, or pincers,
fastened to a little carriage running on the table. The carriage
to the further bench is up close to the cylinders, ready to receive
a strip, which is inserted edgewise. When the end is between
the pincers, the operator touches a foot pedal which closes the
pincers firmly on the strip, and pressing another pedal, forces
down a strong hook at the left end of the carriage, which
catches in a link of the moving chain. This draws the
carriage away from the cylinders, and the strip being connected with it has to follow. It is drawn between the cylinders,

DRAWING BENCH.

which operating on the thick part of the strip with greater power
than upon the thin, reduces the whole to an equal thickness.
When the strip is through, the strain on the tongs instantly
ceases, which allows a spring to open them and drop the strip.
At the same time another spring raises the hook and disengages
the carriage from the chain. A cord fastened to the carriage
runs back over the wheel near the head of the table, and then
up to a couple of combination weights on the wall beyond,
which draw the carriage back to the starting place, ready for
another strip.

THE CUTTING MACHINES.

After being thoroughly washed, the strips are consigned to
the cutting machines. These are in the rear of the rolling mills,

and are several in number, each when in active operation
cutting two hundred and twenty-five planchets per minute.
The press now used, consists of a vertical steel punch, which
works in a round hole or matrix, cut in a solid steel plate.
The action of the punch is obtained by an eccentric wheel.
For instance, in an ordinary carriage wheel, the axis is in the
centre, and the wheel revolves evenly around it. But if the

CUTTING MACHINE.

axis is placed, say four inches from the centre, then it would
revolve with a kind of hobble. From this peculiar motion
its name is derived. Suppose the tire of the wheel is arranged,
not to revolve with, but to slip easily around the wheel, and a
rod is fastened to one side of the tire which prevents its turn-

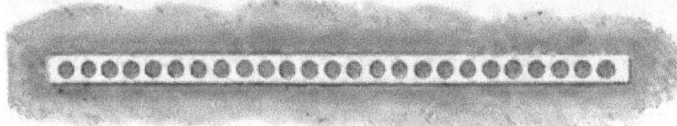

STRIP FROM WHICH PLANCHETS ARE CUT.

ing. Now as the wheel revolves and brings the *long side nearest the rod*, it will push forward the rod, and when the long
side of the wheel is *away from the rod*, it draws the rod with it.
The upper shaft, on which are seen the three large wheels,
has also fastened to it, over each press, an eccentric wheel. In

the first illustration will be seen three upright rods running from near the table to the top. The middle one is connected with a tire around the eccentric wheel, and rises and falls with each revolution. The eccentric power gives great rapidity of motion with but little jerking.

The operator places one end of a strip of metal in the immense jaws of the press, and cuts out a couple of planchets, which are a fraction larger than the coin to be struck. As the strips are of uniform thickness, if these two are of the right weight, all cut from that strip will be the same. They are therefore weighed accurately. If right, or a little heavy, they are allowed to pass, as the extra weight can be filed off. If too light, the whole strip has to be re-melted. As fast as cut the planchets fall into a box below, and the perforated strips are folded into convenient lengths to be re-melted. From a strip worth say eleven hundred dollars, eight hundred dollars of planchets will be cut.

ADJUSTING ROOM.

The planchets are then removed to the adjusting room, where they are adjusted. This work is performed by ladies. After

DELICATE SCALES.

inspection they are weighed on very accurate scales. If a planchet is too heavy, but near the weight, it is filed off at the edges; if too heavy for filing, it is thrown aside with the light ones, to be re-melted. To adjust coin so accurately requires great delicacy and skill, as a too free use of the file would make it too light. Yet by long practice, so accustomed do the operators become, that they work with apparent unconcern, scarce glancing at either planchets or scales, and guided as it were by unerring touch.

The exceedingly delicate scales were made under the direction of Mr. Peale, who greatly improved on the old ones in use. So precise and sensitive are they that the slightest breath of air affects their accuracy, rendering it necessary to exclude every draft from the room.

PROGRESS IN COINING.

The methods of coining money have varied with the progress in mechanic arts, and are but indefinitely traced from the beginning; the primitive mode, being by the casting of the piece in sand, the impression being made with a hammer

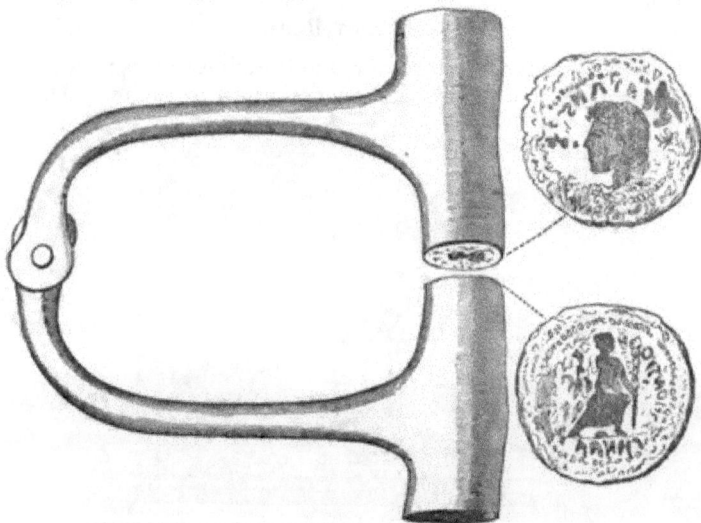

ANCIENT COINING PRESS.

and punch. In the middle ages the metal was hammered into sheets of the required thickness, cut with shears into shape, and then stamped by hand with the design. The mill and screw, by which greater increase in power, with finer finish was gained, dates back to the Sixteenth Century. This process, with various modifications and improvements, continued in use in the Philadelphia Mint until 1836.

The first steam coining press was invented by M. Thonnelier, of France, in 1833, and was first used in the United States Mint in 1836. It was remodeled and rebuilt in 1858, but in 1874 was superseded by the one now in operation, the very

STEAM COINING PRESS.

perfection of mechanism, in which the vibration and unsteady bearing of the former press were entirely obviated, and precision attained by the solid stroke with a saving of over seventy-five per cent. in the wearing and breaking of the dies.

DIES.

The dies for coining are prepared by engravers, especially employed at the Mint for that purpose. The process of engraving them consists in cutting the devices and legends in soft steel, those parts being depressed which, in the coin, appear in relief. This, having been finished and hardened, constitutes an "*original die*," which, being the result of a tedious and difficult task, is deemed too precious to be directly employed in striking coins; but it is used for multiplying dies. It is first used to impress another piece of soft steel,

DIES.

which then presents the appearance of a coin, and is called a *hub*. This hub, being hardened, is used to impress other pieces of steel in like manner which, being like the original die, are hardened and used for striking the coins. A pair of these will, on an average, perform two weeks' work.

TRANSFER LATHE.

The transfer lathe, a very complicated piece of machinery, is used in making dies, for coins and medals. By it, from a large cast, the design can be transferred and engraved in smaller size, in perfect proportion to the original.

THE COINING AND MILLING ROOMS.

This department, the most interesting to the general visitor, occupies the larger portion of the first floor on the east side of the building. The rooms are divided by an iron railing, which separates the visitors, on either side, from the machinery, etc., but allows everything to be seen.

The planchets, after being adjusted, are received here, and, in order to protect the surface of the coin, are passed through the milling-machine. The planchets are fed to this machine

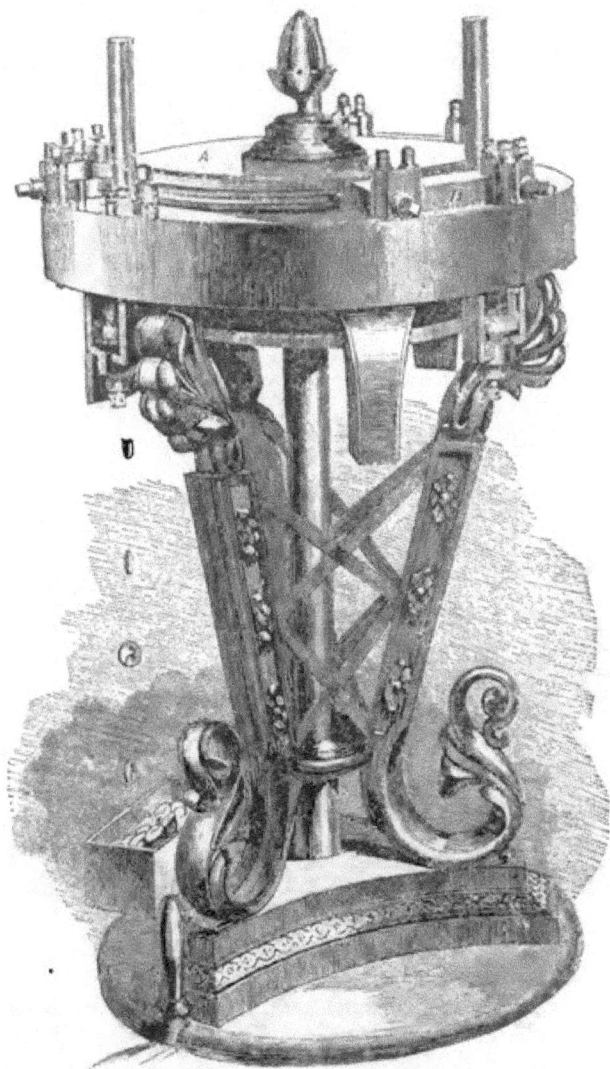

MILLING MACHINE.

through an upright tube, and, as they descend from the lower aperture, they are caught upon the edge of a revolving wheel

and carried about a quarter of a revolution, during which the
edge is compressed and forced up—the space between the wheel
and the rim being a little less than the diameter of the planchet.　This apparatus moves so nimbly that five hundred and
sixty half-dimes can be milled in a minute; but, for large
pieces, the average is about one hundred and twenty.　In this

PERFECTED COINING PRESS.

room are the milling machines, and the massive, but delicate,
coining presses, ten in number.　Each of these is capable of
coining from eighty to one hundred pieces a minute.　Only
the largest are used in making coins of large denominations.
　　The arch is a solid piece of cast iron, weighing several tons,
and unites with its beauty great strength.　The table is also

of iron, brightly polished and very heavy.   In the interior of
the arch is a nearly round plate of brass, called a triangle.   It
is fastened to a lever above by two steel bands, termed stirrups,
one of which can be seen to the right of the arch.   The stout
arm above it, looking so dark in the picture, is also connected

COINING PRESS.

with the triangle by a ball-and-socket joint, and it is this arm
which forces down the triangle. The arm is connected with
the end of the lever above by a joint somewhat like that of the
knee.   One end of the lever can be seen reaching behind the
arch to a crank near the large fly-wheel. When the triangle

is *raised*, the arm and near end of the lever extends outward. When the crank lifts the further end of the lever it draws in the knee and forces down the arm until it is perfectly straight. By that time the crank has revolved and is lowering the lever, which forces out the knee again and raises the arm. As the triangle is fastened to the arm it has to follow all its movements.

Under the triangle, buried in the lower part of the arch, is a steel cup, or, technically, a "die stake." Into this is fastened the reverse die. The die stake is arranged to rise one-eighth of an inch; when down it rests firmly on the solid foundation of the arch. Over the die stake is a steel collar or plate, in which is a hole large enough to allow a planchet to drop upon the die. In the triangle above, the obverse die is fastened, which moves with the triangle; when the knee is straightened the die fits into the collar and presses down upon the reverse die.

Just in front of the triangle will be seen an upright tube made of brass, and of the size to hold the planchets to be coined. These are placed in this tube. As they reach the bottom they are seized singly by a pair of steel feeders, in motion as similar to that of the finger and thumb as is possible in machinery, and carried over the collar and deposited between the dies, and, while the fingers are expanding and returning for another planchet, the dies close on the one within the collar, and by a rotary motion are made to impress it silently but powerfully. The fingers, as they again close upon a planchet at the mouth of the tube, also seize the coin, and, while conveying a second planchet on to the die, carry the coin off, dropping it into a box provided for that purpose, and the operation is continued *ad infinitum*. These presses are attended by ladies, and do their work in a perfect manner. The engine that drives the machinery is of one hundred and sixty horse-power.

After being stamped the coins are taken to the Coiner's room. and placed on a long table—the double eagles in piles of ten each. It will be remembered that, in the Adjusting Room, a difference of one-half a grain was made in the weight of some of the double eagles. The light and heavy ones are kept separate in coining, and when delivered to the treasurer, they are mixed together in such proportions as to give him full weight in every delivery. By law the deviation from the standard weight, in delivering to him, must not exceed three pennyweights in one thousand double eagles. The gold coins—as small as quarter eagles being counted and weighed to verify the count—are put up in bags of $5,000 each. The three-dollar pieces are put up in bags of $3,000, and one-dollar pieces in $1,000 bags. The silver pieces, and sometimes small gold, are counted on a very ingenious contrivance called a "counting-board."

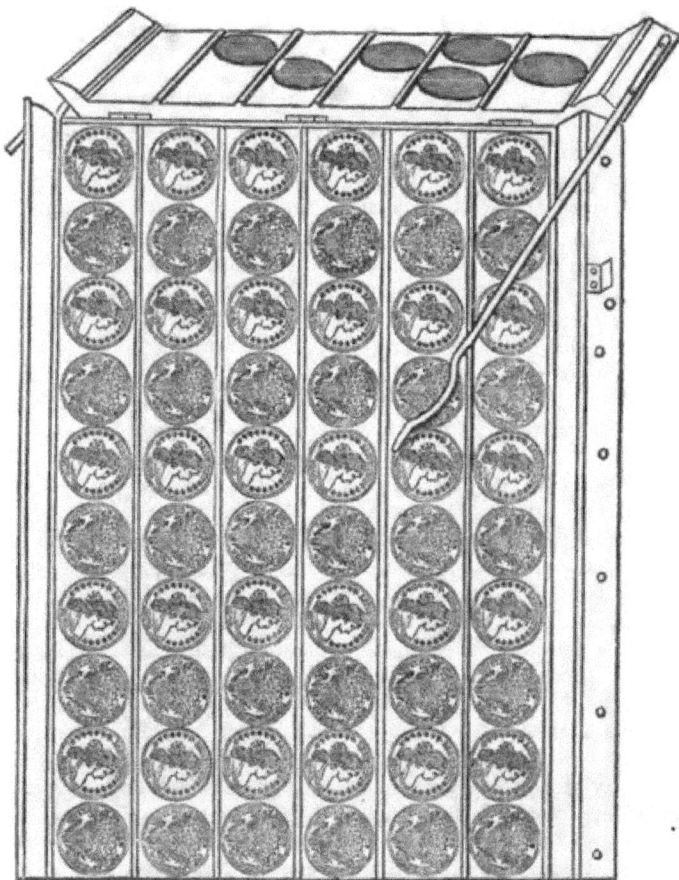

COUNTING BOARD.

By this process twenty-five dollars in five-cent pieces can be counted in less than a minute. The "boards" are a simple flat surface of wood, with copper partitions, the height and size of the coin to be counted, rising from the surface at regular intervals, and running parallel with each other from top to bottom. They somewhat resemble a common household "washing board," with the grooves running parallel with the sides but much larger. The boards are worked by hand, over a box, and as the pieces are counted they slide into a drawer prepared to receive them. They are then put into bags and are ready for shipment.*

* For the various duties of the Mint there are over three hundred persons employed as clerks, workmen, etc.—say about two-thirds men and one-third women—the number depending, of course, upon the amount of work to be done.

THE CABINET.

THE room in the Mint used for the Cabinet is on the second floor. It was formerly a suite of three apartments connected by folding-doors, but the doors have been removed, and it is now a pleasant saloon fifty-four feet long by sixteen wide. The eastern and western sections are of the same proportions, each with a broad window. The central section is lighted from the dome, which is suported by four columns. There is an open space immediately under the dome, to give light to the hall below, which is the main entrance to the Mint. Around this space is a railing and a circular case for coins. The Cabinet of Coins was established in 1838, by Dr. R. M. Patterson, then Director of the Mint. Anticipating such a demand, reserves had been made for many years by Adam Eckfeldt,* the Coiner, of the "master coins" of the Mint; a term used to signify first pieces from new dies, bearing a high polish and struck with extra care. These are now more commonly called "proof pieces." With this nucleus, and a few other valuable pieces from Mr. Eckfeldt, the business was committed to the Assay Department, and especially to Mr. Du Bois, Assistant Assayer. The collection grew, year by year, by making exchanges to supply deficiencies, by purchases, by adding our own coin, and by saving foreign coins from the melting-pot—a large part in this way, at a cost of not more than their bullion value, though demanding great care, appreciation, and study. Valuable donations were also made by travelers, consuls, and missionaries. In 1839, Congress appropriated the sum of $1,000 for the purchase of "specimens of ores and coins to be preserved at the Mint." Annually, since, the sum of $300 has been appropriated by the Government for this object. More has not been asked or desired, for the officers of the Mint have not sought to vie with the long established collections of the national cabinets of the old world, or even to equal the extravagance of some private numismatists; but they have admirably succeeded in their purpose to secure such coins as would interest all, from the schoolboy to the most enthusiastic archæologist. The economic principle upon which the collection has been gathered is a lesson to all governmental departments in frugality, as well as a restraint upon the natural tendency to extravagance which has heretofore distinguished those who have a passion for old coins. There are thousands of coin collectors in the United

---

* Adam Eckfeldt's portrait, by Samuel Du Bois, hangs in the Cabinet. A short sketch of him will be found in the list of Coiners.

States, and fortunes have been accumulated in this strange way. More than one authenticated instance has been known in this country where a man has lived in penury, and died from want, yet possessed of affluence in time-defaced coins.

RELICS.

Having referred to the portraits of the Directors of the Mint, we will cite other interesting subjects of observation, before describing the coins.

The first object in the Cabinet attracting attention is a framed copy of the law of Congress establishing the Mint, with its quaint phraseology with the signature of Thomas Jefferson. (See fac simile on page 11.)

In the first section, near the western window, is the assorting machine, the invention of a Frenchman, Baron Seguier, and which is now in use in the Mint at Paris.

The planchets for coinage are liable to be a little too heavy or too light; it is therefore necessary, at least in the case of gold, to assort them by weighing. This machine is designed to enable one person to do the work of many. "The planchets are thrown into the hopper at the rear, and, being arranged by the action of the wheel, slide down balances. By machinery beneath they are carried one by one to the nearest platforms to be weighed. If too heavy, the tall needle of the beam leans to the right and lifts a pallet-wire, which connects with an apparatus under the table by which the planchet is pushed off and slides into one of the brass pans in front. If the piece be light, the needle is drawn over to the left, and touches the other pallet, which makes a passage to another brass pan. If the piece be of true weight, or near enough, the needle stands perpendicular between the pallets, and the piece finds its way into the third brass pan."

On the opposite wall is a fine cast of Cromwell, a duplicate of one taken shortly after his death. It was placed here by Mr. W. E. Du Bois, who received it from H. W. Field, Esq., late Assayer of the Royal Mint, London, who is a descendant of the great Protector. Below the cast of Cromwell is a case showing progressive "alloys of gold." The plates comprise gold alloyed with copper, gold alloyed with silver, and gold fine.

In the eastern section are the Standard Test Scales, used to test the weights sent to all the mints and assay offices in the United States, and are so delicate as to weigh the *twenty-thousandth* part of an ounce. These scales were manufactured by employees of the Mint, and have been in use more than a quarter of a century. The beam is hollow, and filled with Spanish cedar to guard against the effect of dampness; the bearings are edges of knife-blades, which impinge on a surface of agate plate. These scales are tested by the Annual Assay Committee, which meets on the second Tuesday in February of every year.

CURIOSITIES AND MINERALS.

The most interesting objects of this curious display are three golden images from graves in the Island of Chiriqui, off Central America. They were dug up in 1858, and sent to the Mint as bullion, to be melted. They are of pure gold, but the workmanship is very crude. The images are in the forms of a reptile, a bird, and a man with symbols of power in his hands, not unlike those designating Jupiter. There are also, in the first section, two large cases with choice selections of mineral specimens, carefully classified and labeled. These are from well selected results of years of patient collecting, and are deserving of more study than can be devoted to them by casual visitors. They are chiefly from different parts of the United States, and are an "index book" to the vast mineral wealth of the nation.

Near the exit door of the Cabinet, in a large glass case, is a magnificent American eagle, which is worthy of the visitor's attention. It is superbly mounted, with grand breadth of wing and wondrous piercing eyes. The portrait of this "pet" can be recognized on Reverse of the "Pattern" Silver Dollars of 1836, 1838, and 1839, and on the Obverse of the first nickel cent pieces coined in 1856.

"PETER,"

the name which the noble bird recognized, was an inhabitant of the Mint six years. He would fly about the city, but no one interfered with the going or coming of the "Mint bird," and he never failed to return from his daily exercise before the time for closing the building. In an evil hour he unfortunately perched upon a large fly wheel, and getting caught in the machinery, received a fatal injury to his wing, and this ended rather an unusual career for an eagle.

EASTERN CORRIDOR.

Opening into the eastern corridor are the rooms of the Superintendent, the Chief Clerk, and the library of Historical and Scientific Works, including many valuable books upon the art of coinage. Passing out upon the gallery, we enter the Machinists' and Engravers' rooms. Here are engraved and finished the dies used in this Mint and in all the branch mints. Visitors are not ordinarily allowed access to these rooms, or to the assay office, or to the cellar. (In the latter are a number of immense vaults, and in the main cellar are engines, which supply the power and light used throughout the building.) Here are also blacksmith, carpenter, and paint shops; and in the rear, west side, is the medal-striking room, where medals are struck by a screw press, worked by hand. The cellar also contains the "sweep" grinding rooms. Near this room are the wells, which are receptacles for the water used in washing the precious metals. These wells are cleaned out every few years and the deposit is then treated in the same way as the sweepings.

The little wooden building in the court was formerly the cent-room, where copper cents were exchanged for nickels;* it is now the office of the agent of the Adams Express Company, who brings to the Philadelphia Mint millions of dollars worth of precious metals in the shape of bullion from the far west, to be converted into American Coin, when it is again transported by the same company to various points to be put into circulation.

COINS.

The ancient coins are chiefly arranged in upright cases against the walls in the doorways and the middle section of the saloon. The modern coins are placed in nearly level cases at either end of the room and in the circular or central cases. Of antique coins the portion labeled Cabinet Nos. 97, 98, 99, "Massilia," are interesting as belonging to a Greek colony which settled about six hundred years before Christ upon the coast of Gaul, on the spot now known as Marseilles. This little colony fled their native country and the rule of a governor placed over it by a Persian monarch. They were distinguished for their civilization, and the work upon these small coins is the most palpable witness of that fact in existence to-day.

GREEK COINS.

Their surfaces, of gold, silver, and bronze, bristle with lance and spear, helmet and shield. On one of these coins Jove is seated and bearing an eagle, defying Alexander of Macedon, while on the obverse the same mighty conqueror impersonates Hercules. The oldest coin here is supposed to date back to 550 B.C. It is well to mention the fact that coins were

* The exchange at the present time (1885) is made at the Sub-Treasury in the Custom House.

never dated until the fifteenth century; and previous to that time the ages of coins can only be determined by the legends upon them, as answering to the page of corroborative history and the art era to which they belonged. No. 9 bears on the obverse the Macedonian horse, a favorite animal, which the then war-loving Greeks are said to have deified At this period the haughty royal families began to chronicle in coin their line of descent. The kings of Macedon claimed Hercules for an ancestor, and in proof thereof the lion's skin was a royal insignia. An old historian says, "The kings of Macedon, instead of the crown, the diadem, the purple, bear upon their effigy the skin of a lion." Several pieces of money in this case, upon which are heads of Alexander, have rings in them, and were worn by gracious dames as ornaments. The value of this series of coins is priceless, as furnishing portraits of the heroes of that period which can be received without question as accurate, for the art patronage of the kingdom was regulated by the strictest laws. Alexander was especially jealous of how the future nations should regard his physique, allowing only three artists, during his reign, the privilege of drawing, painting, or modeling his head.* To such royal guardianship may be attributed the perfection to which Greek art attained; and it may well be a matter of regret that the same firmness in this regard was not universal. The last coin of this series is a small bronze coin, and was issued by Perseus, the last king of Macedon.

PERSIAN.

In this case is a collection of Persian coins, very choice, and of no mean workmanship, and, of course, portraying the faith and rites of the fire-worshippers. One era is distinctly Greek in style, and marks the period of Greek supremacy. The oldest gold coin known to the collector is the gold Daric of King Darius, with the head of the king in bold relief; and all Persian coins are so called in remembrance of this monarch. Their money was very fine, so the word *Daric* has become incorporated into numismatic terminology to designate any pure gold coin. Nos. 58 to 67, inclusive, of this series, are silver coins of the Sassanian kings.

EGYPT

is also represented in this case, as is proper, for that nation had no coinage until it was taught the art when conquered by

* Horace says that Alexander the Great ordained that no one should take his portrait on gems but Pyrgoteles; no one should paint him but Apelles; and no one should stamp his head on coins but Lysippus.—*American Bibliopolist*.

Alexander. Here are some very attractive **data of** Egyptian
history, and from these coins are obtained **the only portraits**
of Arsinoe, Cleopatra, and others.

THE SYRIAN COINS

are embraced in the division called "Greek monarchies," and
in them are found many coins **not only** important **in** history,
but of the **very finest** Greek art, **from** the third **to** the first
century B.C. In this period the Syriac and Hebrew coins
become intermingled, **a** fact abundantly sustained by the Jewish **shekel** of Simon Maccabees. The legend of this interesting **relic is** in the language **of** Samaria; on one side the
budding rod of Aaron, legend, "Jerusalem the Holy;" on
the other, a cup of incense or pot of manna, and the inscription, "Shekel of Israel." This shekel is well preserved, and
is one of the most prized coins known. (See Plate and Case
XV., marked "*Selections.*" In this collection are some coins
from Bactria, considered priceless by **savans**. These **are** tro-
phies of recent British explorations, and **are** judged to **be of**
sufficient importance to call forth from an English **professor**
an extended **treatise on** the "Antiquities and Coins of Afghan-
istan." They are **exceedingly rude in** workmanship, and
nearly all of **baser** metal, the most important being a small,
square, brass coin, in the case marked "*Selections.*"

ROMAN COINS.

The collection of Roman coins in this Cabinet numbers
nearly one thousand, and an acquaintance with it is invaluable
for object teaching, as in it is the condensed history, not only
of the glory of Rome, "Mistress of the World," but of her cus-
toms, faith, conquests, wealth, culture, divisions, and *downfall.*
Through this entire section of time—one-third of the known
history of the world—Roman **art,** though high, never reached
the **exalted** purity of Greek lines. In their finest coins we see
no Phidias, no Myron, no Praxiteles, but they deteriorate and
fluctuate visibly when **in or out of contact** with the influence
of the Grecian mind.

GREEK REPUBLIC

will be first in interest, both historic and artistic. It is conceded that to the Greeks the world owes the introduction of
the art of coinage, and though centuries numbered by tens
have passed, some of the old Greek coins equal many modern
productions in purity of lines, and surpass nearly all in poetic

sentiment. On the first coins no earthly potentate was allowed to be pictured, no deed of heroism portrayed. The glory of the gods was considered the only appropriate theme for impressions on the surface of bronze, silver, and gold. The coins of the republic embrace a large variety, as nearly a thousand towns were allowed the privilege of coinage. Upon this varied issue are preserved nearly all the legends of Greek mythology. Upon the coins are the heads of Jupiter, Juno, Minerva, Bacchus, Apollo, and Diana, with many sacred animals, and the work is to-day the standard of artistic perfection. Of course, the collection of this ancient period cannot be extensive. In this case there are, however, more than one hundred and fifty specimens, and these present a study so attractive and so intense that it is almost impossible to imagine what classic poetry would be without it.

Nos. 4, 5, and 6, are silver coins of Ægina, which have on the obverse, for a device, the tortoise, emblematic of the security of the island amid the waves, and the protection of the gods of the sea. On the reverse are the marks of the punches only, probably denoting the value of the coins. These are claimed to belong to an era seven hundred years before Christ. No. 28 is a silver coin of Athens, with a head of Minerva splendidly drawn upon the obverse, while the reverse presents a large owl, the bird sacred to the goddess of Wisdom. The devices upon this coin indicate its age to be from twenty-one to twenty-three centuries. The Greek proverb of "taking owls to Athens" referred to this coin, which was necessarily of great importance to the tradespeople of that city.

FAMILY COINS.

These comprise about one hundred and seventy-five, of which one hundred and twenty-six are in the collection. They were struck to record the heroic deeds which first introduced any notable ancestor to fame, and hence are to-day family charts of respectability for many of the patricians of Rome, albeit some of them have plebeian roots. Be that as it may, they are as much the trusted patents of aristocracy as is the "Book of the Peerage" of England. Here are found the same distinctions between patrician and plebeian which mark all countries, the patricians being always designated by a symbol of warfare, while the plebeians were indicated by the tools and instruments of common trade. The more noticeable of the coins are as follows: No. 16, Acilia; the reverse a female leaning against a pillar, with a serpent clutched in her right hand, indicating the wisdom or courage of some ancestor. No. 20, Æmilia; on the obverse of this curious coin is a figure kneeling by the side of a camel, presenting an olive branch, from which depends a fillet or ancient diadem; on the reverse, a figure guiding a triumphal chariot, a scorpion in the field. Josephus tells us of an invasion of Arabia, and that Aretus, the king of the country, purchased peace of the Romans for five hundred talents. The diadem hanging from the olive branch chronicles the entire humiliation of Aretus, and the scorpion doubtless indicates the month of the Roman triumph. No. 30, Aquillia, a small silver coin; the reverse shows a woman kneeling before a soldier. The motto below the figures (or in the *exergue* of the coin, as is the art term) is "*Sicil.*" This commemorates the suppression of a revolt of slaves in Sicily, which was achieved by Manlius Aquillia. No. 41, Calpurnia, the family of Cæsar's noble wife; reverse, a horseman riding at full speed, a head of wheat above him; legend, L. Piso-Trugi. The coin recalls the fact that in the year 507 B. C. there was a famine in Rome, and Calpurnius Piso was dispatched to Africa to buy corn. This seemingly small service is magnified upon a large number of coins. Nos. 95 and 96, Hostilia, a coin with a sacrifice to *Pallor* and *Pavor* (fear and trembling), offered by Tullus Hostilius in some great emergency. No. 97, Julia; obverse, a helmeted head; legend, Cæsar; reverse, a warrior in a chariot drawn by two horses.

No. 98, Junia; obverse, head of Liberty; reverse, Junius Brutus guarded by lictors, and preceded by a herald, showing that an ancestor of Junius Brutus was the first consul of Rome. Nos. 181, 182, Tituria. The reverse shows two soldiers throwing their shields upon a prostrate female, illustrating the famous story of the "Tarpeian Rock." Reverse represents the Romans carrying off Sabine women—a witness in coin of the fact that the family of Tituria trace their ancestry from the Sabines. To do justice to this case is impossible, for here are coins relating to the ancestors of Antonia, Aurelia, Cornelia, Fulvia, Horatio, Lucretia, Lucilla, Sempronia, Titia Valeria, and many others familiar to the readers of history.

This era of coins terminated about the time of the birth of Christ, when the

IMPERIAL COINS

were introduced. In noticing these, little save the labels on the case can be given.

Division II.

Julius Cæsar to Trajan, inclusive. Beginning 49 B. C., and ending 117 A.D. A simple catalogue of the illustrious names on these coins would convey an idea of their importance. All the victories of Cæsar are marked by coinage; but out of the two hundred belonging to this case reference need only be made to No. 24, a beautiful gold coin, with the undraped head of Augustus, exquisitely severe, the interest attaching chiefly to the legend, "The Son of God," referring to the deification of Cæsar.

Division III.

embraces from Hadrian to Elagabalus, 117–222. In the reign of Hadrian much coin was issued, though it did not bear marks of the disasters and revolts that signalized the foregoing. That he was a merciful ruler is indicated by the coins, especially one—Hispania; the reverse showing the emperor raising Spain—a female figure—from the ground. His travels are also illustrated in coin.

Division IV.

From Severus Alexander to Claudius Gothicus, 222–270. These coins indicate the vicious effect of the rulers immediately preceding.

Division V.

From Aurelian to the end of the Western Empire; includes 270–475. A brilliant succession; Aurelian's busy reign, ending in assassination; the war-like Probus, the slave-emperor; Diocletian's despotism and vindictive persecution of Christians; the usurpation of Carausius; the happy reign of Constantine the Great, Julian, Theodosius, down to Julius Nepos. These are a few of the historic names and events presented in this division.

Division VI.

covers the period of the Byzantine or Eastern Empire, and a lapse of eight centuries; but the coinage is not comparable with that of other eras, nor were events of so stirring and heroic a character. A general decay, painful to contemplate, marked this long lapse of time, which began near the acceptance of Christianity, and extended through the dark ages.

"THE TEMPLE SWEEPERS."

A small case attracts no little attention, because it contains a single coin; and the interest does not decrease when the inscription is read: "Struck in the Philadelphia Mint, at least two thousand years ago." The late Assayer of the Philadelphia

Mint, Mr. W. E. Du Bois, under title of "The Temple Sweepers," wrote, not long since, a valuable sketch of this coin, made in the City of Attalus Philadelphus, Asia Minor, and for which William Penn called his city, because the ancient one was a monument of "brotherly love." Diana was the patroness of Philadelphia.

"On one side, then, we have a head; not a king's nor an emperor's; as yet the free city had a pride and a privilege above that. It is a female head, an ideal, representing the city itself; or rather the dwellers in it, the *Demos.* Here in this head and title, we have the radix of Democracy.

"This is all we can gather from the obverse. On the other side we have a larger variety: a running female figure; a dog also on the trot; a legend of some length and of more significance.

"The half-clad figure is that of the goddess known to the Greeks as Artemis, to the Latins as Diana; and otherwise called Selene, Phœbe, Delia, or Cynthia.

"She was the favorite divinity of the cities of Asia Minor. Once the patroness of chastity and purity. Goddess of the chase."

The legend on the obverse of this coin explains its name: "Friends of Philadelphia's [her] Temple Sweepers."

ORIENTAL.

Oriental coins are not as attractive as other varieties, though there are special coins among them which have no rival in historic importance. Antique coins from the East were usually without device, and, their legends being rudely inscribed in a dead language, proved frequently to be sealed fountains to the thirsting antiquarian. Therefore in cases marked "Oriental" the visitor is undetermined where to begin to study, and often decides to give it but little time.

Those having for device the sacred peacock are from Burmah; there is, however, in the division marked "Selections" a very curious coin belonging to that country, which certainly formed a part of its earliest currency. It is a common gravelstone, encased in a circling band of brass.

Coins of Siam.

The coins of Siam are much sought for. Some of them, known to European travelers as "bullet money," are lumps of gold or silver, hammered by rude implements into a doubtful roundness, and a few Siamese characters stamped irregularly upon them. The sacred elephant is found on a large proportion of their money. A Siamese coin in the Cabinet, of modern date, is quite handsome in both workmanship and design. On the obverse is the sacred elephant in ponderous proportion, which delights the eyes of the devout, and the reverse presents a group of three pagodas, finely drawn. In the case marked "Selections" is a Siamese coin of gold, comparatively modern, called "Tecal," corresponding in some respects to the "Shekel," or "Oxen," of biblical fame.

CHINESE COINS.

On the south side of the first section is a case of seven hundred coins of the Celestial Empire. With but few exceptions these coins are bronzed. Dynasty succeeds dynasty; usurpation, insurrection, are all writ in bronze. The Chinese assert an uninterrupted coinage for forty-one centuries. The manuscript attesting this is in the case, and was prepared under authority. Large numbers of their coins were considered charms, sufficient to protect the owner, against fever, or even the more dreaded horrors of spiritual menace. In this connection it may be said that the Chinese had an exalted reverence for the coin-charm, and a small coin was often placed in the mouth of the dead (now, if a Chinaman dies in California, a small silver United States coin is placed on his tongue). These coins were covered with cabalistic characters, symbolic animals, birds, etc. Two worthy of notice in this regard, and said to be of the oldest issue, are Nos. 1 and 2. The first might be mistaken for an iron safe-key; the second is known as the "razor coin," its form and almost its size being that of a razor.

In another case, appropriately labeled, is the Chinese porcelain money." They are the only people who have made porcelain a "legal tender," though it would appear that almost every part of the three kingdoms of nature has been laid under contribution. The specimen here may be mistaken for the popular Chinese sleeve-button, bought in any bazaar for a few cents. The Chinese, as did also the Africans, utilized the small sea-shells for trade. In the same case are some of the variety legalized. Ten small shells made one "cash." This is a small, round, copper-bronzed coin, with a square hole in the centre. The Chinese dames of high degree wore such strung around their throats. One thousand of them are equal to our dollar. The Japanese, however, *outcount* their neighbors, as they have a bronze coin called the "One-hundredth," of which just seven thousand make one Spanish dollar.

Shell money of pure gold, "or gold beaten into small solid shells, was made by those natives who supplied the Portuguese slave-traders with slaves," and was called by the traders "Spondylus Macutus," from which, some contend, came the *slang* term "spondulics." Forty of those small coins, each worth about a dollar of Spanish money, was a high price for a slave.

There is also in the Cabinet a valuable collection of African ring money. These ornaments are very massive and pure, comprised of elaborately carved "signet-rings, armlets, anklets," etc. One article, more novel and valuable than the others, is a pipe of fine gold, bowl and handle of curious bas-relief figures, and a heavy, square-linked chain attaching a large medallion, on which is the head of a monarch poorly drawn.

The Chinese government, like all despotisms, is very jealous of its coining prerogatives; yet it does not fail to appreciate an advantage when offered, as is evident to us by the following:

Proclamation for general information:

"WHEREAS, The foreign silver (coin) in daily use among the people of the Kwang Tung Provinces has long been in circulation, and is moreover admitted to be advantageous and convenient. In the 5th and 11th years of Tung Chih (1866 and 1872) the Hong Kong Mint coined a new Dollar which, upon comparison with pure silver, bore a proportion of fully ninety per cent., and as the Records will prove. Proclamations were issued notifying the people that it might come into general circulation. There has lately come to Hong Kong a newly coined American Eagle Dollar, called the "Trade Dollar," and Sir Brooke Robinson, the British Consul, having requested that officers might be appointed to assay it, the Viceroy and Haikwan thereupon appointed officers to melt it down and assay it, in concert with (an officer from the British Consulate), when, taking the Haikwan Tael of pure silver as the standard, an outturn was obtained of fully 89. 61—or Taels 111.6 of this new Eagle Dollar are equal to 100 Haikwan Taels of pure silver. Minutes of the assay were drawn up in proof thereof.

"For the convenience of Traders and people, therefore, this coin should be allowed to be tendered in payment of duties at the rate of touch obtained at the assay, and to come into daily circulation. It becomes the duty then of the Viceroy and his colleagues to issue a Proclamation on the subject for general information.

"This Proclamation, therefore, is for the information of you merchants, traders, soldiers, and people of every district.

You must know that the 'Eagle Trade Dollar' that has lately come to Hong Kong has been jointly assayed by officers specially appointed for the purpose, and it can be taken in payment of duties, and come into general circulation. *You must not look upon it with suspicion.* At the same time rogues, sharpers, and the like, are hereby strictly forbidden to fabricate spurious imitations of this new Eagle Dollar, with a view to their own profit.

"And should they dare to set this prohibition at defiance, and fabricate false coin, they shall, upon discovery, most assuredly be arrested and punished. Let every one obey with trembling! Let there be no disobedience!

"A Special Proclamation. Tung Chih 12th year, 9th moon—day (October, 1873.)

" Translated by

" (Signed) WALTER C. HILLIER."

JAPAN.

Perhaps the peculiar adaptability of the Japanese character cannot be better illustrated than by their late monetary revolution, especially as their coinage is hedged around with laws, with penal attachments of no doubtful character. In the small morocco case marked "Japan" are a few specimens of their original coin. Of this series the large gold plate, four inches by three and a half, is known as the "Gold Oban," their most valuable coin, worth about seventy-five dollars. This coin is of perfectly smooth surface, with an elaborate black inscription of Japanese text, burnt in by a chemical process. To take the "Gold Oban" out of the kingdom is *punishable with death;* to remove it by mistake, subjects the offender to imprisonment for life. The other coins in this case are, in their composition and shape, as distinctive as the Japanese are peculiar as a people. The progressive character of the Japanese is exemplified by their recent acceptance of the United States system of coinage.

The mind of the Japanese proletaire has been much troubled in recent years with regard to the coinage of his country; not that he ever has much of the currency in question, but the Japanese proletaire has no pockets, and he finds it awkward to carry in his hands such coins as he contrives to possess. In ancient times his rulers were more considerate. They punched square holes in the centre of the coins, through which he passed a string, and was thus able to carry about his available capital tied around his neck or to his waistband, which in those days was his sole garment. The coins were not large in amount; it took a thousand of them to make a few shillings, while a cart was required to convey five dollars worth. But with civilization came an improved coinage, larger in value, and with no holes, and the pocketless proletaire naturally grumbled that civilization treated him hardly in this respect. Paper currency for small amounts partially satisfied him for a time; but at last his cries have been heard, and the Japanese Government has promised to issue a new coin specially for his behoof. Its value is rather less than one cent, and is to possess the indispensable hole, by which he can string it as a child strings beads, and he is probably content.

TURKEY.

Turkish coins often bear texts from the Koran on either side, so it may be said the tenets of their religion are their circulating medium. The piastres in this collection are generally those now in circulation.

EGYPT.

Egypt's antique coins were of Greek or Roman workmanship, of which the very finest is in the case marked "Selections," and has not its superior for interest or beauty in the world. It was the work of some Greek artist, and presents the head of Arsinoe, wife of Ptolemy. It was found in 1868, and bought by the United States Government at a high price; but as only three had been found, its market value may be named by thousands, though its metal value is not more than twenty dollars.

This notice of Oriental coins may conclude with suggestive reference to the "Cufic coins," of which there are some valuable specimens. The first is the silver dirhem of Walid, the eccentric caliph of Damascus, A. D. 713. There is also in case XV. a coin of the reign of Haroun Alraschid.

FRENCH COINAGE.

The French have the credit of making the greatest improvements in modern coinage. The French coins are a history of that nation, from the small coin issued in the reign of Louis "the Meek" to the last currency of the republic of France, spanning a period of one thousand years.

In design and execution the French coins bear the impress of the national character, and also give assurance of the art patronage in which her rulers, failing in much, have never wavered, but brought all their power and cunning to bear on securing the best artists, as in the instance of Francis I. beguiling from the holy father that exquisite artist Benvenuto Cellini, or the later *enterprise* of Napoleon Bonaparte. No. 83,—a medalet of the unhappy Marie Antoinette,—which is in itself very beautiful, and from its tragic association attracts general interest.

GERMANY.

The collection of Germany is very large and divided and sub-divided by its kingdoms and principalities.

One of the most interesting coins of any age, and excelling in beauty as well, is the gold medallic ducat on which are the heads of Martin Luther and Philip Melanchthon. This coin is very generally admired by visitors to the Cabinet.

COINS OF SWITZERLAND.

Switzerland is modestly represented in all her cantons, each, like the classic Greek town, enjoying the coining privilege. There are several pieces of commemorative and artistic worth, especially the two issues of the republic of 1796.

RUSSIAN COINS.

The double rouble, with a magnificent draped head of Peter the Great, is unexcelled for strength of outline, and valuable as a correct portrait of one of the very greatest and most self-reliant of modern rulers. Turning to another rouble, the features of Elizabeth II. are recognized. It may be assumed, with all due deference to royalty, that this portrayal is the most laughter-provoking figure ever stamped on metal. She is so fat as to have the effect of "spreading herself" all over the coin. Another rouble presents the majestic Catherine II.

Of the coins marked Denmark, Norway, Sweden, there can be only the copper half-daler of Sweden mentioned. This coin is four inches square, weighs about twelve ounces, and is equivalent to a United States silver half-dollar. The daler of Sweden, thaler of Germany, dollar of Spain and America, are all synonymous terms.

ENGLAND.

The first coins of Great Britain were of tin, according to Cæsar's authority, who mentions the "tin money of Britain," which has lately been sustained by the discovery, in some work of excavation, of coins of that metal in antique design. These coins are, however, of little use, by reason of the obscure inscription, or rather the frequent absence of all device.

The English collection in the Cabinet begins with a coin made after the stater of Greece, presenting the head of Minerva, with Greek helmet on obverse, while the reverse gives the figure of a woman most crudely drawn. It is supposed this rude attempt at art was coined about the time of the Roman invasion. Note the contrast presented in placing this relic by the side of the Victorian sovereign, where, on the obverse, is the queen's head superbly cut; on the reverse, Wyon's inimitable figure of Una and the Lion. These two coins are the Alpha and the Omega of British coinage, while the thousands issued between them are progressive links to civilization.

Two small coins are placed here, thought to be contemporary with the Christian era, having no device, but an attempt to portray the sun on one side. No. 2 is the skeattae of Ethelbert I, king of Saxony, and is the first Saxon coin which has yet been appropriated. It bears upon the obverse the head of the king; on the reverse is the figure of a bird.

Next in interest is No. 6, the penny of William the Conqueror. The bust of that famous monarch is attempted; 1068 is about the year it is supposed to have been made. During the three centuries following, the condition of England, whether she was at peace or war, is plainly indicated by her coinage. Every added province is memorialized in coin. The rose, thistle, and fleur-de-lis, all tell in strange language for flowers of bloody battles, long sieges, perils by the sea and land; at last all resistance bowing before the ever-increasing power of Great Britain.

The first coin of English issue was dated in 1553, being either the close of Edward VI.'s or the beginning of Queen Mary's reign. This is claimed by many to be the first coin dated, though old medals of the preceding century have been found with date.

In 1558, the ryal or royal of Queen Elizabeth was issued. On the obverse the queen is grandly enthroned, while the reverse is a large rose, in the centre of which are the Danish arms of Britain, and the arms of Anjou quartered. This coin and the pound sterling of Charles I. are in Case XV., "Selections."

This pound sterling is one of the famous "siege pieces" of that unhappy king,—which were often made on the field with hammer and anvil out of the family plate brought to the closely-pressed Stuart by his faithful followers. It is to be regretted that so much valuable family plate of no mean workmanship was thus sacrificed. This "siege piece" is the largest silver coin known. The legend upon it, rudely inscribed, is, "Let God arise; let his enemies be scattered;" above are three fleurs-de-lis, with date, "1642."

In 1684–88, during the short reign of James II., several varieties of new coins were introduced, notably, "Maundy Money," a small coin made to be distributed by the king on "Maundy Thursday." Beggars, on that day, received from his majesty bags containing as many maundy pieces as the king had lived years.

King James II. also had issued "gun money." This variety was made out of old cannon, after the suppression of an Irish rebellion. Though not even giving a glance towards the interesting series of Queen Anne, it is impossible to pass unnoticed the beautiful bust of George IV., by Chantrey, upon a pattern five-sovereign piece. This well-executed bust of "the handsomest man in Europe," was said to be the means of Sir Francis Chantrey being knighted. That vain monarch was as careful about how his face would appear to future generations as was Alexander of Macedon; and Chantrey well knew if he placed upon the shoulders of sixty years the head of forty years, he had given the cabalistic words which would be the "open sesame" to royal favor.

The gold sovereign of Victoria, Nos. 183–184, has, on the reverse, an evidence of coins as a deposit of law archives. The shield surrounded by a crown, and bearing the arms of Great Britian quartered; but the arms of Hanover *are omitted*. Although Victoria was next heir to William IV., she was prevented by the Salic law from assuming the sceptre of Hanover. On this coin, it may be remembered, are very beautifully presented the rose. the thistle, and the shamrock.

A recent addition has been made to the Mint Cabinet of a very fine sovereign of the times of Oliver Cromwell, purchased at the coin sale of May 14 and 15, 1885.

Scotch moneys of any variety, are very much prized by collectors (see, in Case XV., "Selections," "Groat of Robert Bruce, 1602.") A very rare coin is the penny of Robert II. of Scotland, said to be the only specimen in existence of that monarch's reign. In the seventeenth century the coinage of Scotland merged into that of England.

ENGLISH SILVER TOKENS,

issued in England, Scotland, and Ireland. "During the long suspension of specie payments, occasioned by the wars with Napoleon, the minor currency of England was supplied, not with small paper notes, but with silver tokens, issued by banks and traders. and made redeemable in bank notes. They were of reduced weight, to keep within the premium, and to prevent hoarding. They continued to circulate **until** the return **of** better times and **of** regular silver **coinage.** There **were** many varieties, most **of** which are here.

PORTUGAL AND SPAIN.

The coinage of Portugal and Spain in the fifteenth century, held greater sway than that of other countries. Of their coins, there are many fine specimens in the Mint Cabinet. The "joe and half-joe *" of Portugal are known of all nations, while the Spanish dollar, with its pretentious two globes under a crown, did not claim too much, and only tells the almost limitless rule of the great Philip. The coins of these nations became, through their possessions in the New World, the circulating medium of that portion of the earth. Spanish and Mexican dollars were almost synonymous, while the real and joe of South America was patterned after that of Portugal, which fact can be learned in this Cabinet. As nations decay it will be seen their coins become inevitably less trustworthy ; even a glance at the cases marked "Portugal," "Spain," will give this lesson. In the Mexican collection there are issues which seem to contradict this assertion, for the "Mexican dollar" has, for generations, had a position in the monetary world of almost unchallenged credit, yet not by reason of the recognition given Mexico, but because of the *United States using it so extensively ;* for, until the introduction of the "trade dollar," this country had *no currency* that would meet the demand of the Oriental market.

MEXICO.

The Mexicans use only gold **and silver,** and their national series is full of tragic interest, embracing, as it does, three and a half centuries of Mexican history, from Cortez to Maximilian. The "pillar dollar," "windmill dollar," "cast dollar" (the Mexicans are the only nation that cast money). and the "cob money" (a series so called by **reason** of its clumsiness), are all to be seen in this collection.

COINS OF BRAZIL.

One coin, a gold "half-joe," issued in 1832, with the infant head of Dom Pedro, is very beautiful. By the side of this, in every way a contrast to it, is a series of copper coins of a late issue with the head of the "child" now seated on the throne.

<hr/>

* "In box, three pictures (miniatures), *two half joes,* two small pieces of gold." Dec. 26, 1780.—Martha Washington. These were sent to be used in the manufacture of the miniature cases for the above pictures. This letter is in the possession of R. Coulter Davis, Ph. G., of this city.

The coins of Bolivia proudly present the bust of Simon Bolivar. Among the West Indies are many samples of "cut money." The law permitting money to be quartered had to be repealed, because the traders of the West Indies made the wonderful mathematical discovery that *five* **quarters** make a whole!

* * * * * * *

Leaving both the eastern and the western world and their coins, there is a single piece, of small commercial value, which is yet a light-house in mid-ocean." This is the one cent of the Sandwich Islands, the only venture of that kind made by the enterprising little kingdom. The inscription is " Kamehameha III., one hundredth, Hawaii." The name of the king being interpreted signifies "the solitary one," which is singularly well adapted to the coin.

Colonial Coins.

In 1684, the charter of the Massachusetts Bay Company was revoked, and the governor recalled ; one of the alleged grievances by the crown was a colonial law concerning the Mint. The currency used by the colonies was chiefly from England, Spain, and Portugal, but the supply was limited from these sources, and the mother-country was jealous of any infringement of her prerogative of coinage. There are various specimens of the "pine-tree" money of Massachusetts in the Cabinet. Some doubt has arisen as to the species of tree intended, but it is generally accepted as the emblematic pine. This is claimed to be about the second colonial issue, a kind of semi-official coin. The first was from the Bermudas.* It is a shilling piece, stamped by one John Hall, silversmith, of the city of Boston, 1652, who made a very good speculation of the privilege. There has lately been added to the Cabinet a sixpence of this rare money. The work on this species of coins is so exceedingly simple as to present little save a planchet. On the obverse, a double ring around a pine-tree; legend, "Massachusetts in ;" and on the reverse, a double ring also, containing the legend, "New England An Dom.†"

Charles II., it appears, was easily deceived in regard to the significance of the "pine-tree shilling." Sir Thomas Temple, a friend of the colonies, adroitly presented one of these obnoxious coins to the irate monarch, explaining that the tree

---

* This issue being made at Sommer Islands, gave the name of "Sommer money."

† The old story of the weighing of John Hall's daughter on her marriage-day is recalled in seeing those coins. Her dowry was her weight in "pine-tree" shillings ; and the suggestion is allowable that these specimens formed a part of the portion of the blushing bride two centuries ago.

was the "royal oak" which had saved his majesty's life. Whereupon the king, laughing, denominated his trans-Atlantic subjects "honest dogs," and allowed the coinage to proceed.

During the reign of George I. a new species of coin was issued from the English Mint, denomination half penny, and it is asserted upon good authority that this was the only issue ever authorized by the home government for general circulation in the colonies. It was a coin of mixed metal, resembling brass. The head of the king was on the obverse; inscription, "Georgius Rex." The reverse, a large double rose under a crown; legend, "Rosa Americana." Upon a scroll, "Utile Dulci.*"

"Peltry," we learn, was one of the principal articles of currency, and was known as "pelt," or Massachusetts currency, and was extensively used in trading between Indians and whites, sometimes called "Beaver Money," "Corne, Wheate, Barley, and Rye;" and a still more quaint currency was established, as will be found in an old Massachusetts court order, as follows : " *It is likewise ordered that muskett balletts of a full boare **shall** passe current for a farthing **a peece**, provided that noe man **be compelled** to **take** above 12d. att a tyme of them*"

In Maryland, not only cattle, tobacco, and other produce was accepted as currency, but powder and shot were also included. Lord Baltimore, in 1660, sent over to Maryland the "Baltimore" shilling. In the colonial case there is a series of these exceedingly rare coins. They were a shilling, sixpence, groats, and are all of the same design, differing only in denomination. They were coined in London, and compare favorably with any minting of that age. The bust of Lord Baltimore on the obverse is very well cut; his name "Cecil," is the legend. On the reverse, the coat of arms of Cecil, Lord Baltimore, is given; this device has been re-adopted by the State of Maryland. The substitution of any legal tender seems to be fraught with danger, and at best is jealously scanned by the people; and there was trouble to put this coin into circulation. The people, though demanding coin, did not yield their old currency of "*wheat, corn, tobacco, powder, and shot*," without a demonstration. The Carolinas, Virginia, and New Hampshire all followed Maryland in the introduction of a colonial coinage.

In the interval of the Revolution, known as the Confederacy, the growth of the spirit of independence in the people

---

* This is the coin which caused such excitement and so much feeling in Ireland, and which Dean Swift attacked from the pulpit.

is plainly written on their coins, especially upon their tokens or individual coins. We notice one inscription attributed to Franklin, "*Mind your business;*" and others, such as "*Good copper,*" "*Cut your way through,*" and like characteristic expressions. The "New York Doubloon" was coined in 1787, value sixteen dollars. This coin is highly esteemed by reason of its rarity, and its market value to-day is about five hundred dollars, as only three or four are known to be in existence.

The Washington cent of 1791 (so-called) was not a coin of the United States, but was struck at a private mint in Birmingham, England, (Boulton's), partly, no doubt, to bespeak the "job," and partly to *please Americans* generally.

It has been said that Washington objected to putting his head on the coins, and it may be true; but it was also objected that no man's head should appear on the coin of a republic, which, whether good doctrine or not, is still the prevailing idea. The "cent of 1791" is of two types, one very rare and costly, with a small eagle. The other, with a large eagle, is more common, and perhaps sells for about five dollars at a public coin sale.

UNITED STATES COINS.

The first copper coins made by the United States Mint were one cent and one-half cent issues, of which there were four designs: 1st, the "chain cent;" 2d, the "wreath cent;" 3d, the "flowing hair;" and 4th, the "liberty cap," which was used for a number of years. The "chain" device was not acceptable to the sensitive American mind, and of consequence the accidental breaking of the die was not a subject of regret, but "quite the contrary." The pattern sections of United States coins are very beautiful and varied, especially those in gold.

THE TRADE DOLLAR.

This coin bears on the obverse a female figure seated on bales of merchandise, holding in her left hand a scroll on which is the word "liberty." At her back is a sheaf of wheat; this and the bales of goods indicate the commercial character of the coin. Her right hand, extended, offers the olive branch. On a scroll beneath the figure are the words "In God we trust," and the date below, "1873." The reverse has a circling inscription, "United States of America, Trade Dollar." In the centre is an eagle, in his claws three arrows and a sprig of olive. On a label above are the words "E Pluribus Unum." Below, "420 grains fine," very beautiful in design.

History of the Trade Dollar.

.The coinage of the Trade Dollar was authorized by act of February 12, 1873, and was not intended for circulation in the United States, but for export to China.

It was designed to compete with the Spanish and Mexican dollar. That empire, having no mint for the coinage of gold or silver, depended upon foreign coin for its domestic circulation, and until the institution of the Trade Dollar the principal shipments of coin to China were in the form of Mexican dollars.

The Trade Dollar was made a trifle more valuable than the American and Mexican dollar, thus not only affording a market for the surplus silver of the mines of the Pacific Coast, but furnishing merchants and importers from China with silver in a convenient form for payment for commodities, instead of their being obliged to purchase Mexican dollars for that purpose.

When its coinage was authorized it was inadvertently made a legal tender to amount of five dollars, but this was repealed by section 2, Act of July 22, 1876.

Brief History of the Standard Silver Dollar.

Authorized to be coined, Act of April 2, 1792. Weight, 416 grains, standard silver; fineness, 892.4; equivalent to 371¼ grains of fine silver, with 44¾ grains alloy of pure copper.

Weight changed, Act of January 18, 1837, to 412½ grains, and fineness changed to 900, preserving the same amount of pure silver = 371¼ grains, with $\frac{1}{10}$ alloy.

Coinage discontinued, Act of February 12, 1873.

Total amount coined, from 1792 to 1873, $8,045,838.

Coinage revived, two million dollars per month required to be coined, and issue made legal tender for all debts, public and private, Act of February 28, 1878.

Total amount coined, February 28, 1878, to November 1, 1884, $184,730,829.

Pacific Coast.

The semi-official coins of the Pacific coast present quite a glittering array of monetary enterprise, and signify the great wealth and daring spirit of that part of the world. The fifty-dollar octagon gold piece, issued in 1851, is a very beautiful coin. "Gold slugs" are novelties; are oblong gold pieces, and are valued at sixteen dollars. The Utah coins also attract attention. They are of gold, fine. The device is an "all-seeing eye" and two clasped hands; reverse, "a bee-hive," with inscription, "Holiness to the Lord." Some have for legend, "G. S. L. C. P. G.," which the initiated receive as "Great Salt Lake City, Pure Gold."

The series of the United States coins is complete, and can be readily examined. The changes have been very gradual. The motto, "In God we trust," was introduced in 1866.

There is one specimen which illustrates how a coin may become famous without the least premonition, and also is a witness of the positive law which protects and governs coinage. A law passed Congress in 1849 ordering twenty-dollar gold pieces to be issued. One piece was struck. Something intervened to delay the work, and the year closed; then, of course, the dies had to be destroyed, as no more could be lawfully issued of 1849. The coin just beside this, marked 1850, of same value, is not worth the collector's consideration, while "1849" cannot to be purchased. It is marked "unique," and is really the only one in gold. One specimen exists in brass.

COINS OF THE SOUTHERN CONFEDERACY.

It has been said and repeated as a historical fact that the Southern Confederacy had no metallic currency. After a lapse of eighteen years the following official document from the Confederate archives explains itself, and substantiates the fact that silver to a limited extent was coined at the New Orleans Mint by order of the Confederate Government, in the early days of the rebellion, and only suspended operations on account of the difficulty in obtaining bullion for coinage.

WAR DEPARTMENT,
ADJUTANT GENERAL'S OFFICE,
WASHINGTON, *March* 27, 1879.

DR. B. F. TAYLOR,
New Orleans, La.

DEAR SIR:—The enclosed circular will explain to you the nature of the duties upon which I am now engaged; I would like to have from you, from file with confederate archives, a letter stating when you were appointed Chief Coiner of the Confederate States Mint, instructions received copies of the originals of any official papers, sketches, descriptions, etc.' of all the coins made, etc. This will make a valuable addition to Confederate history, and I know no one but you can give it.

Very truly yours,
MARCUS J. WRIGHT.

NEW ORLEANS, LA., *April* 7, 1879.

To HON. MARCUS J. WRIGHT.

DEAR SIR:—Your favor requesting a statement of the history of the New Orleans Mint, in reference to the coinage under the Confederate

Government, is received. That institution was turned over by the **State** of Louisiana, the last of February, 1861, to the Confederate States of America, the old officers being retained and confirmed by the government, viz.: Wm. A. Elmore, Superintendent; A. J. Guyrot, Treasurer; M. F. Bonzano, M. D., Melter and Refiner; and Howard Millspaugh, Assayer. In the month of April, orders were issued by Mr. Memminger, Secretary of the Treasury, to the effect that designs for half-dollars should be submitted to him for approval. Among several sent, the one approved bore on the obverse of the coin a representation of the Goddess of Liberty, surrounded by thirteen stars, denoting the thirteen States from whence the Confederacy sprung, and on the lower rim the figures, 1861. On the reverse there is a shield with seven stars, representing the seceding States; above the shield is a liberty-cap, and entwined around it stalks of sugar cane and cotton, "Confederate States of America." The dies were engraved by **A. H. M. Peterson**, Engraver and Die Sinker, who is now living in Commercial Place. They were prepared for the coining press by Conrad Schmidt, foreman of the coining room (who is still living), from which *four pieces only* were struck. About this period an order came from the secretary suspending operations on account of the difficulty of obtaining bullion, and the Mint was closed April 30, 1861.

Of the four pieces mentioned, one was sent to the Government, one presented to Prof. Biddle, of the University of Louisiana, one sent to Dr. E. Ames of New Orleans, the remaining one being retained by myself. Upon diligent inquiry I am unable to find but one piece besides my own, that being in the possession of a Confederate officer of this city, who transmitted it to his son as a souvenir of his father's in the Confederate cause.

So soon as copies are made I will take pleasure in sending you a specimen for the archives you represent.

Very respectfully, your obedient servant,

B. F. TAYLOR, M. D.
Formerly Chief Coiner C. S. A.

The most notable and valuable silver coin is the dollar of 1804. It is said that the scarcity of this dollar was owing to the sinking of a China-bound vessel having on board almost the entire mintage of the 1804 dollars in lieu of the Spanish milled dollars. It is believed that there are not more than seven, possibly eight, genuine 1804 dollars extant. The rarity of the piece and the almost fabulous prices offered for it are patent facts.

SKETCH OF THE 1804 DOLLAR.*

This coin among collectors is known as the "king of American rarities." But seven or eight pieces are known to exist. The 1804 dollars are of two classes, to wit: first, originals, which are from but one obverse and one reverse die,—draped bust of Liberty facing right; the head bound with a fillet: hair flowing; 6 stars before and 7 behind the bust above LIBERTY, upper right hand star almost touching letter y; reverse heraldic eagle bearing on his breast a broad shield, in his beak a scroll, inscribed E PLURIBUS UNUM; 12 arrows in right talon, a branch of olive in left; above, an arc of clouds from wing to

* From Chapman's Collection Catalogue, May 14-15, pp. 24-25.

wing of eagle; in field beneath 13 stars; UNITED STATES
OF AMERICA; edge lettered ONE HUNDRED CENTS,
ONE DOLLAR OR UNIT, which are lightly struck in some
parts. The first specimen in the Mint Cabinet weighs 415.2
grs.; second, Mr. M. A. Stickney procured from the Mint in
1843 in exchange for other coins; third, W. S. Appleton
bought, at an advance of $750, in 1868, from E. Cogan, who
purchased it from W A. Lilliendahl, who bought it at a sale
of collection of J. J. Mickley, 1867, for $750; fourth, L. G.
Parmelee bought, at sale of E. H. Sandford's collection, 1874,
for $700, who obtained it in 1868 from an aged lady, who got
it at the Mint many years before; fifth, W. B. Wetmore
bought of Mr. Parmelee, 1868, for $600, from sale of H. S.
Adams' collection, 1876, at $500, from sale of M. J. Cohen's
collection, 1875, at $325 (in fair condition); sixth, present
owner unknown to us, formerly in possession of collection of
Mr. Robert C. Davis, of Philadelphia, and recently sold for
$1200; seventh, S. H. and H. Chapman purchased October,
1884, at a sale in Berlin, and resold to a Mr. Scott, a dealer in
coins, for $1000 at their Philadelphia sale, in May, 1885.

Restrikes. There were struck at the Mint in 1858 restrikes
with plain edges, of which three were recovered after diligent
search; two of these were destroyed in the Mint, and the other
placed in the Cabinet, where it remains. The difference between these and the originals are as follows: obverse, the
original die was re-cut in the word LIBERTY, the stars and date,
which made them larger and deeper, especially noticeable in
the stars, which are broadened; also in the date, it making
the outline sharp and square, whereas in the originals they are
somewhat rounded; reverse, not having the original die, they
used another, which differs in many respects, most easily noticeable in that the A touches the eagle's claw, the OF much
nearer of the end of eagle's wing than S in States (in the
original it is equally spaced); edge, plain; weight, 381.5
grains. One specimen is in the Mint and another in England,
—struck between 1860 and 1869, as in the latter year all dies
remaining were destroyed, same as the above, but endeavors
were made to letter the edges in the absence of a complete
collar by using pieces of collars which did not contain all the
letters, but repeated some of them several times. There was
one of these pieces sold in the Berg collection in 1883 for
$740, and showed all the peculiarities mentioned, and its
weight was said to be inaccurate. The dies were destroyed in
the winter of 1868-69. No counterfeit dies of the 1804 dollar were ever made. After the close of each year all dies are
now destroyed.

DOUBLE EAGLE.

Among the rare coins in the Cabinet at the Mint is a **Double Eagle**. The dies for this piece were made in 1849, and only one was struck. "UNIQUE" and beyond price. There is also a Quarter Eagle of **1842**, and the only one known extant at the Mint.

SELECTIONS.

Having referred many times to this case, it may be as well to append the entire list of its contents, as they, almost without exception, are rare, spanning the world from remotest antiquity to the present day, beginning with the gold Daric of Darius, and ending with the twenty-mark piece of Kaiser William.

GREECE.

1. Four drachma, Athens, B. C. 500; 2. Oboloi of Athens; 3. One-half obolos, 1½ of a cent; 4. Daric, Darius, of Persia, B. C. 520, value, five dollars and fifty cents; 5. Silver Daric; 6. Brass Ob. Berenice, B. C. 284; 7. Ptolemy and Berenice, copy; 8. Manch of Ptolemy Philadelphus, B. C. 284, value, $17.70; 9. Drachma, Cyrene, B. C. 322; 10. Coin of Syracuse, copy, about B. C. 300; 11. Silver coin, Bactria, B. C. 126; 12. Brass of Bactria, B. C. 180; 13. Cleopatra, B. C. 30; 13a. Denarius of Cleopatra and Mark Antony; 14. Alexander the Great, B. C. 36; 15. Philip, B. C. 323; 16. Stater of Seleucus; 17. Alexander Balas, B. C. 150; 18. Antiochus VI; 19. Philip, King of Syria, B. C. 93.

ROME.

20. Roman aes, B. C. 500; 21. Denarius of Augustus, B. C. 31; 22. Tiberius, A. D. 14; 23. Simon, Bar Cochab, false Christ, A. D. 133; 24. Vespasian, A. D. 49; 25. Gold bezants, A. D. 610; 26. Justinian, A. D. 527; 26a. Kingdom of Cyprus and Jerusalem, Peter 1, 1361 to 1372, testoon, Kingdom of Jerusalem; 26b. Amaury II., 1194 to 1205.

ENGLISH.

27. **Gold** of Britain; 28. Carausius, Roman Emperor of Britain, A. D. 287; 29. Penny of **Ethelbert**, King of Kent, 858

A. D.; 30. Harold the Dane, A. D. 1036; 31. William the Conqueror, 1066, A. D.; 32. Edward the Confessor, A. D. 1041; 33. Robert the Bruce, A. D. 1306; 34. Elizabeth, Double Ryal, A. D. 1558; 35. James I, 1603, Ryal (30 shillings) and sovereign; 36. Charles I, sovereign; 37. Siege pound of Charles I, 1642; 37a. Gold sovereign of Oliver Cromwell; 38. Crown, and half crown and shilling, Oliver Cromwell, 1658; 38a. Farthing, Queen Anne; 39. George IV; 40. Coins of Australia.

FRANCE.

41. Deniers of Charlemagne 806; 42. Medalet, Marie Antoinette; 43. Five francs, Napoleon I; 44. Gold, Napoleon I, 1851; 45. Five francs, Paris Commune.

GERMANY.

46. Bracteats; 47. German Crown, Ob. St. Stephen; 48. Ducat, Ob. Luther and Melancthon, 1730; 49. Crown, Maximilian, A. D. 1615; 50. Ducat, Nuremburg; 51. Ducat Hamburg; 52. Monument, Bavaria; 53. King's family, Bavaria; 54. Coins of Prussia; 55. Silver piece, Frederick William and Augusta.

SPAIN.

56. Ferdinand and Isabella; 57. Charles II., Spain; 58. Alphonso, Spain.

ITALY.

59. Silver of Venice under the Doges, twelfth century; 60. Ducat of Venice; 61. Copper of San Marino; 62. Silver piece of Lombardy; 63. Gold twenty lira piece; 64. Swiss crown, ob. St. Vincent; 65. African shell money; 66. African ring money.

ORIENTAL.

67. Siamese coins; 68. Chinese tael; 69. Widow's mite; 70. Jewish shekel; 70a. Herod the Great, 37 B. C.; 70b. Herod Archelaus, 4 B. C.; 71. Glass coin, Egypt; 72. Gold of Alnaser, A. D. 1222; 73. Dirhem of Mahomet V., A. D. 854; 74. Dirhem of Walid, Caliph of Damascus, A. D. 713;

75. Haroun Alraschid, Koran text, 806; **76.** Fire Worshippers, A. D. 300; 77. **Gold** of Japan, 1634; 78. Gravel stone of Burmah; **79.** Late **coin** of Turkey; **80.** Mexican dollar used in China; 81. Coin **of** Cochin China.

The most notable coin in this case, and perhaps the most celebrated coin in the world, is the "Widow's Mite." Its name bespeaks its commercial insignificance. Yet visitors every day, upon entering the Cabinet of the Mint, ask first to see the "Widow's Mite."

The following letter from Wm. E. Du Bois, will be found of interest to the reader.

THE WIDOW'S MITE.

SIR: **The** curators of the mint cabinet do not consent to the intimation in a statement recently made that their widow's mite is not the real coin.

The expression of a doubt as to any received fact is thought to be a sign of superior insight. Hence we have so much "destructive criticism," a good deal of it being fatal to the critic himself.

The widow's mite in our showcase of specialties, always attracting much attention, is precisely what the Scriptures speak of—a *lepton*, the smallest of Greek and Syriac coins. The name comes from *leptos*, very small. The word "mite" is English, and was formerly a weight representing the twentieth part of a grain, but has long fallen into disuse. It was employed in the translation of the New Testament **to** represent the word *lepton*, simply because it was so **very** small.

It is pretty certain **that there was no Jewish or Hebrew** coin so small **as the** *lepton;* that people **depended very much upon outside** coins for their circulation. Even their **money terms had changed to those** of the Syrian-Greek Empire **and** of Rome, **as we see from all the** instances in the New Testament. What few **copper or bronze pieces** they had, struck by local princes for a limited time, and **now very rare,** were large enough to bear a **show** of devices and inscriptions, for **which** the *lepton* was too minute. The **one** in our cabinet has a diameter **of** only three-tenths of an inch, and weighs but ten grains. On **one** side nothing is discernible, on the other a **mint** monogram, **such as** were common in that era, occupies the space. It **is** much like the letter x, with **a** line crossing it near the top. Whether it **is** Samaritan, or Syriac, **or** Greek, we cannot be sure, nor is it of any consequence. It is enough **to** show that it **is** a coin, and belongs to the age shortly before and after the advent of **Christ,** and its size proves it to be a *lepton.*

It is an interesting and confirmatory fact, that this piece **was** found among the rubbish of the Temple grounds, by Dr. Barclay, long resident in Jerusalem, and author of "The City of the Great King." By him it was presented to the mint cabinet. The objector may soberly doubt whether this was one of the identical mites offered by the widow; for the rest of his doubts they are of no value.

We are often asked how much this famous offering amounted **to**? There **is** some obscurity and confusion about their coin-tables, and, therefore, some variety in the estimation. We may say, however, that the current value of the *lepton,* **or** mite, was about one-fifth of a cent in our money; being eighty to **the drachma** or denarius, which was 16 or 15 cents.

But **as the** purchasing or paying power of a drachma was probably **as great in that** day and country as a dollar is in ours, we may say that the **value of a** lepton, judged by our ideas, was about one cent. As the treasurer **would not** take a less gift than two *lepta,* it follows that the poor but **very liberal** woman contributed fully two cents, which is more than some persons—neither poor **nor** in widowhood—throw into **the** church basket.

It is worth while to add that a visitor at the mint saw a similar piece in Jerusalem, and tried to obtain one, but on account of its rarity did not succeed.

W. E. D.

DONATIONS OF OLD COINS.

Extract from the American Journal of Numismatics, April, 1884.

Under the head of *donations*, we have from Quartermaster General Meigs, a half-dollar and pistareen of Carolus and Johana of Spain. These pieces were presented to General Meigs at Corpus Christi, Texas, in 1870. The special interest attached to them, is their having been found on the beach of Padre Island, off the southerly coast of Texas. The supposition is that they were washed up from a sunken treasure ship wrecked on the coast, while carrying funds to the Army of Cortez, who entered the City of Mexico in 1519. Their good condition may warrant our accepting this briny romance *Cum grano salis.* Antiquarian stories must expect to stand the test of the chemist, as well as of the historian. This reminds me, however, of some specimens of the Mint Cabinet, from the wreck of the San Pedro, some account of which may not be uninteresting here.* "Early in 1815, a naval armament was fitted out in Spain, by Ferdinand VII., for the purpose of reducing the Rebellious Colonies in South America. The military force of this expedition amounted to ten thousand men, of whom two thousand were on board the flag ship "San Pedro." The vessel was also freighted to a large amount with gunpowder, cannon balls and specie."

The account then goes on to state that the fleet touched at the Island of Marguerita near the coast of Venezuela. After leaving the island, the vessel took fire, burnt four hours until the magazine caught and exploded, and the wreck went down with four hundred men. The right of working the wreck, was granted about thirty years after, to a Baltimore Company, known as the "San Pedro Company." Divers were set to work, and the wreck found in sixty feet of water on a hard bed of coral. Over this there was a deposit of mud, and again over this a layer of coral, which had to be pierced to arrive at the treasure.

The Spanish dollars recovered were sent to Philadelphia, and (up to September, 1848) about seventy-five thousand dollars had been recovered and re-coined. The dollars were much corroded and encrusted, the coating having first to be removed, to bring the pieces into fit condition for minting; the loss from corrosion was considerable; one dollar with the impression still visible, being reduced to thirty-four cents in value. In the light of these and other facts, it is difficult to conceive how the pieces found in Texas, could have come so clean from their reputed berth, of over three hundred years, but they are worth keeping for all that, and General Meigs has the thanks of the Republic for them.

---

* From the proceedings of the American Philosophical Society, reported by Wm. E. Du Bois, in October, 1845.

PLATE I.

NOVA CONSTELLATIO
"QUINT." 1783.

NOVA CONSTELLATIO
"MARK." 1783.

NOVA CONSTELLATIO,
IMMUNE COLUMBIA.

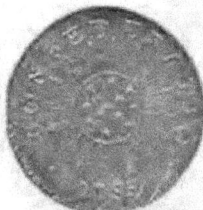

SOMMER ISLAND
SHILLING. "HOGGIE."

NEW JERSEY
IMMUNIS.

CONFEDERATIO
INIMICA, ETC.

See description.

PLATE II.

CONNECTICUT CENT,
1787.

NEW ENGLAND
ELEPHANT TOKEN.
VERY RARE. 1694.

GOOD SAMARITAN
SHILLING, MASS.

MASSACHUSETTS
HALF CENT. 1787.

MASSACHUSETTS
CENT.

NEW YORK.

See description.

COLONIAL COINAGES.

Nova Constellatio.

Obverse: An eye, the center of a glory, thirteen points cross, equidistant; a circle of as many stars. Legend: "NOVA CONSTELLATIO."

Reverse: "U. S. 500" inscribed in two lines, a wreath surrounding. Legend: "LIBERTAS JUSTITIA 1783." Border, beaded; edge, leaf work. Known as the "Quint."

No. 2.—Obverse: An eye, around which a narrow, plain, circular field; outside a glory, thirteen points cross, equidistant; a circle of as many stars. Legend: "NOVA CONSTELLATIO."

Reverse: "U. S. 1000" inscribed in two lines, a wreath surrounding. Legend: "LIBERTAS JUSTITIA 1783." Border, a wreath of leaves; edge, leaf work; silver; size, 21; weight, 270 grains. Known as the "Mark."

THE IMMUNE COLUMBIA.

Obverse: An eye, on a small, plain, circular field; from the outside of the field radiates a glory of thirteen blunt points, crossing, equidistant, the spaces between as many stars in a circular constellation. Legend: "NOVA CONSTELLATIO." Border, serrated.

Reverse: The Goddess of Liberty, seated upon a paneled cubic pedestal, facing right; her left hand is well extended and balances the scales of justice. A short liberty staff, crowned with a cap and bearing a flag, rests against her right shoulder, and is supported by the right hand. Legend: "IMMUNE COLUMBIA." Exergue: the date 1785. Border, serrated; edge, plain or milled; size, 17; weight, gold, 128.8 grains; silver, 92 grains; copper 148 grains.

BERMUDA SHILLING—("HOGGE-PENNY").

Obverse: Device—A hog, standing, facing left, above which are displayed the Roman numerals "XII.," the whole surrounded by a beaded circle. Legend: "SOMMER ISLANDS" around which is a beaded circle like that enclosing the device.

Reverse: Device—A full-rigged ship under sail to the left, a flag flying from each of her four masts—enclosed in a beaded circle, the beads larger than on the obverse. Copper; size, 19; weight, 177 grains.

New Jersey Immunis.

Obverse: Goddess of Liberty, seated upon a globe, facing right; in her extended left hand the scales of justice; right hand staff of liberty bearing a flag and crowned with a cap. Legend: "IMMUNIS COLUMBIA." Exergue: "1786." Border, serrated; edge, plain; size, 18; weight, 160 grains.

Reverse: A shield argent, six pales gules, a chief azure. Legend: "E PLURIBUS UNUM." Border, serrated; edge, plain; size, 18; weight, 160 grains.

Confederatio and Inimica Tyrannis.

Obverse: A circular central field, size 6, covered with a cluster of thirteen small stars; around this device a glory of fine rays, presenting a corrugated outline of sixteen points. Legend: "CONFEDERATIO 1785." Border, serrated.

Reverse: An Indian, standing beside an altar or pedestal, his right foot upon a crown, an arrow in his right hand, a bow in his left; at his back a quiver full of arrows. Legend: "INIMICA TYRANNIS AMERICA." Border, serrated; edge, plain; size, 18; weight, 112 grains.

Connecticut Cent, 1788.

Obverse: Identical with one of 1787.

Reverse: The same as one of the coins of Vermont. Another Connecticut coin of this year, has the same reverse as the "GEORGIVS III REX" issue of Machin & Co., from the mint established by them in the State of New York.

'Note.—The obverse and reverse dies of the Connecticut cents are too numerous to mention, there being no less than one hundred and sixty-four of the first, and eighty-four of the latter.

New England Token.

Obverse: Same as that of the common type of the Carolina Token of 1694, and from the same die as that and the "London Halfpenny."

Reverse: An inscription, in five lines, occupying the whole field, "GOD PRESERVE NEW ENGLAND 1694." Borders, milled; edge, plain; copper; size, 18½; weight, 133 and 236 grains.

Good Samaritan Shillings.

The same general type and variety as the Pine Tree Shilling, but bearing upon the obverse a well-executed device, illustrating the parable of the Good Samaritan; but two or

PLATE III.

LARGE PATTERN CENT.
NOT ISSUED.

BAR CENT.
VERY RARE.

FUGIO.
"MIND YOUR BUSINESS."
FIRST.

INIMICA TYRANNIS
AMERICANA.

See description.

FUGIO.
"MIND YOUR BUSINESS."
SECOND.

PLATE IV.

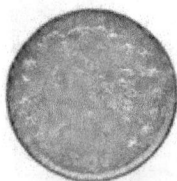

HALF CENT.
1836.

CONFEDERATE
C. S. A. HALF DOLLAR.

HALF CENT.
1840.

HALF CENT.
1845.

"JEFFERSON HEAD"
CENT.

See description.

HALF CENT.
1846.

three specimens of this coin have been known, two of which are in existence and of unique varieties; they are supposed to have been pattern pieces, struck at the origin of the Mint of Massachusetts Colony.

MASSACHUSETTS HALF CENT, 1787.

Obverse: Same general description as the Cent of 1787.

Reverse: Same in general as the Cent of 1787, except that the shield upon some specimens, bears only "HALF CENT." Borders, milled; edge plain; size, 15 to 15½; weight, 75 to 83 grains.

The "Cent," 1788. Twelve Types. Thirteen Varieties.

MASSACHUSETTS CENT, 1788.

Obverse: A clothed Indian, standing, facing left, in his right hand a bow, in his left an arrow. Legend: "COMMON-WEALTH."

Reverse: A spread eagle, a broad shield upon his breast, six pales gules (upright), a chief azure (open or plain). Upon the chief, or upper part of the shield, the word "CENT," in bold Roman lettering. In exergue, beneath a heavy horizontal bar, the date 1787. Borders, milled; edge, plain; size, 16½ to 19; weight, 146 to 165 grains.

FUGIOS OR FRANKLIN CENTS.

The Fugios or Franklin Cents are the earliest coins issued by authority of the United States. They being all dated 1787, and made in conformity with resolution of Congress, dated July 6, 1787:

"*Resolved*, That the Board of Treasury direct the contractor for the copper coinage to stamp on one side of each piece the following devices, viz.: Thirteen circles linked together, a small circle in the middle, with the words 'UNITED STATES' round it, and in the centre the words, 'WE ARE ONE'; on the other side of the same piece the following device, viz.: a dial with the hours expressed on the face of it; a meridian sun above, on one side of which is to be the word 'FUGIO,' and on the other the year in figures '1787'; below the dial the words 'MIND YOUR BUSINESS.'"

THE BAR CENT, OR U S A COPPER.

This coin, presumed to have belonged to the same issue as the Nova Constellatio Coppers, was probably made in Birmingham, England, by Thomas Wyon, for circulation in America. The "U S A" Copper was first passed as money in the City of New York, in November, 1785. The device was taken from an old Continental button, to which fact and the light weight of the piece, has been attributed the disfavor shown the coinage and the limited circulation given the same.

Obverse: Large Roman "U S A" in a monogram, on a plain field.

Reverse: Thirteen horizontal bars. Border, serrated; Edge, plain; size, 15½; weight, 85 grains. Two pairs of dies.

MARYLAND PENNY.

The Maryland Penny. One Type. One Variety. Unique.
Obverse: Similar to that of the sixpence.

Reverse: A Ducal Coronet, upon which are erected two masts, each bearing a flying pennant. Legend: "DENARIVM TERRE-MARIÆ." Copper; size, 13.

The only specimen of this piece extant was imported into America from England, at a cost of £75, and was sold for $370 with the collection of J. J. Mickley, Esq., of Philadelphia.

ROSA AMERICANA HALF-PENNY, 1722.

Obverse: Laureated head of King George I, facing right. Legend: "GEORGIUS DEI GRATIA REX."

Reverse: A full double rose; from this project five barbed points. Legend: "ROSA AMERICANA UTILE DULCI 1722" which encircles the piece. Border, beaded; edge, plain; "Bath Metal;" size, 16 to 18; weight, 139 grains.

Devices: Same as those of the Penny of this coinage. Legends: Same import as those upon the Penny, but varied by abbreviations and in punctuation. Border, beaded; edge, plain; "Bath Metal;" size, 13 to 14; weight, 75 grains.

LIBER NATUS LIBERTATEM DEFENDO—*First.*

Reverse: Arms of the State of New York. Upon an oval shield at the center is shown the sun rising from behind a range of hills, the sea in the foreground; left of the shield, Justice, with sword and scales; right, Liberty, with staff and cap. Upon a hemisphere, above the shield, stands an eagle, wings outspread, facing right. Exergue: 1787; beneath this, next the border, "EXCELSIOR." Border, serrated; edge, plain; size, 17; weight, 157 grains.

PLATE V.

MARYLAND
PENNY.

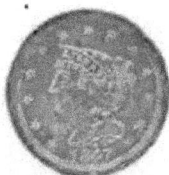

HALF CENT.
1847.

ROSA AMERICANA
HALF PENNY.
1722.

LIBER NATUS
LIBERNATUM DEFENDO.
FIRST.

GRANBY OR HIGLEY
TOKEN. 1737.

See description.

LIBER NATUS
LIBERNATUM DEFENDO.
SECOND.

PLATE VI.

WASHINGTON CENT.
1783.

WASHINGTON LIVERPOOL
HALF PENNY.
1793.

"NAKED BUST,"
WASHINGTON CENT.
1792.

NON DEPENDENS
STATUS.

HALF CENT.
1842.

PATTERN CENT.
1792.

See description.

Liber Natus Libertatem Defendo.—*Second.*

Obverse: An Indian, standing, crowned with feathers, and facing left; in his right hand he wields a tomahawk, his left supports a bow, the end of which rests on the ground near his feet; over his right shoulder appears the top of a quiver of arrows, which is borne upon his back. Legend: "LIBER NATUS LIBERATEM DEFENDO."

Reverse: A hemisphere of the globe, marked by longitudinal and meridianal lines; upon this stands a large heavy-bodied eagle, wings spread, somewhat drooping, beak toward the right. Legend: "NEO-EBORACUS 1787 EXCELSIOR." Border, serrated; edge, plain; size, 17; weight, 153 grains.

Granby or Higley Token, 1737.

Obverse: A deer, standing, facing left, occupying the whole field. Legend: "VALVE ME AS YOU PLEASE." Exergue: The Roman numerals III upon a small scroll; a little crescent is shown below.

Reverse: Three hammers, each bearing a crown upon the head. Legend: "I AM GOOD COPPER 1737."

Washington Cent, 1783.

Obverse: Large laureated bust of Washington, draped, facing left. Legend: "WASHINGTON & INDEPENDENCE 1783."

Reverse: A figure of a female, facing left, seated upon a rock; right hand holds an olive branch; left, staff of liberty, with cap. Legend: "UNITED STATES." Exergue: T. W. I. E. S. Border, beaded; edge, plain; size, 17½; weight, 120 grains. Two obverse and three reverse dies.

Washington Liverpool Half-Penny.

Obverse: Bust of Washington, in uniform, facing left, hair in a queue. Legend: "WASHINGTON PRESIDENT."

Reverse: A ship, under sail, to the right: Legend: "HALFPENNY" under the ship, waves, and in the foreground, on a panel, the date 1793. Border, milled; edge, lettered: "PAYABLE IN ANGLESEY LONDON OR LIVERPOOL." Size, 19; weight, 163 grains.

Washington Naked Bust Cent, 1792.

Obverse: A classical bust of Washington, undraped, facing right; the head is encircled by a fillet, confining the hair, which is cut short and is curly; the fillet is tied at the back of the head by a bow knot with long pendent ends. Legend: "WASHINGTON PRESIDENT 1792."

Reverse: A small eagle, displayed, wings upraised; on his breast a shield argent, six pales gules; right talon, an olive branch, fourteen leaves, six berries; left talon, thirteen arrows; about the head of the eagle are six mullets, and above is the word "CENT." Border, milled; edge, plain, or inscribed: "UNITED STATES OF AMERICA." Size, 19; weight, 198 grains. Some six or eight specimens only are known.

NON DEPENDENS STATUS.

Obverse: A full bust, facing right; flowing hair to the shoulders. Upon the drapery of the bust a small oval shield as an epaulet, emblazoned with a staff bearing a flag; across the staff, saltierwise, rests a naked sword. In each angle of this device is displayed a fleur de lis. Upon the breast of the bust is a head with spreading wings. Legend: "NON-DEPEN-DENS STATTS."

Reverse: An Indian, seated upon a globe, facing left; nude, except a cap or bandeau upon his head, and a feather tunic around the lower part of the body. In his extended right hand he holds a bunch of tobacco; the left reaches behind him and rests upon a shield, bearing the same emblems displayed upon the epaulets upon the bust on the obverse. Legend: "AMER ICA," divided by the figure of the Indian. Exergue: 1778. Border, plain; edge plain; size, 19.

Some coin dealers advertise the Non Dependens Status as "a rare copper, worth $100."

PATTERN CENT, 1792.

Obverse: A bust of Liberty, facing to right, the hair confined by a fillet. Above is inscribed the word "LIBERTY," and beneath the date "1792."

Reverse: A portion of a globe, on which stands an eagle, with raised wings. Legend: "UNITED STATES OF AMERICA." This cent has a grained edge, like the cents of 1793. Some numismatists give it the preference as the first cent.

GEORGE CLINTON COPPER, 1787.

The George Clinton Copper has the bust of Governor Clinton facing right, with legend "GEORGE CLINTON."

Reverse: The State arms of New York, and in the exergue, "1787 EXCELSIOR." This last reverse is found also combined with the Liber Natus, which has an Indian standing, facing left, with tomahawk in the right hand and bow in the left, a bundle of arrows also at his back. Legend: "LIBER NATUS LIBERTATEM DEFENDO." This latter obverse is also found combined with another reverse, as follows: An eagle stands upon a section of the globe. Legend: "NEO EMBORACUS 1787 EXCELSIOR."

PLATE VII.

GEORGE CLINTON
COPPER. 1787.

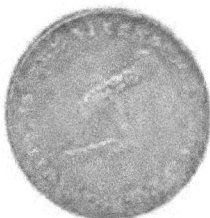

KENTUCKY TOKEN.

IMMUNIS COLUMBIA.
1787.

MASSACHUSETTS
PINE TREE SHILLING.
1652.

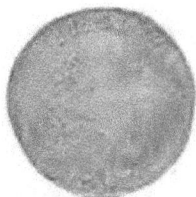

CHAIN CENT.
1793.

See description.

MYDDELTON TOKEN.

PLATE VIII.

GREEK EGYPTIAN COIN.
PTOLEMAUS SOTER.
285-300 B. C.

ROMAN COIN.
FAUSTINA, DAUGHTER
OF ANTONINUS PIUS,
WIFE OF MARCUS
AURELIUS.
DIED, 175 A. D.

MACEDONIAN SILVER
COIN.
ALEXANDER THE GREAT.
300 YEARS B. C.

SILVER SHEKEL OF
JUDEA.
SIMON MACCABEES,
143 B. C.

PERSIAN SILVER COIN.
VOLOGESES III.
148-190 A. D.

JUDEAN COPPER COIN.
SIMON MACCABEES
145 B. C

See description.

KENTUCKY TOKEN OR CENT

Has a hand holding a scroll inscribed "Our Cause is Just." Legend: "UNANIMITY IS THE STRENGTH OF SOCIETY." Reverse: A radiant pyramid, triangular in shape, of fifteen stars united by rings, each star having placed in it the initial of a State, Kentucky being at the top. Legend: "E PLURIBUS UNUM."

SHEKEL (SIMON MACCABEES).

The Shekel was originally a weight. The first form in which money was used by the Jews, and by all other nations of which we have any knowledge, was the pieces without any regular shape or any marks or devices upon them. Precious metals passed by weight. Thus it is said of the purchase made by Abraham of the cave and field of Machpelah, "And Abraham hearkened unto Ephron; and Abraham weighed to Ephron the silver, which he had named in the audience of the sons of Heth, four hundred shekels of silver, current with the merchant." Gen. xxiii. 16. .

The weight of a shekel was a little less than one-half an ounce troy. The term "current with the merchant," probably refers to the purity of the silver, which was about ninety-five per cent. fine, and the value in our money was fifty-eight cents. It first appeared as a coin in the time of the Maccabees, who lived about 140 B. C. The amount of silver in the coin is the same as was contained in the piece of silver denominated a shekel. It will be seen that on one side is the golden cup that had manna (see Exod. xvi. 33, and Heb. ix. 4), with the inscription in old Hebrew character, "SHEKEL OF ISRAEL;" on the other side appears Aaron's rod that budded with the legend in the same character, "JERUSALEM THE HOLY." This specimen is in the Mint cabinet; one of the most rare and interesting coins in the collection.

IMMUNIS COLUMBIA, 1787.

Obverse: The Goddess of Liberty, seated upon a globe, facing right; in her fully extended left hand she balances the scales of justice; the right hand supports a liberty staff, bearing a flag and crowned with a cap. Legend: "IMMUNIS COLUMBIA." Exergue: 1787.

Reverse: An eagle, displayed; right talon, an olive branch, thirteen leaves; left talon, thirteen arrows. Legend: "E PLURIBUS UNUM." Borders, serrated; edge, plain; size, 16½; weight, 135 grains.

MASSACHUSETTS PINE TREE SHILLING.

"John Hull and Robert Saunderson were equal officers in the 'gainful business' of the Mint. How much they coined in all for the colony, or the exact amount of their profits under the contract they carried out, cannot be determined." The coinage was certainly large in amount, and they, as was well understood, became men of wealth and substance. When the daughter of John Hull was married to Judge Samuel Sewall, the founder of the town of Newbury, Mass., the prosperous mint-master gave the bride a dowery of her weight in silver. At the conclusion of the wedding ceremony, a large steel-yard was brought into the room, and the blushing bride placed upon one of the platforms of the same, while into a tub upon the other side were poured the Pine Tree Shillings, until the steel-yard balanced.

CHAIN CENTS.

These have a bust with flowing hair, looking right, with the date below and word "LIBERTY" above it; on the reverse side, in the centre, is "ONE CENT," with "₁₀₀" below it, enclosed in an endless chain of fifteen links, typifying the number of States then in the Union. The legend is "UNITED STATES OF AMERICA" in all excepting one die, which reads "UNITED STATES OF AMERI," the engraver evidently not having room to complete the word.

THE MYDDLETON TOKENS.

Obverse: A figure, representing Hope, beside an anchor; she presents two children to a female, the last extending her right hand in reception of the charge; the left hand supports a liberty staff, which is crowned with a cap; in front of the figure with the staff is an olive branch and a wreath, to the rear a cornucopia. Legend: "BRITISH SETTLEMENT KENTUCKY."

Reverse: Brittania, seated disconsolate amid the down-cast emblems of her power, and facing left; her head is bowed; she holds in her right hand an inverted spear, the head of which penetrates the ground; at her right side a bundle of fasces or lictors' rods have fallen near the cap of Liberty; upon the ground, before the figure, are the scales of justice, upon which Brittania has set her left foot and the sword of justice, with broken blade; the left arm of the figure rests upon a large shield, bearing the cross of the British ensigns. Legend: "PAYABLE BY P. P. P. MYDDLETON."

PLATE IX.

HALF CENT.
1802.

WREATH CENT.
1793.

HALF CENT.
1794.

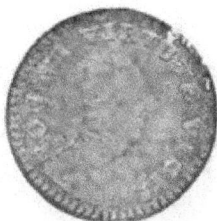

WASHINGTON MEDAL,
1789.

HALF CENT.
1847.

See description.

NEW YORK CENT.

PLATE X.

GREEK EGYPTIAN COIN.
PTOLEMY.

WIDOW'S MITE.
COPPER COIN.

ROMAN BRONZE COIN.
TRAJAN AUGUSTUS.
98–117 A. D.

ANTIOCHUS EPIPHANES.

COUNTERFEIT JUDEAN SHEKEL.
DATING ABOUT THE TIME
OF CHRIST.

See description.

MACEDONIAN COIN.
PHILIP III.
317–324 B. C.

THE SMALL PATTERN CENT.

Obverse: A head, facing right, hair unconfined, floating backward in flowing locks. Legend: "LIBERTY PARENT OF SCIENCE & INDUST." Exergue: Beneath the head the date 1792.

Reverse: A wreath, two olive branches crossed at the lower ends and tied with a ribbon; within the wreath a field bearing an inscription "ONE CENT" in two lines. Legend: "UNITED STATES OF AMERICA." Exergue: "¹⁄₁₆₀." Border, milled; edge, reeded; size, 14; weight, 65 grains. Extremely rare.

THE DOUBLE HEAD WASHINGTON

A small head on both obverse and reverse. The former has the legend, "WASHINGTON;" the latter the legend "ONE CENT." No date.

NEW YORK WASHINGTON CENT.

Bust of Washington with a wig, and with military draping, face right. Legend: "NON VI VIRTUTE VICI."

Reverse: The Goddess of Liberty, seated, with liberty pole and scales of justice. Legend: "NEO EBORACENSIS." Date, 1786.

CAROLINA ELEPHANT (TOKEN.)

A token much prized by collectors is known as the Carolina Elephant. The obverse is from a rather common English token known now as the London Elephant. The animal is standing with his head down. There is no legend.

Reverse: "GOD PRESERVE CAROLINA AND THE LORDS PRO-PRIETERS 1694."

COPPER HALF-CENT OF 1794.

In 1794 and 1795 similar device to that of 1793; but face Liberty facing to the right. Weight, 104 grains.

CENT, 1799.

The liberty cap is omitted, as is the lettering on the edge, not to reappear on the American cent. Liberty Cap Cents are very rare.

In the year 1798 a slight change was made in the obverse of the cent, giving some of the curls a different termination from those of 1796, 1797, and the early part of 1798. The latter device was continued each year, until and including 1807. The reverse remained unchanged during the same time, excepting some slight variations, probably unintentional, if not positive mistakes. For instance, in 1797 and 1802 we find some without stems to the wreaths, and in one case only

one stem. In 1801 and 1802 some have $\frac{1}{10}$ instead of the
fraction $\frac{1}{100}$. In addition to this error, a variety of the cent of
1802 has "Iinited," instead of "United." In 1796 we have
in one instance "Liherty," instead of "Liberty."

LIBERTY CENT, 1809.

In 1809 an obverse head of Liberty; forehead encircled by
a band, "LIBERTY" inscribed upon it, surrounded by thirteen
stars. Exergue: "1809."

Reverse: Wreath in a circular garland inclosing the words
"ONE CENT." No change took place during the issues of 1808
to 1814, inclusive.

HALF-CENT OF 1793.

The first half-cent was issued in 1793, having on obverse:
Bust of Liberty, facing to the left; staff surmounted by
liberty-cap over right shoulder. Legend: "LIBERTY." Exergue: "1793."

Reverse; Inscription, "HALF CENT," surrounded by a
wreath, tied with a ribbon. Weight, 132 grains.

WREATH CENT.

Obverse: Bust of Liberty, hair flowing. Legend: "LIB-
ERTY." Exergue: "1793."

Reverse: A wreath with berries, the stems of wreath tied in
a bow with a ribbon. Inscription: "ONE CENT." Legend:
"UNITED STATES OF AMERICA." Exergue: "$\frac{1}{100}$."

Third. Known as the "Liberty Cap Cent."

LIBERTY AND SECURITY WASHINGTON COIN.

Obverse: A bust of Washington, in uniform, facing right,
hair in a queue. Legend: "GEORGE WASHINGTON."

Reverse: A shield with sixteen argent and gules impaling
argent, fifteen mullets; above the shield an eagle, left talon,
an olive branch, right talon, six arrows. Legend: "LIBERTY
AND SECURITY." Exergue: "17 95," divided by the point
of the shield. Border: A plain circle, and outside of the
same, milled edge, lettered "AN ASYLUM FOR ALL NATIONS."
Size, 20½; weight, 310 grains. This piece is extremely rare.

VIRGINIA HALF-PENNY.

The well-known Virginia half-pennies seem to have been
very plentiful. A number of different dies were used. A laureated bust of George the Third is surrounded, as on the English half-penny, with his title, "GEORGIVS III. REX." The
reverse has an ornamental and crowned shield, emblazoned
quarterly: 1, England empaling Scotland; 2, France; 3, Ireland; 4, the electoral dominions. Legend: "VIRGINIA."

PLATE XI.

CENT, 1809.　　　　HALF CENT.　　　　CHAIN CENT.
　　　　　　　　　　　1793.　　　　　　　　1793.

PATTERN　　　　CENT, 1799.　　　　SMALL
"TWO CENT" PIECE.　　　　　　　　PATTERN CENT.　1792

　　　　　　　　See description.

PLATE XII.

DOUBLE HEAD
WASHINGTON.

LIBERTY AND SECURITY
WASHINGTON MEDAL. 1795.

GRANBY OR HIGLEY
COPPER TOKEN.

N. Y. COLONIAL CENT.
1787.

CAROLINA
ELEPHANT TOKEN. 1694.
See description.

VIRGINIA
HALF CENT.

PLATE XIII.

MEDAL OF 1776, COMMEMORATIVE OF THE NATION'S INDEPENDENCE.

"KITTANNING MEDAL," ONE OF THE EARLIEST MEDALS EXECUTED
IN AMERICA.

PLATE XIV.

1795 SILVER DOLLAR.   OBVERSE AND REVERSE.

1798 SILVER DOLLAR.   OBVERSE AND REVERSE.

PLATE XV.

ROSA AMERICANA.

MASSACHUSETTS
HALF CENT.

RHODE ISLAND MEDAL.

PITT MEDAL.

IMMUNIS COLUMBIA.

See description.

NEW YORK TOKEN.

PLATE XVI.

PATTERN HALF DOLLAR.
1859.

PATTERN CENT.
1854.

LIBERTY CENT.
1793,

LIBERTY HALF CENT.
1795.

PATTERN CENT,
COPPER AND SILVER.
1850.

PATTERN CENT.
1855.

PLATE XVII.

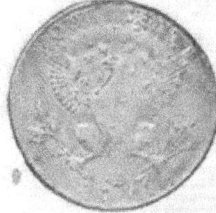

PLATE XVIII.

TRIBUTE MONEY.   CONSTANTINE THE GREAT.

COUNTERFEIT SHEKEL,
OF EUROPEAN MANUFACTURE.

JEWISH.
LEPTON, B. C.

JEWISH.
LEPTON, A. D.

SYRIAN.

GRECIAN.

MAXIMUS PHILLIPUS.

PLATE XIX.

DOUBLE EAGLE, 1849. "Unique," beyond price.

GOLD DOLLAR, 1849.

DOUBLE EAGLE. 1885.

HALF EAGLE, 1849.

TEN DOLLAR EAGLE, 1795.

HALF EAGLE, 1885.

EAGLE, 1849.

HALF EAGLE, 1795.

EAGLE, 1885.

THREE DOLLARS. Gold Piece, 1885.

QUARTER EAGLE, 1847.

QUARTER EAGLE, 1885.

GOLD DOLLAR, 1885.

PLATE XX.

RHODES.   ANTIOCHUS VII.   SYBARIS.

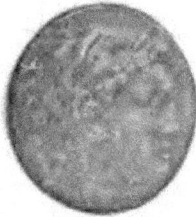

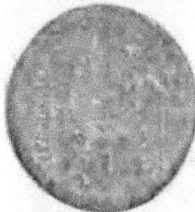

GREEK COIN.
ALEXANDER THE GREAT.
300 B. C.   ATHENS.   HEROCLEA.

PLATE XXI.

1804 DOLLAR,
"The King among Rarities."

PATTERN DOLLAR,
None issued.

PATTERN DOLLAR OF 1871,
Rejected.

PATTERN PIECE KNOWN AS THE
BARBER DOLLAR. Rejected.

PLATE XXII.

SILVER DOLLAR, 1840.

STANDARD DOLLAR, 1885.

HALF DOLLAR, 1840.

DIME, 1840.

HALF DOLLAR, 1885.

HALF DOLLAR, 1794.

QUARTER DOLLAR, 1885.

QUARTER DOLLAR, 1840.

HALF DIME, 1840.

DIME, 1885.

HALF DIME, 1794.

DIME, 1796.

PLATE XXIII.

LIBERTY CAP CENT, 1793.

CHAIN CENT, 1793.
First issue.

CHAIN CENT, 1793.
Second issue.

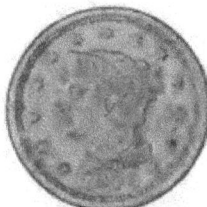

HALF CENT, 1793.

CENT, 1849.

PATTERN TWENTY CENT
PIECE, Rejected.

CENT, 1885.

THREE CENT NICKEL.
1885.

HALF CENT, 1849.

THREE CENT PIECE,
1885.

PLATE XXIV.

ANTIOCHUS VII.   ABDERA.   PRUSIAS.

ANTIOCHUS VIII.   PANORMUS.   ALEXANDER
EPIPHANES,   THE GREAT.

Grecian Coins about 300 years B. C.

Coins issued at the United States Mint at Philadelphia, from its establishment in 1792 to 1888.

Gold.

Double Eagle.

Authorized to be coined, Act of March 3, 1849. Weight, 516 grains; fineness, 900 ; size, 21

1850 to 1865, inclusive. No. 1. Obverse: Liberty head, facing left, hair tied behind, a coronet on the forehead inscribed " LIBERTY," thirteen stars and date.

Reverse: An eagle with shield upon its breast, and an olive branch a· three arrows in its talons; in its beak, an elaborate scroll, inscribed ". PLURIBUS UNUM." Above, a circle of thirteen stars and a curved line of rays extending from wing to wing. "UNITED STATES OF AMERICA." "TWENTY D."

1866 to 1876, inclusive. No. 2, same, with the motto "IN GOD WE TRUST" inscribed within the circle of stars on the reverse.

1877. No. 3. Same, with "TWENTY DOLLARS" for "TWENTY D."

Eagle.

Authorized to be coined, Act of April 2, 1792. Weight, 270 grains; fineness, 916⅔. Weight changed, Act of June 28, 1834, to 258 grains. Fineness changed, Act of June 28, 1834, to 899.225. Fineness changed, Act of January 18, 1837, to 900.

1795. Obverse: Liberty head, wearing a cap, facing right. Fifteen stars. Above, "LIBERTY;" beneath, "1795;" size, 21.

Reverse: An eagle with displayed wings, standing on a palm branch; in beak, a laurel wreath. "UNITED STATES OF AMERICA."

1796. Same, with sixteen stars.

1797. No. 1. Same, with sixteen stars.

1797. No. 2. Obverse: Same, with sixteen stars.

Reverse: An eagle with the United States shield upon its breast, a bundle of arrows in the right talon, and an olive branch in the left; in its beak, a scroll inscribed "E PLURIBUS UNUM." Around the head are sixteen stars; above, is a curved line of clouds extending from wing to wing. "UNITED STATES OF AMERICA."

1798 to 1801, inclusive. Same, with thirteen stars on the obverse. Of 1798, two varieties with four stars facing.

1802. None issued.

1803 and 1804. Same as No. 2 of 1797. Thirteen stars.

1805 to 1837, inclusive. None issued.

1838 to 1865, inclusive. Obverse: Liberty head facing left, hair tied behind, a coronet on the forehead inscribed "LIBERTY," thirteen stars, and date.

Reverse An eagle with the United States shield upon its breast, and an olive branch and three arrows in the talons. "UNITED STATES OF AMERICA." Size, 17.

1866. Same, with a scroll above the eagle inscribed "IN GOD WE TRUST."

Half Eagle.

Authorized to be coined, Act of April 2, 1792. Weight, 135 grains; fineness, 916⅔. Weight changed, Act of June 28, 1834, to 129 grains.

Fineness changed, Act of June 28, 1834, to 899.225. **Fineness changed,** Act of January 18, 1837, to 900.
　　1795. No. 1. Same type as the Eagle; size, **16.**
　　1795. No. 2. Obverse: Same.

　　Reverse: An eagle, wings extended upwards, with the United States shield upon its breast, a bundle of thirteen arrows in the right talon, and an olive branch in the left. In its beak, a scroll inscribed " E PLURIBUS UNUM." Around the head are sixteen stars, and above is a curved line of clouds extending from wing to wing. "UNITED STATES OF AMERICA."
　　1796. Same as No. **1** of 1795; fifteen stars on obverse.
　　1797. No. 1. Same as No. 1 of 1795.
　　1797. No. **2.** Same, with sixteen stars on **obverse.**
　　1797. No. **3.** Obverse: Same, with fifteen **stars.**

　　Reverse: Same as No. 2 of 1795, sixteen stars around the eagle.
　　1798. No. 1. Same as No. 1 of 1795, with thirteen stars.
　　1798. No. 2. Obverse Same.

　　Reverse: Same as No. 2 of 1795, thirteen stars.
　　1799 and 1800. Same as No. 2 of 1795, with thirteen stars on the obverse.
　　1801. None issued.
　　1802 to 1806, inclusive. **Same** as No. 2 of 1795, with thirteen stars on the obverse.
　　1807. No. **1. Obverse:** Same as No. 1, 1795, with thirteen stars.

　　Reverse: Same as No. 2, 1795.
　　1807. No. 2. Obverse: Liberty head, facing left; bust, draped, wearing a kind of turban with a band in front inscribed " LIBERTY," thirteen stars, and date.

　　Reverse: An eagle, **with the** United States **shield upon** its breast, an **olive** branch and three arrows in the talons. **Above, a** scroll, inscribed **"E** PLURIBUS UNUM."　United States of America **"5. D."**
　　1808 to 1812 inclusive. Same as No. 2 of 1807.
　　1813 to 1815, inclusive. Obverse: Liberty head, facing left, wearing a kind of turban, a band in front inscribed "LIBERTY."　Thirteen stars and date. No shoulders.

　　Reverse: Same as No. 2 of 1807
　　1816 and 1817, inclusive. None issued.
　　1818 to 1828, inclusive. Same as 1813.
　　1829. No. 1. Same as 1813; size, 16.
　　1829. No. 2. Same, but smaller; size, 15.
　　1830 to 1833, inclusive. Same as No. 2 of 1829.
　　1834. No. 1. Same as No. 2 of 1829.
　　1834. No. 2. Obverse: Liberty head, facing left, hair confined by a band inscribed "LIBERTY."

　　Reverse: Same as **No. 2 of 1807,** without the motto **"E** PLURIBUS UNUM" omitted; size, 14.
　　1835 to 1838, inclusive. Same as No. 2 of 1834.
　　1839 to 1865, inclusive. Same type as the Eagle of 1838.
　　1866. Same type as Eagle of same date.

Three-Dollar Piece.

　　Authorized to be coined, Act of February 21, 1853. Weight, 77.4 grains; fineness, 900.
　　1854. Obverse: An Indian head, wearing a crown of eagle feathers, on band of which is inscribed " LIBERTY "—" UNITED STATES OF AMERICA."
　　Reverse: "3 dollars 1854" within a wreath of corn, wheat, cotton, and tobacco. Size, 12.

Quarter-Eagle.

Authorized to be coined, Act of April 2, 1792. **Weight,** 67.5 grains; fineness, 916⅔. Weight changed, Act of June 28, **1834,** to 64.5 grains. Fineness changed, Act of June 28, 1834, to 899.225. **Fineness** changed, Act of January 18, 1837, to 900.

1796. No. 1. Obverse: Liberty **head,** facing right, above "LIBERTY"— sixteen stars.

Reverse: **Same** type as No. **2** half-eagle of 1795, size **13.**
No. 2. Same, with no stars on obverse.
1797-1798. Same as No. 1 of 1796, with thirteen stars.
1799-1801, inclusive. None issued.
1802. Same as 1798.
1803. None issued.
1804 to 1807, inclusive. Same as 1798.
1808. **Same** type as No. **2** half-eagle of 1807, with "2½ D."
1809 **to 1820,** inclusive. None issued.
1821. **Obverse:** Same type as the half-eagle of **1813, size 12.**
Reverse: Same type as No. 2 half-eagle of 1807.
1822 and 1823. None issued.
1824-1827, inclusive. Same **as 1821.**
1828. None issued.
1829 to 1833, inclusive. **Same** as 1821.
1834. No. **1.** Same **as 1821.** No. 2. Same type as No. **2 half-eagle of** 1834, size 11.
1835 to 1839, inclusive. Same as No. 2 of 1834.
1840 to 1865. Same type as the eagle of 1834.
1866. Same type as eagle of 1866.

Dollar.

Authorized to be coined, Act of March **3,** 1849. Weight, 25.8 grains; fineness, 900.

1849 to 1853, **inclusive. Obverse:** Same type as the eagle, without date.
Reverse: **"1 DOLLAR 1849"** within a laurel wreath, "UNITED STATES OF AMERICA." Size 8.
1854. No. 1. Same. No. 2. Same type as the three-dollar piece, size 9.

SILVER.

Dollar.

Authorized **to** be coined, Act of April 2, 1792. **Weight,** 416 grains; fineness, 892.4. Weight changed, Act of January 18, 1837, to 412½ grains. Fineness changed, Act of January 18, 1837, to 900. Coinage discontinued, Act of February 12, 1873. Coinage reauthorized, Act of February 28, 1878.

1794. Obverse: Liberty head, facing right, flowing hair, fifteen stars. **above, "LIBERTY;"** beneath, "1794."

Reverse: **An** eagle with raised wings, encircled by branches of laurel crossed; "UNITED STATES OF AMERICA." On the edge, "HUNDRED CENTS, ONE DOLLAR OR UNIT." Size, 24.
1795. No. 1. Same.
1795. No. 2. Bust of Liberty, facing right, hair bound by a ribbon, shoulders draped, fifteen stars.

Reverse: An eagle with expanded wings, standing upon clouds, within a wreath of palm and laurel, which is crossed and tied. "UNITED STATES OF AMERICA."
1796. Same **as No. 2, of** 1795.

1797. No. 1. Same as No. 2 of 1795, with sixteen stars, six of which are facing.

1797. No. 2. Same, with seven stars facing.

1798. No. 1. Same as No. 2 of 1795, with fifteen stars.

1798. No. 2. Same, with thirteen stars.

1798. No. 3. Obverse: Same, with thirteen stars.

Reverse: An eagle with raised wings, bearing the United States shield upon its breast, in beak, a scroll inscribed "E PLURIBUS UNUM." A bundle of thirteen arrows in the right talon, and an olive branch in the left. Above, are clouds, and thirteen stars. "UNITED STATES OF AMERICA." Size, 25.

1799 to 1804, inclusive. Same as No. 3, of 1798.

1805 to 1839, inclusive. None issued.

1840 to 1865, inclusive. Obverse: Liberty seated upon a rock, supporting with her right hand the United States shield, across which floats a scroll inscribed "LIBERTY," and with her left the staff and liberty cap; beneath, the date.

Reverse: An eagle with expanded wings, bearing the United States shield upon its breast, and an olive branch and three arrows in its talons. "UNITED STATES OF AMERICA." "ONE DOLL." Reeded edge; size, 24.

1866 to 1873, inclusive. Same, with a scroll above the eagle, inscribed, "IN GOD WE TRUST."

1874 to 1877, inclusive. None issued.

1878. Obverse: Liberty head facing left, upon which is a cap, a wheat and cotton wreath, and a band inscribed "LIBERTY;" above, "E PLURIBUS UNUM;" beneath, the date. Thirteen stars.

Reverse: An eagle with expanded wings pointing upwards; in right talon an olive branch with nine leaves; in the left, three arrows. In the field above, "IN GOD WE TRUST;" beneath, a semi-wreath, tied and crossed, reaching upwards to the wings; "UNITED STATES OF AMERICA." Some pieces of the above date (1878) were coined with eight feathers in the tail during the year, but seven have been adopted.

SILVER.

Trade Dollar.

Authorized to be coined, Act of February 12, 1873. Weight, 420 grains; fineness, 900.

1873. Obverse: Liberty seated upon a cotton bale, facing left; in her extended right hand an olive branch; in her left a scroll incribed "LIBERTY;" behind her a sheaf of wheat; beneath, a scroll inscribed "IN GOD WE TRUST;" thirteen stars; "1873."

Reverse: An eagle with expanded wings; in talons three arrows and an olive branch; above, a scroll inscribed "E PLURIBUS UNUM;" beneath, on field, "420 grains;" "900 fine." "UNITED STATES OF AMERICA. Size, 24.

Half Dollar.

Authorized to be coined, Act of April 2, 1792. Weight, 208 grains; fineness, 892.4. Weight changed, Act of January 18, 1837, to 206¼ grains. Fineness changed, Act of January 18, 1837, to 900. Weight changed, Act of February 21, 1853, to 192 grains. Weight changed, Act of February 12, 1873, to 12½ grammes, or 192.9 grains.

1794 and 1795. Same type as the dollar of 1794. On the edge, "FIFTY CENTS OR HALF A DOLLAR." Size, 21.

1796. No. 1. Same type as No. 2, dollar of 1795, with the denomination, "½," inscribed on the base of the reverse. No. 2. Same, with sixteen stars on the obverse.

1797. Same as No. 2, of 1796.
1798 to 1800, inclusive. None issued.
1801 to 1803, inclusive. Same type as **No. 3, dollar of 1798.**
1804. None issued.
1805 and 1806. Same as **No. 3, dollar of 1798.**
1807. No. 1. Same.
No. 2. Obverse: Liberty head facing left, wearing a kind of turban, with
"LIBERTY" inscribed upon the band. Thirteen stars and date.

Reverse: An eagle with expanded wings pointing downwards, bearing
upon its breast, the U. S. Shield, an olive branch and three arrows in its
talons; above, in the field, a scroll inscribed "E PLURIBUS UNUM;" beneath
50 c. "UNITED STATES OF AMERICA."
1808 to 1835 inclusive, same as No. 2 of 1807.
1836. No. 1. Same as No. 2 of 1807.
No. 2. Obverse: Same.

Reverse: An eagle with expanded wings pointing downwards, the U. S.
shield upon its breast, an olive branch and three arrows in its talons,
"UNITED STATES OF AMERICA," reeded edge.
1837. Same as No. 2 of 1836.
1838. Obverse: Same as No. 2 of 1836.
Reverse: Same; "HALF DOL." for "50 c."
1839. No. 1. Same as 1838.
No. 2. Same type as dollar of 1840.
1840 to 1852 inclusive, same.
1853. Obverse: Same with an arrow head on each side of the date.

Reverse: Same, with a halo of rays around the edge.
1854. Same, without the rays.
1855. Same.
1856 to 1865 inclusive, same, without the arrow heads.
1866 to 1872 inclusive, same, with scroll above the eagle inscribed "IN
GOD WE TRUST." (Some have been occasionally met with, which have been
issued by the San Francisco Mint, *without* this legend in 1866.)
1873. No. 1. Same.
No. 2. Same, with arrow heads on each side of the date.
1874. Same.
1875. Same, without the arrow heads.

SILVER.

Quarter Dollar.

Authorized to be coined, Act of April 2, 1792. Weight, 104 grains;
fineness, 892.4. Weight changed, Act of January 18, 1837, to 103½ grains.
Fineness changed, Act of January 18, 1837, to 900. Weight changed,
Act of February 21, 1853, to 96 grains. Weight changed, Act of February 12, 1873, to 6⅛ grammes, or 96.45 grains.
1796. Same type as No. 2 dollar of 1795, with reeded edge; size, 18;
fifteen stars.
1797 to 1803. None issued.
1804 to 1807, inclusive. Same type as No. 3 dollar of 1798, beneath,
"25c."
1808 to 1814, inclusive. None issued.
1815. Same type as No. 2 half dollar of 1807.
1816 and 1817. None issued.
1818 to 1825, inclusive. Same type as No. 2 half dollar of 1807, size 17.
1826. None issued.
1827 and 1828. Same type as No. 2 half dollar of 1807.
1829 and 1830. None issued.

1831 to 1837, inclusive. Same type as half dollar of 1807, with the diameter reduced from size 17 to size 15, and a corresponding increase in thickness and decrease of the size of devices, and the omission of the scroll, inscribed "E PLURIBUS UNUM."

1838. No. 1. Same as 1837. No. 2. Same type as the dollar of 1840, with "QUAR. DOL." for "ONE DOLL."

1839 to 1852, inclusive. Same as No. 2 of 1838.

1853. No. 1. Same. No. 2. Same, with arrow heads on each side of date, and a halo of rays around the edge.

1854 and 1855. Same, without the rays.

1856 to 1865. Same, without the arrow heads.

1866 to 1872, inclusive. Same, with the scroll above the eagle, inscribed "IN GOD WE TRUST."

1873. No. 1. Same. No. 2. Same, with an arrow head on each side of the date.

1874. Same.

1875. Same, without the arrow head.

Twenty-Cent Piece.

Authorized to be coined, Act of March 3, 1875. Weight, 5 grammes, or 77.16 grains; fineness, 900. Coinage discontinued, Act of May 2, 1878.

1875 to 1878, inclusive. Obverse: Same type as the dollar of 1840.

Reverse: An eagle with displayed wings, three arrows, and an olive branch, two of the leaves of which nearest the stem, together with those drooping from the centre, overlap; the terminating leaves on the end of the branch, however, do not. On each side a star. Plain edge. "UNITED STATES OF AMERICA." "TWENTY CENTS." Size, 14.

Dime.

Authorized to be coined, Act of April 2, 1792. Weight, 41.6 grains; fineness, 892.4. Weight changed, Act of January 18, 1837, to 41½ grains. Fineness changed, Act of January 18, 1837, to 900. Weight changed, Act of February 21, 1853, to 38.4 grains. Weight changed, Act of February 12, 1873, to 2½ grammes, or 38.58 grains.

1796. Same type as the No. 2 dollar of 1795; size 13; fifteen stars.

1797. No. 1. Same, with sixteen stars on the obverse. No. 2. Same, with thirteen stars on the obverse.

1798. No. 1. Same type as No. 3 dollar of 1798, with sixteen stars. No. 2. With thirteen stars on the obverse.

1799. None issued.

1800 to 1805, inclusive. Same as No. 3 of 1798.

1806. None issued.

1807. Same as No. 2 of 1798.

1808. None issued.

1809. Same type as No. 2 half-dollar of 1807 ; size, 12.

1810. None issued.

1811. Same as 1809.

1812 to 1813, inclusive. None issued.

1814. Same as 1809.

1815 to 1819, inclusive. None issued.

1820 to 1825, inclusive. Same as 1809.

1826. None issued.

1827 to 1836, inclusive. Same as 1809.

1837. No. 1. Same as 1809. No. 2. Obverse: Liberty seated. No stars. Reverse: "ONE DIME" within a wreath of laurel. "UNITED STATES OF AMERICA." Size, 11.

1838. No. 1. Same as No. 2 of 1837. No. 2. Same, with thirteen stars.

1839 to 1852, inclusive. Same as No. 2 of 1838.

1853. No. 1. Same. No. 2. Same, with an arrow head on each side of the date.
1854 and 1855. Same as No. 2 of 1853.
1856 to 1859, inclusive. Same, without arrow heads.
1860 to 1872, inclusive. Obverse: Same, with "UNITED STATES OF AMERICA" instead of stars.
Reverse: "ONE DIME" within a wreath of corn, wheat, cotton, and tobacco.
1873. No. 1. Same. No. 2. Same, with an arrow head on each side of the date.
1874. Same as No. 2 of 1873.
1875. Same, without arrow heads.

Half Dime.

Authorized to be coined, Act of April 2, 1792. Weight, 20.8 grains; fineness, 892.4. Weight changed, Act of January 18, 1837, to 20⅝ grains. Fineness changed, Act of January 18, 1837, to 900. Weight changed, Act of February 21, 1853, to 19.2 grains. Coinage discontinued, Act of February 12, 1873.
1794 and 1795. Same type as the half dollar; size, 10.
1796. Same type as No. 2 dollar of 1795; fifteen stars.
1797 No. 1. Same, with fifteen stars. No. 2. Same, with sixteen stars. No. 3. Same, with thirteen stars.
1798 and 1799. None issued.
1800 to 1803, inclusive. Same type as No. 3 dollar of 1798.
1804. None issued.
1805. Same as 1800.
1806 to 1828, inclusive. None issued.
1829 to 1873. See dime.

Three Cent Piece.

Authorized to be coined, Act of March 3, 1851. Weight, 12⅜ grains; fineness, 750. Weight changed, Act of March 3, 1853, to 11.52 grains. Fineness changed, Act of March 3, 1853, to 900. Coinage discontinued, Act of February 12, 1873.
1851 to 1853, inclusive. Obverse: A star bearing the United States shield. "UNITED STATES OF AMERICA."
Reverse: An ornamented "c," within which is the denomination "III;" around the border, thirteen stars; size, 9.
1854 to 1858. Obverse: Same, with two lines around the star.
Reverse: An olive branch above the "III," and three arrows below, all within the "c."
1858 to 1873, inclusive. Same, with one line around the star.

MINOR COINS.

Five cent piece. (Nickle.)

Authorized to be coined, Act of May 16, 1866. Weight, 77.16 grains; composed of 75 per cent. copper, and 25 per cent. nickle.
1866. Obverse: A United States shield surmounted by a cross, an olive branch pendent at each side, back of the base of the shield are two arrows, the heads and feathers are only visible; beneath, "1866;" above, in the field, "IN GOD WE TRUST."
Reverse: "5" within a circle of thirteen stars, and rays, "UNITED STATES OF AMERICA." Size, 13.
1867. Same. No. 2. Same, without the rays
1868. Same as No. 2 of 1867.
1869 to 1882. Same as No. 2 of 1867.

1883. No. 1. Same. No. 2. Obverse: Liberty head wearing a coronet which is inscribed "LIBERTY," thirteen stars, and date, "1883."

Reverse: A "V" within a wreath of corn and cotton. Legend, "UNITED STATES OF AMERICA." Exergue, "E PLURIBUS UNUM." No. 3, Obverse: Same as No. 2.

Reverse: Same, with "CENTS" as the exergue, and "E PLURIBUS UNUM" above the wreath.

1884. Same as No. 3 of the preceding.

Three cent piece. (Nickle.)

Authorized to be coined, Act of April 3, 1865. Weight, 30 grains; composed of 75 per cent. copper, and 25 per cent. nickle.

1865. Obverse: Liberty head, facing left, hair bound by a ribbon, on the forehead a coronet inscribed "LIBERTY;" beneath, the date, "UNITED STATES OF AMERICA."

Reverse: "III" within a laurel wreath.

MINOR COINS.

Two Cent Piece (bronze).

Authorized to be coined, Act of April 22, 1864. Weight, 96 grains, composed of ninety-five per cent. copper and five per cent. of tin and zinc. Coinage discontinued, Act of February 12, 1873.

1864 to 1873, inclusive. Obverse: The United States shield, behind which are two arrows, crossed, on each side a branch of laurel; above, a scroll inscribed "IN GOD WE TRUST"; beneath, the date.

Reverse: "2 CENTS" within a wreath of wheat. "UNITED STATES OF AMERICA." Size, 14.

Cent (copper).

Authorized to be coined, Act of April 22, 1792. Weight, 264 grains. Weight changed, Act of January 14, 1793, to 208 grains. Weight changed by proclamation of the President, January 26, 1796, in conformity with an Act of March 3, 1795, to 168 grains. Coinage discontinued, Act of February 21, 1857.

1793. No. 1. Obverse: Liberty head, facing right, flowing hair. Above, "LIBERTY": beneath, "1793."

Reverse: A chain of fifteen links, within which is inscribed "ONE CENT" and the fraction "$\frac{1}{100}$." United States of America; reeded edge; size, 17.

No. 2. Same, with the abbreviation "AMERI." in the Legend.

No. 3. Obverse: Same as No. 1, with a sprig beneath.

Reverse: "ONE CENT" within a wreath of laurel. "UNITED STATES OF AMERICA. Reeded edge.

No. 4. Obverse: A bust of Liberty, facing right, with pole and liberty cap. Above, "LIBERTY"; beneath, "1793."

Reverse: Same as No. 3; on the edge, "ONE HUNDRED FOR A DOLLAR." Size, 18.

1794 and 1795. Same as No. 4 of 1793.

1796. No. 1. Same. No. 2. Same, with hair bound by a ribbon, and without pole and liberty cap on the obverse. Plain edge.

1797 to 1807 inclusive. Same as No. 2 of 1796.

1808 to 1814, inclusive. Obverse: Liberty head, facing left, hair confined by a band; inscribed "LIBERTY." Thirteen stars and date.

Reverse: "ONE CENT," within a laurel wreath. "UNITED STATES OF AMERICA." The fraction "$\frac{1}{100}$" is omitted.

1815. None issued.

1816. Obverse: **Liberty** head, facing left, the hair is **confined by a roll, and tied by a cord, whilst he** forehead is bedecked with **a tiara, inscribed** "LIBERTY."

Reverse: **Same** as 1808.

1817. No. 1. **Same.** No. 2. **Same, with fifteen stars.**

1818 to 1836. Same as No. 1 of 1817.

1837. No. 1. Same. No. 2. **Same, with the hair tied by a string of beads** instead of a cord.

1838 to 1857, inclusive. Same as No. 2 of 1837.

Cent (Nickle).

Authorized to **be coined, Act of** February 21, 1857. Weight 72 grains; composed of 88 per cent. copper and 12 per cent. nickle. Coinage discontinued, Act of April 22, 1864.

1857 and 1858. Obverse: An eagle **flying to the** left. "UNITED STATES OF AMERICA."

Reverse: "**ONE CENT,**" **within a wreath of corn,** wheat, cotton, **and to**bacco. Size, 11.

1859. Obverse: An Indian-head, **facing left, bedecked with eagle plumes,** confined. "UNITED STATES OF AMERICA." **Beneath, the date.**

Reverse: "ONE CENT." within a wreath of **laurel.**

1860 to 1864, inclusive. Obverse: Same.

Reverse: "ONE CENT," within an oak **wreath and shield.**

Cent (Bronze).

Coinage authorized, Act of April 22, 1857. Weight, 48 grains; composed of 95 per cent. copper and 5 per cent. of tin and zinc.

1864. Same type as nickle cent of 1860. Size, 12.

Half Cent (Copper).

Authorized to **be coined, Act** of April 2, 1792. Weight, 132 grains. Weight changed, Act of January 14, 1793, to 104 grains. Weight changed by proclamation of the President, January 26, 1796, in conformity with Act of March 3, 1795, to 84 grains. Coinage discontinued, Act of February 21, 1857.

1793. Same type **as cent No.** 4, 1793, with head facing **left. On the** edge, "TWO HUNDRED FOR A DOLLAR." Size, **14.**

1794. Same type as the cent of 1794.

1795 to 1797, inclusive. Same, with plain edge.

1798 and 1799. None issued.

1800. Same type as No. 2 cent of 1796, with the fraction "$\frac{1}{100}$" on the base of the reverse.

1801. None issued.

1802 to 1808, **inclusive.** Same as 1800. **From 1808,** the fraction "$\frac{1}{200}$" omitted.

1809 to 1811, inclusive. Same type as cent of **1808.**

1812 to 1824, inclusive. None issued.

1825 and 1826. Same type as cent of 1808.

1827. None issued.

1828. No. 1. Same **type as cent** 1808, with thirteen stars. No. 2. Same, with **twelve stars.**

1829. Same, with **thirteen stars.**

1830. None issued.

1831 to 1836, inclusive. Same type as cent of 1808.

1837 to 1839, inclusive. None issued.

1840 to 1857, inclusive. Same type as No. 2 cent of 1837; size, 14.

THOMAS JEFFERSON,

an eminent American Statesman, and third President of the United States, was born April 2, 1743, at Shadwell, Virginia, near the spot which afterwards became his residence, with the name of Monticello. He was the oldest son in a family of eight children. His father, Peter Jefferson, was a man of great force of character and of extraordinary physical strength. His mother, Jane Randolph, of Goochland, was descended from an English family of great note and respectability. Young Jefferson began his classical studies at the age of nine, and at seventeen he entered an advance class at William and Mary College; on his way thither, he formed the acquaintance of Patrick Henry, who was then a bankrupt merchant, but who afterwards became the great orator of the Revolution. At college, Jefferson was distinguished by his close application, and devoted, it is said, from twelve to fifteen hours per day to study, and we are told became well versed in Latin, Greek, Italian, French, and Spanish, at the same time proficient in his mathematical studies. After a few years course of law under Judge Wythe, he was admitted to the bar in 1767. His success in the legal profession was remarkable; his fees during the first year amounted to nearly three thousand dollars. In 1769, Jefferson commenced his public career as a member of the Virginia House of Burgesses, in which he had while a student of law, listened to Patrick Henry's great speech on the Stamp Act. In 1773 he united with Patrick Henry and other revolutionary patriots in devising the celebrated committee of correspondence for disseminating intelligence between the Colonies, of which Jefferson was one of the most active and influential members. He was elected in 1774 to a convention to choose delegates to the first Continental Congress at Philadelphia, and introduced at that convention his famous " Summary view of the rights of British America." On the 21st of June, 1775, Jefferson took his seat in the Continental Congress. His reputation as a Statesman and accomplished writer at once placed him among the leaders of that renowned body. He served on the most important committees, and among other papers drew up the reply of Congress to the proposal of Lord North, and assisted in preparing in behalf of the Colonies, a declaration of the cause of taking up arms against the Mother Country. The rejection of a final petition to King George, destroyed all hope of an honorable reconciliation with England. Congress, early in 1776, appointed a committee to draw up a Declaration of Independence, of which Jefferson was made Chairman; in this capacity he drafted, at the request of the other members of the committee, (Franklin, Adams, Sherman, and Livingston), and reported to Congress, June 28, the great Charter of Freedom, known as the "Declaration of American Independence," which, on July 4, was unanimously adopted, and signed by every member present, with a single exception. "The Declaration of Independence," says Edward Everett, "is equal to anything ever borne on parchment, or expressed in the visible signs of thought." "The heart of Jefferson in writing it," adds Bancroft, "and of Congress in adopting it, *beat for all humanity.*" After resigning his seat in Congress, Jefferson revised the laws of Virginia; among other reforms, he procured the repeal of the laws of entail, the abolition of primogeniture, and the restoration of the rights of conscience, a reform which he believed would abolish "every fibre of ancient or future aristocracy;" he also originated a complete system of elementary and collegiate education for Virginia. In 1779, Jefferson succeeded Patrick Henry as Governor of Virginia, and held the office during the most gloomy period of the Revolution, and declined a re-election in 1781. In 1783, he returned to Congress, and reported the treaty of peace, concluded at Paris, September 3, 1783, acknowledging the independence of the United States. He also proposed and carried through Congress a bill establishing the present Federal system of coinage, which took the place of the English pounds, shillings, pence, etc., and also introduced measures for establishing a Mint in Philadelphia, (the first public building built by the general Government, still standing on Seventh street, east side, near Filbert). In 1785, he succeeded Dr. Franklin as resident Minister at Paris. In organizing the Government after the adoption of the Constitution, he accepted the position of Secretary of State, tendered him by President Washington during his first term. Jefferson was Vice-President of the United States from 1797 to 1801, and President for the two consecutive terms following. After participating in the inauguration of his friend and successor, James Madison, Jefferson returned to Monticello, where he passed the remainder of his life in directing the educational and industrial institutions of his native State and entertaining his many visitors and friends. His death occurred on the same day with that of John Adams, July 4, 1826.

ALEXANDER HAMILTON,

Statesman, orator, and financier, born in the West Indian island of Nevis, 11th of January, 1757. His father was a Scotch merchant, and his mother was the daughter of a French Huguenot. He was educated at King's College, N. Y. When he was 18 years of age he surprised the people by his public speeches and pamphlets in favor of American independence. He was commissioned Captain of a Company of Artillery in March, 1776, and served with distinction at the battles of Long Island, White Plains, Trenton, and Princeton, and was appointed Aid-de-camp and Private Secretary to General Washington in March, 1777, and gained his special favor and confidence in planning campaigns and devising means to support the army. In 1782 he was elected a member of the Continental Congress, and Washington expressed the opinion that no one excelled him in probity and sterling virtue. He was an active member of an anti-slavery party in New York, and offered a resolution in 1784, that every member of that society should liberate his own slaves. He was a delegate to the convention which met in Philadelphia in May, 1787, to form a Federal Constitution and to promote the Union of the States, and it appears was the principal author of the movement. Hamilton was appointed Secretary of the Treasury in 1789, at the time the nation was burdened with a heavy debt, almost destitute of credit, and on the verge of bankruptcy. The results of his financial policy were the restoration of public credit, protection to American industry, and a rapid revival of trade and commerce. He resigned his office to resume his practice of law, January 31, 1795: He declined the position of Chief Justice of the Supreme Court of the United States previously tendered him. Washington testified his great esteem for Hamilton by consulting him in the preparation of his Farewell Address, as well as in many other acts of his noble career.

In 1804, Aaron Burr, presenting himself as a candidate for Governor of New York, but Hamilton opposed his election expressing the opinion that "Burr was a dangerous man and unfit to be trusted with power." The election of Gen. Lewis blasted the ambitious projects of Burr, who insolently demanded an explanation of Hamilton, and finally challenged him, Hamilton accepted the challenge, was mortally wounded at Weehawken, and died July 12, 1804. His death was profoundly lamented throughout the country.

NOTE.—His eldest son had been killed in a duel by a political adversary about 1802. Mr. Hamilton was the principal author of the Federalist, and the real father of our financial system. Immediately after adopting the constitution, he strongly advocated the establishment of a Mint, so that the New World would not be dependant on the Old for a circulating medium.

HON. JAMES PUTNAM KIMBALL,

PRESIDENT DIRECTOR OF ALL THE MINTS,

was born in Salem, Mass., April 26, 1836. After graduating at the High School of his native town in 1854, he entered the Lawrence Scientific School of Harvard University. In the summer of the following year he went to Germany, and matriculated at the University of Frederick Wilhelm, Berlin, in the Fall of the same year, and was graduated at the University of George Augusta, at Gottingen, in the Autumn of 1857, with the degrees of Master of Arts and Doctor of Philosophy. Upon his graduation he entered upon a practical course in Mining and Metallurgy, at the Mining School of Freiburg, in Saxony.

After making a tour of the Continent and England, he returned home and engaged as the Assistant of Prof. J. D. Whitney, now of Harvard University, in the State Geological Surveys of the States of Wisconsin and Illinois, embracing the Upper Mississippi lead region. He continued with Prof. Whitney during the survey, comprising the southeastern part of Iowa.

On the establishment of the New York State Agricultural College at Ovid, the foundation of which was subsequently merged with that of Cornell University, Dr. Kimball was appointed to the Chair of Professor of Chemistry and Economic Geology. Upon the appointment of the President of the college, Gen. Patrick, as Brigadier-General of Volunteers, Dr. Kimball became that officer's Chief of Staff, with a commission from the President of the United States, as Assistant Adjutant-General of Volunteers, with the rank of Captain. This was in 1862. His first service in the field was with the Army of the Rappahannock, under Gen. McDowell. He took part in numerous engagements, notably, those of Groveton, Manassas, Chantilly, South Mountain, Antietam, Fredericksburg, Chancellorsville, and Gettysburg. General Patrick having been assigned to duty as Provost-Marshal of the Army of the Potomac, Capt. Kimball accompanied him, and served on the General Staff of that army under Generals McClellan, Burnside, Hooker, and Meade, successively.

When the army went into winter quarters, Capt. Kimball, whose health had become impaired, resigned from the army, and settled in New York. He resumed the practice of his profession as Mining Engineer and Metallurgist. Upon his marriage, in 1874, he accepted an honorary Professorship in Lehigh University, Bethlehem, Pa., removing from New York to one of the houses in the beautiful park and grounds of that

institution, though retaining his office and business in New
York City.

Dr. Kimball has been largely identified with the mineral
development of Bedford County, Pa., and at the time of his
appointment as Director of the Mints, was President of the
Everett Iron Company, whose blast furnace, built in 1883–84,
is one of the largest and finest in this country. As a scientist
he is a contributor to various scientific journals at home and
abroad, and among others the *American Journal of Science*,
published at New Haven. Several of his papers have appeared
in the proceedings of the American Institute of Mining Engi-
neers, of which he has been Vice President. Dr. Kimball has
traveled extensively in the United States, Mexico, and the
West Indies, in prosecuting his professional practice, and as a
man of scientific accomplishments and of affairs, bears a de-
servedly high reputation.

Dr. Kimball comes of Revolutionary stock. His paternal
great-grandfather, William Russell, of Boston, was associated
with the Sons of Liberty, and the leaders in public affairs in
the times that tried men's souls. He was present, disguised as
as an Indian, and assisted in the famous Tea Party in Boston
harbor on the memorable 16th of December, 1773. Later,
Mr. Russell was adjutant of the Massachusetts Artillery, raised
for the defense of Boston, and which served in the Rhode
Island campaign of 1777–78. Still later, while serving as
Secretary to Commander John Manley, of the U. S. war vessel
Jason, Russell was captured by the British frigate Surprise,
and confined in Mill prison till June 24, 1782, when he was
exchanged. But so sturdy a patriot could not rest unemployed,
and twenty days after his liberation, found him again in the
naval service. He was again made prisoner by the British, in
November following, and consigned to the notorious British
prison ship, Jersey, lying off New York.

An anecdote is related by Mr. James Kimball, father of the
subject of this sketch, in a memoir on the Tea Party in Boston
harbor furnished the Essex Institute Historical collections
(1874), which illustrates the temper of Mr. Russell as a patriot.
Returning to his home after the destruction of the tea, he took
off his shoes, and carefully dusted them over the fire; he then
took the tea canister and emptied its contents. Next morning
he had printed on one side of the canister, "Coffee," and on
the other, "No Tea." This was the brief decree of banish-
ment promulgated by the Tea Destroyers, and the prohibited
luxury disappeared from their tables.

HON. JOHN JAY KNOX.

Late Comptroller of the Currency, now President of the Na-
National Bank of the Republic, New York City, we are
indebted to *The Financier, August, 1885,* for the following
biographical sketch:

Hon. John Jay Knox was Comptroller or Deputy Comptroller of the National currency for seventeen years. He was
born in Oneida county, New York, March 19, 1828. His ancestors were Scotch Irish, and came originally from Strabane,
County Tyrone, Ireland, in 1759. He received his early education at the Augusta Academy and the Watertown Classical
Institute, and was graduated from Hamilton College in the Class
of 1849. Among those in college with him were Senator Hawley
of Connecticut, and Chas. Dudley Warner. After leaving college he became teller in a bank at Vernon, of which his father
was President, at a salary of $300 a year, where he remained
from 1850 to 1852. He spent some time in the Burnet Bank
at Syracuse, and was afterwards cashier of the Susquehanna
Valley Bank at Binghampton. He and his brother, Henry
M. Knox, established a banking house at St. Paul, Minnesota,
in 1857, shortly before that State was admitted into the Union.

The first steamboat launched on the Red River of the North,
establishing a most important communication for the business
interests of Minnesota, was transported in the dead of winter
across country on runners, from Sauk Rapids to Breckenridge,
and Mr. Knox was one of the few who paid the expenses of
the enterprise.

In the financial discussions which preceded the establishment of the National banks, Mr. Knox took a prominent part,
and made many valuable suggestions on the currency question.
He advocated a safe and convertible currency, the issue of a
uniform series of circulating notes to all the banks, and the
guarantee by the Government of circulation secured by its
own bonds.

In 1862 he was introduced to Secretary Chase and the Hon.
Hugh McCulloch, then Comptroller of the currency. The attention of the Secretary had previously been attracted to the
financial articles of Mr. Knox, published in *Hunt's Merchants'
Magazine.*

He was shortly afterward appointed to a clerkship under
Treasurer Spinner, and was subsequently transferred to the
office of Mr. Chase, as disbursing clerk, at a salary of $2,000
a year. After three years in this position he became cashier
of the Exchange National Bank at Norfolk, Va., but finding

the southern climate uncongenial, after a year he returned to
Washington. He was commissioned by Secretary McCulloch
to examine the mint at San Francisco, and to select a site there
for a new one. His report upon the Mint service of the
Pacific Coast was printed in the Finance Report of 1866, with
a complimentary notice by the Secretary. The site selected
was purchased from Eugene Kelly of New York for $100,000.

He subsequently visited New Orleans and discovered a de-
ficiency of $1,100,000 in the office of the Assistant Treasurer.
He took possession of that office, and for some weeks acted as
Assistant Treasurer of the United States.

The promotion of Mr. Knox to the office in which he was
able to do himself the most credit, and perform those services
to the country which are part and parcel of its financial progress, occurred in 1867. At this time a vacancy was brought
about in the Deputy-Comptrollership of the Currency, and
Secretary McCulloch appointed him to fill it. Until May 1,
1884, he remained as Deputy or head of the Bureau, his terms
of office being as follows: Five years as Deputy-Comptroller,
from 1867 to 1872; five years as Comptroller, from 1872 to
1877, appointed by General Grant; five years, second term
as Comptroller, from 1877 to 1882, by President Hayes, on
the recommendation of Secretary Sherman—the reappoint-
ment being made without his knowledge, before the expiration
of the preceding term, and confirmed by the Senate without
reference to any committee. He was again reappointed, by
President Arthur, April 12, 1882.

In 1870 he made an elaborate report to Congress (Senate
Mis. Doc., No. 132, XLI. Cong., 2d Sess.), including a codification of the Mint and Coinage laws, with important amendments, which was highly commended. The bill which accompanied the report comprised, within the compass of twelve
pages of the Revised Statutes, every important provision contained in more than sixty different enactments upon the Mint
and Coinage of the United States—the result of eighty years
of legislation. This bill, with slight amendments, was subsequently passed, and is known as "The Coinage Act of 1873;"
and the Senate Finance Committee, in recognition of his services, by an amendment, made the Comptroller of the Currency an *ex-officio* member of the Assay Commission, which
meets annually at the Mint in Philadelphia for the purpose of
testing the weight and fineness of the coinage of the year.

Through his official reports, twelve in number, and his
addresses on the currency question, Mr. Knox has indirectly
exercised great influence in financial legislation, and he took

an active, though quiet and unassuming part, in the great financial *coup d'etat* of the resumption of specie payment.

In April, 1878, he accompanied Secretary Sherman and Attorney-General Devens to New York, and arranged a meeting between these two members of the Cabinet and the officers of ten of the principal banks of the city at the National Bank of Commerce, with the view of negotiating the sale of $50,000,000 of 4½ per cent. bonds, the avails of which were to be used for resumption purposes. The Presidents of the banks, who were present, gave Secretary Sherman no encouragement as to the purchase of the bonds at the rates proposed by him. Upon the return of the Secretary and Comptroller to the Fifth Avenue Hotel, in the evening, they were met by August Belmont, who had a cable dispatch from the Rothchilds, authorizing a purchase of the whole amount at a premium of one and one-half per cent. for the account of the syndicate. Upon the following day the Secretary and the Comptroller returned to Washington, after an absence of three days, and the success of the negotiation was announced, much to the chagrin of some members of the Finance Committee of the House of Representatives, who were then bitterly opposing the scheme proposed by the Secretary for the resumption of specie payments. This negotiation was the first of a series of brilliant financial transactions preceding and following resumption on January 1, 1879.

Subsequently he arranged a conference, which was held in the Treasury at Washington, in the evening, between leading bank officials of New York and Secretaries Sherman and Evarts, which resulted in the admission of the Assistant Treasurer as a member of the clearing house, and the receipt by the banks of legal tender notes on a par with gold; and in 1881, by request of President Garfield, he attended a conference in New York between the leading financial men of the city and Secretary Windom and Attorney-General McVeagh, which resulted in the issue and successful negotiation of three and one-half per cent. bonds.

At the time of his resignation, Mr. Knox was the oldest officer in term of service in the department. One of the leading financial writers in the country, in noticing his retirement, in the *Nation* said:

"The retirement of Mr. John Jay Knox from the office of Comptroller of the Currency is a loss to the public service of no common kind. The intelligence which he has brought to the complicated duties of his office has never been surpassed in any similar station, and has not been equalled in the par-

ticular station which he has so long filled. The National
banking system owes much of its present carefulness in detail
management to his mastery of all the facts and principles of
sound finance. His annual reports embrace perhaps the most
complete and satisfactory arrangement of information needful
to the business-man, the student, and the legislator that has
ever been furnished in this country on any economical subject.
Mr. Knox resigns the Comptrollership to take the Presidency
of the National Bank of the Republic of New York City."

In a speech before the Merchants' Club of Boston, in February, 1885, Mr. Knox alluded to the subjects of civil service
reform and the coinage of silver in the following trenchant
language :

"The platforms of both parties in the late campaign contained nothing but platitudes upon the silver question, which
should have been the burning issue. The candidate of the
Republicans seemed to avoid the issue in his letter of acceptance, rather than to express the sentiments of the best men in
his party. The candidate of the Democrats said nothing.
Yet I am told by good authority that Governor Cleveland is
earnest in his desire to stop the coinage, and that nothing
would please him more than to have a clause inserted in an
appropriation bill which would repeal the law which was passed
in the interest of silver miners when the whole production is
not equal, according to Edward Atkinson, who is an authority
upon such subjects, to the production of eggs by the hens of
this country! If Governor Cleveland has the bottom and
pluck to carry out these two reforms, his administration will
be one of the most memorable in the annals of the country.
It will elevate not only every branch of the civil service, but
will greatly improve the character of the representatives sent
to Congress from every State of the Union, and will serve to
lift the depression which now burdens every industrial interest.
It will require some intellect to work out these reforms. But
it will require more bottom than brains, and if he has the grit
to stand by his pledges, he will have the united support of all
intelligent, upright, and honest men everywhere without distinction of party."

Mr. Knox has written a valuable book, which is justly popular, entitled "United States Notes." It is published by the
Scribners, and republished in London, and is a history of the
various issues of paper money by the Government, and is said
by George Bancroft to be "a clear, thorough, able, accurate
and impartial work on United States Notes."

THE COINAGE ACT OF 1873.

The enactment of the Mint Law of 1873 marks an era in the Mint Service of the United States. Prior to this, the Director of the Mint at Philadelphia was the Director of all the Mints—the institution at Philadelphia being regarded as the "Mother Mint," and the others, at San Francisco, New Orleans, etc., were called Branch Mints. Each branch had its Superintendent, reporting direct to Philadelphia. But the authors of the Act of 1873 regarded the Mint Service as so large and important a part of the Government, that it should be constituted a separate Bureau of the Treasury, with the Director located at Washington. One of the promoters of this Act was the Hon. John Jay Knox, late Comptroller of the Currency, and now President of the National Bank of the Republic, New York. The following sketch of the origin and history of the new law may prove of interest. It was originally published in Rhodes' Journal of Banking, July, 1884. Referring to Mr. Knox, the author says:

"In 1870 he made an elaborate report to Congress (Senate Mis. Doc. No. 132, XLI. Cong., 2d Sess.), including a codification of the Mint and Coinage laws, with important amendments, which was highly commended. The method adopted in this codification was, first, to arrange in as concise a form as possible the coinage laws then in existence, with such additional sections and suggestions as seemed valuable. The proposed bill was then printed upon paper having a wide margin, and transmitted to the officers of the different Mints and Assay offices, and to such other gentlemen as were known to be conversant and intelligent upon the subject of the coinage, with the request that the printed bill should be returned with such notes as experience and education should dictate. In this way the views of many gentlemen who were conversant with these subjects were obtained, with but little inconvenience to such correspondents. This correspondence was subsequently published by order of Congress, in H. R. Ex. Doc. No. 307, XLI. Cong., 2d Sess. Having received these suggestions, the bill, which comprised within the compass of eight or ten pages of the Revised Statutes every important provision contained in more than sixty different enactments upon the Mint and Coinage of the United States—the result of eighty years of legislation—was prepared and submitted to Congress. This bill, with but slight amendments, was subsequently passed, and was known as 'The Coinage Act of 1873;' and the Senate Finance

Committee, in recognition of the services of the Comptroller of the Currency, by an amendment, made that officer an *ex-officio* member of the Assay Commission, which meets annually at the Mint in Philadelphia for the purpose of testing the weight and fineness of the coinage of the year. Upon his suggestion the coinage of the silver dollar was discontinued, and the paragraph in the report upon this subject was as follows:

" The coinage of the silver dollar-piece, the history of which is here given, is discontinued in the proposed bill. It is by law the dollar unit; and, assuming the value of gold to be fifteen and one-half times that of silver, being about the mean ratio for the past six years, is worth in gold a premium of about three per cent., its value being $1.03.12, and intrinsically more than seven per cent. premium in our other silver coins, its value thus being $1.07.42. The present laws consequently authorize both a gold dollar unit and a silver dollar unit, differing from each other in intrinsic value. The present gold dollar-piece is made the dollar unit in the proposed bill, and the silver piece is discontinued."

The first Director of the Mint under this new law, was the Hon. Henry R. Linderman. The title of the chief officer at Philadelphia being changed to Superintendent—the first incumbent with that title was the Hon. James Pollock.

Biographical notices of these officers will be found in their appropriate place in this volume.

DIRECTORS OF THE MINT.

DAVID RITTENHOUSE,
FIRST DIRECTOR OF THE MINT.

Entering the Cabinet, the portraits of the different Directors attract attention. That of David Rittenhouse is the copy of a painting by Charles Willson Peale. Mr. Rittenhouse was appointed by Washington, April 14, 1792, and remained in charge of the Mint until June, 1795, when his declining health compelled him to resign.

At an early age he indicated mechanical talent of a high order in the construction of a clock, and his studies from that time were principally mathematical. His genius soon attracted attention, and he was appointed by the colonial governor a surveyor, and in that capacity determined the famous Mason and Dixon line. He succeeded Benjamin Franklin as President of the American Philosophical Society. Mr. Barber, late Engraver of the Mint, executed a bronze medal of Dr. Rittenhouse. Possibly, excepting Duvivier's head of Washington after Houdon, it cannot be surpassed in the Cabinet. The engraver had a very fine subject, and treated it in the highest style of art. On the obverse is "David Rittenhouse," with date of birth and death. On the reverse, inscription, "He belonged to the whole human race."—"Wm. Barber." This beautiful memento is highly prized.

HENRY WILLIAM DESAUSSURE,
SECOND DIRECTOR OF THE MINT.

The portrait of Henry William Desaussure, now in the cabinet, was painted by Samuel Du Bois, from a daguerreotype taken from a family picture. This Director was distinguished for his legal ability, as well as his strict integrity. He entered upon his duties with a protest, as he claimed no knowledge of the requirements of the position, having long been a practicing lawyer; but he was reassured by Alex. Hamilton, then Secretary of the Treasury, and proved himself a fine officer for the short term of his service. He was appointed by Washington, July 8, 1795, but resigned in the following October. Washington not only expressed regret at losing so valuable an officer, but consulted him as to the selection of a successor.

ELIAS BOUDINOT,

THIRD DIRECTOR OF THE MINT,

was appointed October 28, 1795, and remained in office eleven years. In the summer and autumn of 1797 and the two following years, and also of 1802 and 1803, the Mint was closed on account of the ravages of the yellow fever. Mr. Boudinot resigned in 1805, and devoted the remainder of his life to benevolent and literary pursuits. He died on the 24th of October, 1821, at the advanced age of eighty-two. The fine portrait of this venerable Director seen in the Cabinet was presented by a relative, and is a good copy of a painting by Waldo and Jewett.

ROBERT PATTERSON, LL. D.,

FOURTH DIRECTOR OF THE MINT,

was appointed by President Jefferson, January 17, 1806. He was a native of Ireland, distinguished for his acquirements and ability. He held the office of Director for an exceptionally long term of service. His portrait, which hangs in the Cabinet, is a copy of a fine original by Rembrandt Peale.

SAMUEL MOORE, M.D.

FIFTH DIRECTOR OF THE MINT,

was appointed by President James Monroe, July 15, 1824. He was a native of New Jersey, and the son of a distinguished Revolutionary officer. He was one of the first graduates of the Penn University, in 1791, and was afterwards a tutor in that institution. During his directorship the Mint was removed to the present building. His portrait was painted from life by B. Samuel Du Bois, now in the Cabinet.

ROBERT MASKELL PATTERSON, M.D.

SIXTH DIRECTOR OF THE MINT,

son of a former Director, was appointed by President Andrew Jackson, May 26, 1835. His term of office was marked by an entire revolution in the coinage, and the ready acceptance of those improvements which followed so rapidly upon the introduction of steam. Dr. Patterson possessed the advantage of foreign travel; and having become familiar with the discoveries which had been adopted in the French Mint, he inaugurated and perfected them, also introducing improvements, which are still in use, in the machinery of the Mint. His portrait is in the Cabinet.

GEORGE N. ECKERT, M. D.
SEVENTH DIRECTOR OF THE MINT,

was appointed by President Fillmore, July 1, 1851. He served nearly two years, and, resigning, was followed by

THOMAS M. PETTIT,
EIGHTH DIRECTOR OF THE MINT,

who was appointed by President Pierce, April 4, 1853. He died a few weeks after his appointment. No portrait of him in the Cabinet. He was succeeded by

HON. JAMES ROSS SNOWDEN, LL.D.
NINTH DIRECTOR OF THE MINT.

Mr. Snowden, who was appointed by President Pierce, June 3, 1853, was formerly a member of the State Legislature, and served two terms as Speaker; was afterwards elected for two terms as State Treasurer. During his official term the building was made fire-proof, the large collection of minerals was added, and nickel was first coined.

Mr. Snowden has placed the numismatic world under many obligations, by directing the publication of two valuable quarto volumes.—one of them a description of the coins in the Cabinet, under the title of "The Mint Manual of Coins of all Nations," the other "The Medallic Memorials of Washington," being mainly a description of a special collection made by himself. In the preface to the former work he gives due credit to the literary labors of Mr. George Bull, then Curator, and also to a reprint of the account of the ancient collection, by Mr. Du Bois, who also furnished other valuable material. These books are valuable as authority, and by reason of the national character of the last mentioned.

JAMES POLLOCK, A.M., LL.D.,
TENTH DIRECTOR AND FIRST SUPERINTENDENT,

was appointed by Abraham Lincoln in 1861, and was re-appointed by President Grant to succeed Dr. Linderman in 1869 to 1873. Born in Pennsylvania in 1810; graduated at Princeton College, New Jersey, in 1831, and commenced the practice of the law in 1833; he served in Congress three terms; was elected Governor of Pennsylvania in 1854, and in 1860 was a peacedelegate to Washington from his State to counsel with representatives from different parts of the Union as to the possibility of amicably adjusting our unhappy national troubles. His portrait, by Winner, hangs in the eastern section of the Cabinet.*

* After the resignation of ex-Governor Pollock the title of Director was changed to Superintendent. The Director of all the Mints is now located at Washington.

HON. HENRY RICHARD LINDERMAN, M. D.,

DIRECTOR OF THE MINTS AND ASSAY OFFICES OF THE UNITED STATES,

was the eldest son of John Jordan Linderman, M. D., and Rachel Brodhead. He was born in Pike county, Pennsylvania, the 25th of December, 1825. The elder Dr. Linderman was one of the most noted physicians in northeastern Pennsylvania, and practiced medicine for nearly half a century in the valley of the Delaware, in this State, and New Jersey. He was a graduate of the College of Physicians and Surgeons, of New York, where he had studied under the famous Dr. Valentine Mott. Dr. Linderman's grandfather, Jacob von Linderman, came to this country during the disturbed period of the Austrian War of Succession, during the first half of the last century, and settled in Orange county, where he purchased a tract of land. The property is still in the possession of the family. Jacob von Linderman was the cadet of an ancient and honorable family of Saxony, which had been distinguished for two centuries in the law and medicine, several of his ancestors having been counsellors and physicians to the Elector. He was a descendant of the same family as Margaretta Linderman, the mother of the great Reformer, Martin Luther. Of this paternal stock, Dr. Henry R. Linderman was, by his mother, a nephew of the late Hon. Richard Brodhead, Senator of the United States from Pennsylvania; grandson of Richard Brodhead, one of the Judges of Pike county, and great-grandson of Garrett Brodhead, an officer of the Revolution, and a great-nephew of Luke Brodhead, a Captain in Col. Miles' Regiment, and of Daniel Brodhead, Colonel of the 8th Pennsylvania Regiment of the Continental Line; the latter was afterwards a Brigadier-General, was one of the original members of the Cincinnati of this State, and Surveyor-General of the Commonwealth when the war closed. His only son Daniel was a First Lieutenant in Colonel Shee's Battalion, was taken prisoner by the British, and died after two years' captivity. General Brodhead married Governor Mifflin's widow, and died in Milford, Pike county, in 1803. The nephew of these three brothers, Charles Wessel Brodhead, of New York, was also in the Revolutionary army, a Captain of Grenadiers. They all descended from Daniel Brodhead, a Captain of King Charles II.'s Grenadiers, who had a command in Nichol's expedition, which captured New York from the Dutch in 1664. Captain Brodhead was of the family of that name in Yorkshire, which terminated in England so recently as 1840 in the person of Sir Henry T. L. Brodhead, baronet.

Dr. Henry R. Linderman, after receiving an academic education, entered the New York College of Physicians and Surgeons. When barely of age he graduated, returned to Pike county and began practice with his father, and earned a reputation as a skillful and rising physician.

In 1855 his uncle, Richard Brodhead (United States Senator), procured his appointment as chief clerk of the Philadelphia Mint. He held this position until 1864, when he resigned and engaged in business as a banker and broker in Philadelphia. In 1867 he was appointed Director of the Mint by President Johnson. In 1869 he resigned. In 1870 he was a commissioner of the Government to the Pacific coast to investigate the San Francisco and Carson Mints, and to adjust some intricate bullion questions. In 1871 he was a commissioner to Europe, to examine the coinage systems of the Great Powers. In 1872 he was a commissioner, with the late Dr. Robert E. Rogers, of the University of Pennsylvania, for fitting up the Government refinery at the San Francisco Mint. In the same year he wrote an elaborate report on the condition of the gold and silver market of the world. " In this report he called attention to the disadvantages arising from the computation and quotation of exchange with Great Britain on the old and complicated Colonial basis, and from the undervaluation of foreign coins in computing the value of foreign invoices and levying and collecting duties at the United States Custom Houses." He was the author of the Act of March 9th, 1873, which corrected the defects above referred to. His predictions in this report on the decline in the value of silver as compared to gold were fulfilled to the letter.

He was thoroughly familiar with the practice, science, and finance of the Coinage Department of the Government, and about this time he wrote the Coinage Act of 1873, and secured its passage through Congress. General Grant, then President, considered him as the fittest man to organize the new Bureau, and, though a Democrat, appointed him first Director under the new Act; the Director being at the head of all the Mints and Assay Offices in the United States.

For the remainder of his life until his last illness, which began in the fall of 1878, he worked incessantly. Under his hands the Bureau of the Mints and the entire Coinage and Assay service were shaped in their present form. Much is due to his official subordinates, but his was the master mind, his the skillful and methodical direction, the studious and laborious devotion to the duties and obligations of his high position at the head of the Coinage Department of this great nation,

which have given the United States the best coinage system in
the world. It was Dr. Linderman who projected the "trade
dollar," solely for commerce, and not intended to enter into
circulation here. It was a successful means of finding a
market for our great surplus of silver, which Dr. Linderman
sought to send to Oriental countries rather than flood our own
and depreciate its fickle value. The old silver dollar by the
Coinage Act of 1873 was abolished. The codification of all
the legislation of Congress since the foundation of the Mint in
1792 was thus accomplished. Other needed legislative enactments were passed by Congress on his recommendations.

In 1877 Dr. Linderman wrote, and Putnam published,
"Money and Legal Tender in the United States," a valuable
and interesting contribution to the science of finance, which
was favorably received abroad as well as here. The same year
his official report presented one of the most exhaustive, profound, and able efforts which has ever emanated from the
Government press. The fact that several of his reports were
in use as text books of technical information in some of the
technical schools (notably that at Harvard University), will
serve to show the estimation in which the late Dr. Linderman
was held as an authority upon coinage, mining, and finance.
When the Japanese established their mint, that government
made him the liberal offer of $50,000 to stay in their country
one year and organize their mint service.

When M. Henri Cernuschi, the eminent financier and the
Director of the French Mint, was in this country in 1878, he
said, "Dr. Linderman's name is as celebrated on the continent
of Europe in connection with his opinions on the double standard of metallic currency, as that of Garibaldi in connection
with the Italian revolution."

In 1877 Dr. Linderman was appointed a commissioner, with
power to name two others, to investigate abuses in the San
Francisco Mint and Custom House. He appointed ex-
Governor Low, of California, and Mr. Henry Dodge, and this
commission sat as a court of inquiry in San Francisco in 1877.
He returned to Washington in the autumn of that year. His
report of the commission was duly approved, and all the changes
it advised were made by the Government authorities.

In 1856 Dr. Linderman married Miss Emily Davis, a highly
accomplished and talented lady, daughter of George H. Davis,
one of the pioneer coal operators of the Wyoming and Carbon
districts. Dr. Linderman died at his residence in Washington
in January, 1879, after a long illness superinduced by his
self-sacrificing care and solicitude for public interests. His

conscientious and valuable aid and advice in counsel, his conception of public duty, which so entirely guided his conduct in all his official relations connected with our present monetary system, established through his efforts, justly entitle him to be held in grateful remembrance for the benefits he conferred upon his fellow countrymen.*

COL. A. LOUDON SNOWDEN,
SECOND SUPERINTENDENT.

was born in Cumberland County, Pennsylvania, and descends from one of the old families of Pennsylvania.

He was educated at the Jefferson College in Washington, Pennsylvania. On the completion of his collegiate course he studied law, but on May 7, 1857, just before being admitted to the bar, accepted the position of Register, tendered him by his uncle, the late Hon. James Ross Snowden, then Director of the United States Mint.

In 1866, a vacancy having occurred in the office of Coiner of the Mint, he was appointed by the President, and entered upon the duties of this office October 1, 1866.

At the request of President Grant, in 1876, he was induced to accept the Postmastership of Philadelphia.

He assumed the duties of that office January 1, 1877, with much reluctance, but soon manifested as Postmaster the same capacity for thorough discipline and organization which had distinguished him in the Mint. President Hayes, in December, 1878, tendered him the position of Director of all the Mints of the United States, made vacant by the expiration of the commission of Dr. Linderman. After the death of Dr. Linderman the President again sent for him and urged his acceptance of the place, which he was believed to have declined previous to Dr. Linderman's death from motives of delicacy, having long been the friend of the late Director.

This offer he again declined, as the acceptance of it would necessitate his removal from Philadelphia to Washington.

In the following February the President again made a tender of office. This time it was the superintendency of the Philadelphia Mint, and, as its acceptance of it restored him to a service agreeable to him in every particular, and permitted him to remain among his friends in Philadelphia, he promptly accepted, and assumed control of the Mint on the 1st of March, 1879, and continued in charge of the "Parent Mint" of the United States until June, 1885, when he resigned his commission.

---

* Dr. Linderman's widow and only son, Henry R. Linderman (named for him), a prominent lawyer of Stroudsburg, Penna., are the only survivors of his family.

In January, 1873, he was elected vice-president of the Fire Association, one of the oldest and largest fire insurance companies of the United States. In 1868 he was elected its president. In October, 1880, he was elected president of the "United Fire Underwriters of America," an organization embracing the officers of more than one hundred and fifty of the leading American and foreign companies doing business in the United States, representing a capital of over $118,000,000.

DANIEL M. FOX.

Hon. Daniel M. Fox, the new Superintendent of the United States Mint, was born in this city on the 16th of June, 1819. His ancestors, both on his father's and mother's side, are not without fame, many of them having figured more or less conspicuously in the early history of the country. Daniel Miller, his maternal grandfather, took quite a prominent part in the Revolutionary war, being present with Washington at Germantown, Pa., New Brunswick, N. J., the Highlands, N. Y., Valley Forge, Pa., the siege of Yorktown, and witnessed the surrender of Lord Cornwallis at Yorktown. During the campaign in New Jersey he was taken by the British as a spy and brought to Philadelphia, but effected his escape and rejoined the army. At the termination of the war he finally settled with his family in the old Northern Liberties, where Mr. Fox's grandfather, by the father's side, John Fox, resided. Here Daniel's father and mother were born, and here he himself first saw the light, and was reared and educated.

His parents were possessed of very little of this world's goods, but that did not prevent them from giving their son a liberal education, which he was not backward in taking advantage of. After leaving school the first two years were employed as clerk in a store, after which he turned his attention to conveyancing, as he intended to make that his permanent profession. He devoted the next five years to the close study of all its intricate details in the office of the late Jacob F. Hoeckley, who at that period stood at the head of the profession in this city, and graduating with eminent credit he commenced practice for himself.

The profession is one affording many temptations to men who are not well grounded in strict integrity, and sustained in

Daniel M Fox

the paths of rectitude and **virtue** by a conscientious regard **for** the *meum* and *tuum* of a well-ordered business life; but Mr. Fox, looking upon his profession as one of dignity and trust, soon commanded and permanently secured the confidence of the public, **by** avoiding those speculative ventures which have brought so much disrepute upon it, and by a scrupulous regard for the **interests** of those who placed their property in **his** keeping. **In consequence**, the business entrusted to him **has** increased **to such an extent** from **year** to year that it is said **he has more estates in his charge** for settlement, as administrator, **executor**, or trustee, than any other single individual in Philadelphia. **His** practice constantly increasing as **time** rolled on, the laws touching real **estate operations** becoming more complicated year by year, and appreciating the necessity in many cases for court proceedings to secure perfection of title, he submitted himself to a legal **examination, and was admitted to** the Philadelphia **bar in** November, **1878.**

His Public Career.

His first step in public life was **at the** age **of** twenty-one, when he was elected a member of the Board of School Directors of the district in which he then lived, and for many years prior to 1854, when the city was consolidated, and the law in that regard changed, he was President of the Board. For **many** years he had taken an active interest in the public **schools**, and **was** a pioneer **in** the night-school system for **adults**. He was chosen **two** consecutive terms by the City **Councils as a Director of Girard** College, and also represented **the Northern Liberties** in the Board of Health, having charge **of the sanitary matters and the** quarantine regulations of the city, and was quite active and efficient in the abatement of the cholera, **which was epidemic here twice** during the **nine years** he served in that Board.

For **three years he represented** his ward in the Select Council of **Philadelphia with credit and** ability. **In 1861 he** retired from **Councils, and in** the year following was unanimously **nominated for the** Mayoralty by **the Democratic party.** The city at that time was strongly Republican, and he was defeated by Hon. Alexander Henry, although he ran largely **ahead of** his **ticket.** In 1865 he again received a unanimous nomination for the same **office,** and ran against Hon. Morton McMichael and with the same result. His personal popularity, however, **was** in the ascendant, and when he was placed in nomination **in 1868** against General Hector Tyndale, he was duly elected.

On January 1, **1869, he** was inaugurated, **and** his first official duty as Mayor was to formally receive on behalf of the city authorities General Grant as President-elect. The reception took place in Independence Hall, in the presence of Councils and a large number of prominent citizens, and was conducted on the part of the new Mayor with ease, grace, and elegance. **His municipal** administration was marked by many reformatory **and sanitary measures,** especially in those portions of the city **where the impurity of** the denizens hazarded the health of more respectable neighborhoods. It was during his official term that the Volunteer Fire Department ceased to exist. It had been his practice during its closing days to attend all conflagrations for the double purpose of holding a moral check on the lawless and to stimulate the police in their duties of keeping the streets clear for the free exercise of those whose business it was to extinguish the flames. The passage by Councils of the ordinance establishing a Paid Fire Department created a profound sensation in the city, arousing the bitter feelings of many of the volunteer firemen, and kindling an intense anxiety on the part of the people generally as to the fate of the bill when it reached the hands of the Mayor. He retained it for a fortnight, unsigned, evidently desiring to soften the feeling engendered by its passage, and also to perfect such arrangements as would be necessary to meet any emergency in carrying the act into effect. The latter being accomplished, he formally approved the ordinance and it became a law. This course was very unpalatable to the riotous element of the volunteers, who manifested their feelings in various ways, such as suspending the effigy of the Mayor in several engine houses, but no other violent demonstrations of any moment occurred, as the steps taken by his officers proved effective and rigorous; these, coupled with the co-operation of many of the discreet firemen, enabled the new "Paid Department" to go into operation without any disturbance whatever, and the city has ever since rejoiced in an efficient system without any of the former accompaniments of noise, riot, and public disturbance.

A startling attempt at assassination occurred during Mayor Fox's incumbency, in the shooting of United States Revenue Detective James Brooks, in open day, in a Front street store, by some miscreants. The case was at once taken in hand by the Mayor, who by stimulating the police and offering heavy rewards caused the arrest of the parties. Their conviction soon followed. Whenever any question of grave public importance presented itself, it was his practice to invite conferences with the most prominent citizens at his office, as to the best course to be pursued; thus, while showing a true devotion to the public interests, he was enabled to act with great sagacity; he also brought to his support the power of eloquence, which he possesses in an eminent degree; this added much to his popularity. He did not hesitate to use the veto whenever he differed with Councils, and during his term he transmitted to these bodies thirty-two messages of this character, the majority of which were sustained. His official term ended in a most gratifying manner, both chambers of Councils unanimously passing resolutions of thanks for his able and energetic administration of the city's affairs. This was followed by a grand banquet at the Academy of Music, tendered to him by our most distinguished citizens, irrespective of party. In two successive State conventions he received complimentary votes for the Gubernatorial nominations.

The great International Exposition in commemoration of the centennial anniversary of the birth of our nation was held in this city in 1876. In the preparation for this grand demonstration, in its opening and down to its close, in the autumn of that year, Mr. Fox took a leading part, the incipient step having been taken in the Mayor's Office during his administration, in a consultation with a committee from the Franklin Institute, who waited upon him for that purpose. As an active and earnest member of the Centennial Board of Finance, which had charge of all the funds for the Exposition, Mr. Fox contributed his time, his means, and his voice greatly to its promotion and final success.

Once more Mr. Fox was called to the discharge of an important public duty. For a number of years a controversy had existed between the general Government and the railroad corporations with reference to the transportation of the United States mails, the former complaining that the service was not satisfactorily rendered, and the latter that they were not adequately compensated.

On the 12th of July, 1876, Congress passed a bill authorizing the President to appoint a Commission of three civilians to investigate the subject and make report upon it. Mr. Fox was one of the appointees, his colleagues being selected from other States. The Commission, in the exercise of its functions, visited every section of the country, embracing a distance of travel of over twenty-eight thousand miles. Sessions were held in all the principal cities, much testimony taken, and when its labors were completed a report of great value was prepared and presented, which went far towards a satisfactory settlement of the controversy.

[From The History of the Philadelphia Police.]

One of the most important occurrences during Mr. Fox's term as Mayor was the abolition of the old Volunteer Fire Department. The ordinance for the erection of a Paid Fire department was passed December 29, 1870, after a series of hot debates. The old volunteers were a power in politics, but their acts of violence and incendiarism made it imperative in the opinion of a majority of citizens that they should be superseded. The passage of the ordinance caused a sensation because it was not believed that Councils would dare to abolish the volunteers. Feeling ran high. The firemen held meeting after meeting in their engine-houses. All attention was directed towards the Mayor. Would he sign the ordinance and make it a law? He had ten days in which to consider the bill. He was known to favor it; but day after day passed and he took no action. Meanwhile he was not asleep. He had perfected police arrangements whereby the whole force could be called out at once on the outbreak of any violence, and the excitement was so great that the rowdy element and the firemen were expected to sally forth at any moment. There were two or three isolated outrages, but no general riot. The ten days drew towards a close and the excitement became less intense every day. It was with this object in view that the Mayor delayed signing the ordinance. He waited until the last day before putting his signature to the bill. The volunteers had become in a degree reconciled to the measure, and some of them hoped to resume work with engine and hook-and-ladder under the new system.

The old volunteer firemen now hold Mr. Fox in high esteem. At the great fire in Newhall, Borie & Co.'s sugar refinery, which stood at the corner of Race and Crown streets, the lives of a number of the volunteers were endangered through their own stubbornness, and only saved through determined action on the part of the Mayor. The engine-house of the refinery was a single story building facing on Crown street; over it was a projection five or six stories in height containing the hoisting apparatus and other machinery of great weight.

His Watchful Care Saves Many Lives.

About a score of the firemen took up a position on the roof of the engine-house and directed a stream of water against the main building. Unknown to them the flames were rapidly eating their way to the machinery in the projection over them. The Mayor made it a point to attend all important fires, and frequently his vigilance at great conflagrations re-

sulted in the detection of gangs of thieves who operated in
the uniform of firemen. On this occasion he observed the
danger which threatened the men. It was evident to him
that the machinery would soon be reached, and the projection
fall. A serious disaster would be the consequence unless the
men removed. The Mayor sent the Chief of Police to inform
them of their danger, and endeavored to induce them to retire
from their perilous position. They angrily declared they
would occupy whatever place they pleased, and said the Mayor
should mind his own business as he had no authority over
them. The Mayor saw that prompt and decisive action was
necessary if the lives of the men were not to be sacrificed.
He ordered Chief Mulholland to drive the headstrong fellows
from the roof by force. All the policemen in the neighbor-
hood of the fire were collected and they charged the volunteers, who were routed with some difficulty and came clamor-
ing around the Mayor, demanding to know by what authority
he had interfered with them, execrating and threatening him
with personal violence.

"Wait five minutes and I will give you an answer," said
Mr. Fox, quietly.

A moment later the projection with all the heavy machinery
fell, crushing the engine-house. The men who a moment
before had reviled the Mayor were silent for a moment, then
they gathered around him and gave three prolonged and hearty
cheers for Daniel M. Fox.

Mr. Fox was the first Mayor who directed the roping off
the streets during large conflagrations, thereby keeping away
not only the crogds who drawn by idle curriosity went simply
to look on but also those persons who may have been attracted
for purposes of theft. It aided considerably, too, in giving
the Fire Department a clean working space, thus adding to
their efficiency, and also avoiding the chance of accidents from
falling embers or walls. This plan so wisely begun has been
followed with advantage by every successive Mayor.

Mr. Fox's participation in the philanthropic and benevolent
movements of the city has always been unlimited. As President of the Pennsylvania Society for the Protection of Children from Cruelty, Trustee of the Pennsylvrnia Institution for
the Deaf and Dumb, and in his connection with many other
charitable works, his constant aim has been the alleviation of
the sufferings and the general welfare of his fellow men.

Personally, Mr. Fox is of dignified and distinguished presence, yet in manner affable, courteous, and kind. Always

interested in his fellow men, he draws men towards him and impresses them with the sincerity of his nature and the unselfishness of his purpose. Love of justice is one of the strong characteristics of the man, and his life has been singularly free from the petty strifes which disfigure the lives of so many who have had to fight their battle against odds. His selection for the Superintendency of the Mint, being unsought, was a just tribute to his unquestioned integrity and his eminent abilities as a public man. The country is fortunate in his preferment, and his administration of the affairs of the Mint will fitly crown an honored career.

Superintendent Fox has greatly improved the immediate surroundings of the Mint since his entrance upon duty. The areas have been cleared of rubbish, temporary wooden structures demolished, where it is possible to dispense with them, and a systematic policing of the premises has been adopted. But perhaps the most notable of the improvements which Superintendent Fox has made is the removal of the old steam plant from the body of the basement and the creation of a new and much more efficient plant in vaults prepared outside of the walls. This has had the effect to render the atmosphere of the building cool and pure, and at the same time has actually increased the working space nearly forty per cent. Another story has also been added to the adjusting room, with appliances for cooking and toilet, thus increasing the comfort of the ladies employed in that department. The plots on either hand of the entrance on Chestnut street show some happy efforts to please the eye, in a renewal of the sward and landscape gardening in colors. The fine specimens of American cyress in the centre of these plots seem to have borrowed fresh attractions from their new and beautiful setting, and their foliage contrasts pleasingly with the clumps of foliage plants and exotics beneath. Throughout the premises the supervision of a thorough business man is apparant; nothing seems to escape the eyes of the vigilant Superintendent.

COINERS.

HENRY VOIGT, the first Chief Coiner, was appointed by President Washington, January 29, 1793. He was selected on account of his mechanical knowledge and skill, being a closkmader by trade. Many of our old families bear witness to the skill of Mr. Voigt in the affection they have for many an "old clock on the stairs," for the manufacture of which timekeepers he was quite famous. Mr. Voigt held office until removed by death in February, 1814.

ADAM ECKFELDT was born in Philadelphia, June 15, 1769. He was trained to mechanical pursuits by his father, who was a large manufacturer of edge-tools and implements. On the establishment of the Mint he was engaged to construct some of the machinery for it. He built the first screw-coining presses. The contrivance for ejecting the piece from the collar, together with some other mechanical appliances, were his invention.

In an old pay-roll of 1795 (see page 12), we find the name of "Adam Eckfeldt, Die Forger and Turner." His official connection dates from January 1, 1796, when he was appointed Assistant Coiner by Director Boudinot, with the consent of President Washington. Upon the death of Henry Voigt, Mr. Eckfeldt was appointed to succeed him as Chief Coiner, and remained in that position until he resigned, in 1839. He continued to visit the Mint for some years after; and he is yet remembered as a hard worker in the Mint, without compensation. For half a century he was one of the central figures of the Mint service. His mechanical skill, his zeal, energy, and uprightness, brought him many distinctions, both as an officer and a citizen.

In his letter of resignation he warmly recommends the appointment of Franklin Peale, in the following terms: "I feel it my duty, in leaving office, to recommend that my place be filled by Mr. Franklin Peale, the present Melter and Refiner. Our close association as fellow-officers has made me acquainted with his peculiar qualifications, and I therefore know him to be fitted for the situation; and I do not know any other person that is." He had a high ideal of what a chief coiner should be.

Mr. Eckfeldt died February 6, 1852, in his 83d year.

FRANKLIN PEALE was the son of Charles Willson Peale, the eminent artist and founder of Peale's Museum. Born in the Hall of the American Philosophical Society, October 15, 1795, he was presented to the society by his father, when four months old, as "the first child born in the Philosophical Hall," and with a request that the society should name him. He was accordingly named after the chief founder and first President of the Society—Franklin.

Young Peale early showed a taste for mechanics, and his father gave him every facility to improve himself in any direction in which nature seemed to lead him. Part of his general education was received at the University of Pennsylvania and part at the Germantown Academy. At the age of seventeen he entered the machine shop of Hodgson & Bro., Delaware.

He soon grew to be a skilled mechanic and draughtsman. Some time after he became manager of his father's Museum. He assisted Baldwin in the construction of the first locomotive built in this country. In 1833 Mr. Peale entered the Mint service, and was sent to Europe by Director Moore to examine into foreign Mint methods. He brought with him valuable apparatus for the Assay Department, together with other important improvements and suggestions. He was appointed Melter and Refiner in 1836 and Chief Coiner in 1839. He introduced the first steam coining press, the milling machine and some other of our more modern forms of Mint machinery.

Mr. Peale's administration as Chief Coiner may be said to mark an era in the mechanic arts of Minting. Being specially fitted, by natural genius as well as education, for the position which he adorned, his mildness, integrity, gentlemanly bearing and high moral and mental culture constituted him a model officer. His connection with the service lasted until 1854. He died on the 5th of May, 1870.

GEORGE K. CHILDS, appointed December 12, 1854.

LEWIS R. BROOMALL, appointed June 30, 1861.

JOHN G. BUTLER, appointed November 30, 1863.

A. LOUDON SNOWDEN, appointed October 1, 1866.

(For sketch of A. Loudon Snowden, see list of Directors and Superintendents, page 92.)

COLONEL O. C. BOSBYSHELL. On the 4th of May, 1869, Ex-Governor Pollock, then Director of the Mint, appointed Col. Bosbyshell Register of Deposits. His course in the Mint was so satisfactory that, without solicitation, he was made assistant coiner by Col. A. L. Snowden, the then coiner, on the 1st of October, 1872. Upon Col. Snowden's appointment as Postmaster of Philadelphia, Col. Bosbyshell was appointed Coiner of the Mint by President Grant, on the 15th of December, 1876, and remained in that capacity until January, 1885, when, to the regret of all parties having business relations with him, he tendered his resignation to accept a responsible position in the Controller's Office, tendered him by his friend, Col. Robert P. Dechert.

WILLIAM S. STEEL was born in the City of Philadelphia, on the 1st of March, 1841. He received a good common school education, and in 1856 entered the office of David Cooper & Co., at Girard's wharves, remaining engaged in mercantile pursuits till 1861. At 19 years of age he was appointed by Colonel James Ross Snowden, then Director of the United States Mint, First Assistant Weigh Clerk. In this position he served continuously through Colonel J. Ross Snowden, ex-Governor Pollock, and Colonel A. Loudon Snowden's administrations. In September, 1862, just before the battle of Antietam, Mr. Steele entered the State service, and served with the Thirty-second Regiment, Pennsylvania Volunteers, until discharged by expiration of term. When Colonel A. Loudon Snowden was transferred to the Post Office, January, 1877, Mr. Steele, upon the recommendation of the then Coiner, Colonel O. C. Bosbyshell, became Assistant Coiner, a position he filled in a most acceptable manner, until Colonel Bosbyshell's retirement in February, 1885, when he was made Coiner.

HARRY A. CHESTER, Assistant Coiner, was born in Philadelphia (Northern Liberties), September 10. 1852, and educated in the North East School, Sixth Section. He was an attachee of the National House of Representatives from 1876 to 1882, clerk in Register of Wills' Office from January 1, 1883, until May, 1885, when he was appointed by Colonel A. Loudon Snowden as Assistant Weigh Clerk, and promoted by Hon. Daniel M. Fox in October, 1886.

DR. HENRY LEFFMANN was appointed Chief Coiner at the Philadelphia Mint January 10, 1888, by President Cleveland. Dr. Leffmann was born in Philadelphia September 9, 1847, and was educated in the public schools of Philadelphia, including four years at the Central High School. He devoted three years in practical study in the laboratory of Dr. Charles M. Cresson, and graduated at Jefferson Medical College in 1869, having been for some years assistant to the Professor of Chemistry at the College, and in 1875 was elected Lecturer on Toxicology, which position he held for a number of years. In 1876 he was elected to take charge of the laboratory of the Central High School, and remained in that position for four years. In 1883 he was elected Professor of Chemistry and Metallurgy in the Pennsylvania College of Dental Surgery, a position which he still holds; and he has been for a number of years Professor of Chemistry and Mineralogy in the Wagner Free Institute of Science. Dr. Leffman has been engaged as chemical expert in patent and criminal cases, notably in the Goerson poisoning case and the chrome-yellow poisoning cases. He is a member of several American and foreign scientific societies, has contributed papers to current scientific literature, and has for the past five years been editor of *The Polyclinic*, a monthly medical journal. In 1880 he was a candidate for Coroner on the Democratic ticket, but was defeated, and in 1884 was appointed Port Physician for Philadelphia by Governor Pattison, and held that position until October, 1887.

ASSAYERS.

JACOB R. ECKFELDT, Sixth Assayer, was born in Philadelphia, 1846. He entered the Assay Department as Second Weigher, in 1865. By regular promotions he reached the position of Assistant Assayer, in 1872, and upon the death of his superior he was appointed and confirmed as Assayer, December 21, 1881. The position of Assayer is one of great responsibility, and demands not only scientific training but wide and special knowledge and experience upon subjects relating to the history and arts of Coinage. Since the foundation of the Mint there have been but six official heads of this department.

WILLIAM McINTIRE was born in Delaware in **1831**. He entered the Assay Department of the Mint as an assistant in September, 1853, which position he held, with the exception of a short interim while he was engaged in mercantile business, until October, 1887, when by regular promotion he was appointed Assistant Assayer.

JACOB R. ECKFELDT.

EXTRACT FROM AN OBITUARY NOTICE BY MR. DU BOIS.

(Read before the American Philosophical Society, Oct. 4th, 1872.)

Jacob R. Eckfeldt, late Assayer of the Mint, was the son of Adam and Margaretta Eckfeldt, and was born in Philadelphia, March —, 1803. He was, therefore, in his seventieth year, at the time of decease, August 9th, 1872.

In the Spring of 1832, Mr. John Richardson, who had been Assayer about one year, and did not find the employment congenial to his tastes, informed Mr Eckfeldt that he intended to resign, and wished him to prepare to take the place. Mr. E. shrank from this responsibility, and declined. But some of his friends who had influence with President Jackson, presented his name with a strong recommendation and he was appointed without being asked as to his party preferences. This occured on the 30th of April, 1832. He therefore held the office *over forty years.*

When he entered upon the work, he had to encounter some embarrassments. The apparatus was old-fashioned, and not calculated for nice results. The silver assay had been well performed, without going to a close figure, for many years; but gold was little known in the country or at the Mint, and it is not surprising that its assay was incorrectly performed. Add to this, there was the coarse and cumbrous nomenclature, brought from the old country, of carats and grains for gold fineness, and so many grains to the pound for silver fineness.

Close upon all this, that is to say, in June, 1834, came the celebrated reduction in the standards of our gold coin, one of the chief measures of the Jackson administration. This changed gold from a curiosity to a currency; bullion and foreign coin flowed to the mint, and accuracy of assay was more than ever needful. Mr. Eckfeldt was equal to the emergency, and resolutely introduced reforms, which, at first, made the older officers stand in doubt.

In those days, about the time the new mint edifice on Chestnut street was finishing, Mr. Peale was sent to London and Paris to observe the methods of assaying and refining, and to procure a new apparatus. We were thus supplied with French beams, weights, and cupel furnaces, and with the appliances of Gay-Lussac's humid assay, and the printed details of the process. Soon after, Mr. Saxton, famous for his skill in constructing balances and other delicate instruments, returned from a long schooling in that line in London, and was employed in the Mint. Thus furnished, Mr. Eckfeldt felt himself "set up," and able to compete with the foreign assayers, and if he was ever more precise, it was because he disregarded certain allowances which had become a time-honored custom.

A large importation of fine gold bars from France, known as the French Indemnity, and which came because President Jackson declared he "would submit to nothing that was wrong," gave a fine opportunity for testing and comparing foreign assays; and it was generally found that these bars were somewhat below the alleged fineness. A still more important discovery, was the fact that British Sovereigns ran below their standard of fineness. This happened when he had been in office less than three years, and the Director was unwilling to set the finding of young Eckfeldt against the experience of Old England. The Assayer being assured and re-assured of the accuracy of his results, Director Moore consented to notify the British Government of their error. The result was a closer scrutiny in the London Mint, and a final acknowledgement that they were wrong. This was no less a triumph for Mr. Eckfeldt, than it was a contribution to exact science, and an honor to the American Government.

It is not surprising, that he felt at first the inconvenience of passing from one form of nomenclature to another, though to a better one. A friend remarks, "I recall conversations with Mr. Eckfeldt, showing how seriously he felt the revolution. He would *think* in carats, and *report* in decimals. And I often recur to this as illustrating the kind of difficulties which would arise in case of a decimalising of weights and measures."

For some years prior to 1842, Mr. Eckfeldt and his Assistant, in addition to their ordinary duties, engaged in the preparation of an original and comprehensive work on the Coins of all Nations; on the Varieties of Gold and Silver Bullion; on Counterfeit Coins, and on other subjects related thereto. This was published in 1842, and has long been regarded as a standard authority. In 1850, they issued a supplementary smaller work, and again in 1852.

As the United States increased in commerce, wealth and population, the Mint of course increased in work. In particular, Mexican dollars came in great quantities for recoinage. Not only were our vaults full, but our entries and corridors were at times crowded with rows of kegs. Every day, for years, we had the constant task of sixteen melts of silver ingots to melt and assay; and it was a great advantage and satisfaction to be supplied with the *humid* apparatus.

The success of gold mining in our Southern States, and the increasing commerce of New Orleans, gave rise to the establishment of three branch mints at the South, in 1837; and it devolved upon Mr. Eckfeldt to become schoolmaster, and educate the three assayers appointed for those places. The same had to be done again at a latter date for other mints and assay offices.

In December, 1848, came the first lot of gold grains from California; and with the opening of the next year the tide set in most powerfully. I shall not here speak of this great turning-point in metallic currency any further than as it affected the mint, or rather the labor which it laid upon Mr. Eckfeldt and his department. As is well known, the lots were numerous, and the aggregate amount was enormous. Instead of making gold assays by dozens, we had to go through with hundreds every day, following the arrival of each steamer. We procured young men as operators in the weigh-room and additional workmen in the laboratory; and in spite all the help we were all overworked. Here let me say that the persons who have been educated by Mr. Eckfeldt to this profession have done credit to the selection that was made, not only by skill, diligence, and good character while here, but wherever they are now scattered to other mints and assay offices, or to different pursuits.

The gold pressure continued for about five years, when it was relieved by the creation of a Government assay office in New York, and a branch mint at San Francisco. But directly sequent to this came the change of standard in silver coin, causing an immense recoinage in small pieces. Thus our daily assays continued to count by hundreds. This lasted for some years. When it began to slacken off, a law was passed for calling in the large copper coins and issuing in their stead pieces of copper-nickel alloy of much smaller size.

The analysis of Nickel alloys was not well laid down in the books, and the European or other assays which came with purchased lots showed an incorrect determination. Mr. Eckfeldt was therefore obliged to study out and perfect this assay, which is more tedious and laborious, though of less consequence, than the assay of the precious metals.

But it was his habit to be as scrupulous in minor matters as in major; and after the routine was well settled it went on with the same clock-work regularity as the other branches of assaying. I need not say that this nickel coinage imposed another heavy pressure upon the mint for years.

After this came the substitution of the Bronze alloy; and this called for another process of assay, and brought us a great deal of work.

I thus hastily review this sequence of gold, silver, nickel, and bronze, not only as an interesting part of Mint History, but to show the varied and abundant services of the untiring, energetic Principal Assayer, and the masterly skill with which he met every obligation.

His skill and success as an Assayer and Analyst largely consisted in his power of finding out what was defective or erroneous, and in applying the proper remedy. It often seemed that what was a puzzle to others was to him a matter of quick insight.

In the assays of certain complex alloys, and of low grades of gold and silver, he contrived various methods which are not in print, but which are of great use in the daily manipulations.

And here I may state that he not only introduced great accuracy and precision in the assays, but carried special investigations to a delicacy almost incredible. Thus, much interest was excited by a publication some years ago, both in this country and across the Atlantic, of his experiment upon the brick-clay which underlies our city. Taking two samples from the center of the town and the suburbs he found they contained gold at the rate of nearly 12 grains (say fifty cents) to the ton of clay in its ordinary moisture. Other experiments went to prove the very general diffusion of gold, in infinitesimal proportions.

Some analysts, through want of exactitude, or for the pleasure of making a sensation, may produce very curious results; but Mr. Eckfeldt was conscientious, I may say, nervously scrupulous, about stating anything he was not sure of. Partly for that reason, partly for the very love of work, he was laborious to a fault, all his life long.

UNITED STATES MINT OFFICERS.

Washington, D. C., James P. Kimball, Director of the Mint.................................. $4,500
Philadelphia, Pa., Daniel M. Fox, Superintendent... 4,500
Boisé City, Idaho, Norman H. Camp.. 2,000
Carson City, Nevada, James Crawford, Superintendent....................................... 3,000
Charlotte, N. C., Calvin J. Cowles, Assayer... 1,500
Denver, Colorado, Herman Silver, Assayer.. 2,500
Helena, Montana, Russell B. Harrison, Assayer.. 2,500
New Orleans, La., Andrew W. Smyth, Superintendent.. 3,500
New York, N. Y., Andrew Mason, Superintendent... 4,500
San Francisco, Cal., Edw. F. Burton, Superintendent.. 4,500
St. Louis, Mo., Eliot C. Jewett, Assayer... 2,500

WILLIAM E. DU BOIS.

Extract from an obituary notice by Robert Patterson.

(Read before the American Philosophical Society, November 18, 1881.)

William Ewing Du Bois was born at Doylestown, Pennsylvania, December 15, 1810. Through his father, Rev. Uriah Du Bois, he was descended from Louis Du Bois, a French Huguenot of honorable extraction, who emigrated to America in 1660, seeking freedom of religious worship, and, in connection with others of his countrymen, formed the settlement of New Paltz, Ulster County, New York. Through his mother, Martha Patterson, daughter of Professor Robert Patterson, of the University of Pennsylvania, he inherited the Scotch-Irish element which has exerted so marked an influence in the development of our country

The father of Mr. Du Bois was a Presbyterian clergyman, in charge of churches in and near Doylestown, and was principal of the Union Academy at that place, a classical school then and afterwards of high reputation. He was greatly respected, both as preacher and teacher.

The bright and studious mind of Mr. Du Bois gathered every advantage from his opportunities, and he was well furnished in the classics and mathematics, and in English literature. While yet a boy he developed a freedom and capacity as a writer quite remarkable.

His oldest brother was an eminent member of the bar, and it seemed fitting that Mr. Du Bois should, under his guidance, adopt the law as his profession. He accordingly pursued the usual course, in the meantime aiding to support himself by literary work and conveyancing, and was admitted to practice in September, 1832. But his health failing him on account of a bronchial affection, he accepted an appointment in the Mint at Philadelphia, and thus began the life-work by which his reputation was established.

Mr. Du Bois entered the Mint in September, 1833, and was first employed in the office of the Director, Dr. Moore. In 1835, at the request of the Assayer, Mr. Jacob R. Eckfeldt, he was transferred to a more congenial position in the assay department. Here he continued for the remainder of his life. In 1836 he was appointed Assistant Assayer. In September, 1872, he succeeded Mr. Eckfeldt as Assayer, and remained at the head of the department until his death, July 14, 1881, thus completing nearly forty-eight years of Mint service.

Mr. Du Bois early took rank as an accomplished assayer, and long before his death had reached the head of his profession.

The close intimacy between Mr. Du Bois and Mr. Eckfeldt developed into warm friendship. The tie was made closer by the marriage of Mr. Du Bois, in 1840, to Susanna Eckfeldt, the sister of his chief. I shall have to speak of published works and scientific communications appearing under the names of Eckfeldt and Du Bois. Although it was understood that Mr. Du Bois was the sole literary author, yet no separate claim of authorship was made by either. Whatever of reputation was earned, each was contented that it might be shared by the other, and jealousy never for a moment weakened a union that bound them for life.

In the year 1834 a change took place in the ratio of gold to silver in the standard of U. S. coins, the effect of which was to bring large deposits of gold to the Mint. The coinage previously had been chiefly of silver. The more equal supply of the precious metals gave active employment in the assay of each of them, and was, of course, most valuable as an experience to Mr. Du Bois, who about this time became connected with the assay department.

In 1837, on revision of the Mint laws and standards brought about by Dr. Robert M. Patterson, then Director, a reform was effected in the method of reporting assays, the millesimal system taking the place of the time-honored but cumbrous method of carats and grains. About this time, also, the older plan of assaying silver was abandoned, the humid assay being substituted, and largely worked under the direct supervision of Mr. Du Bois.

About 1838 branch mints were organized in the States of Louisiana, Georgia, and North Carolina. The labors and responsibilities of the Philadelphia assay department were increased by this development, partly from the necessity of instructing assayers for the new branches, and partly in testing the correctness of the assays made there.

In 1848 the great discovery of gold in California was made known. This brought a tremendous pressure on every department of the Mint, and not the least on the assayers. The gold coinage was, in three years, raised from a little over three million dollars to more than sixty-two millions. The assays were often counted by hundreds in a day. But whatever the pressure in the office, accuracy ruled, and the correctness of the assays was never impeached.

In 1853 a change was effected in the law for providing subordinate silver coins. This brought about, for some years succeeding, an unprecedented coinage of that metal, and still further increased the labors of the assay department.

He instituted the Cabinet of coins which now adorns the Mint. This was commenced in 1838. A small annual appropriation was procured from Congress for this purpose, and the work of collection committed entirely to Mr. Du Bois. He brought to it all the enthusiasm which animates most numismatists, sobered, however, by good judgment. His expenditures were always judicious. Some of the best of the specimens were culled from the Mint deposits for the bullion value, merely, of the pieces. After the collection had taken good shape, and been well classified, he wrote and published, in 1846, a description of it, under the title "Pledges of History," etc. The title thus selected intimated his opinion as to the real value of such collections. He thought that a coin should be prized for its historical teaching, or artistic merit, and discouraged the rage to possess a piece simply because of its rarity. Mr. Du Bois acted as curator of the Cabinet until his death.

Another important labor undertaken by Mr. Du Bois (in connection with Mr. Eckfeldt) was the preparation and publication, in 1842, of a "Manual of the Gold and Silver Coins of all nations, struck within the past century." This was a work of very great labor, and, from its expense, of some risk also to the authors. It is admirably arranged, the information clear, and it embraced every subject of interest at that date as to coins, bullion, counterfeits, etc. Subsequently, in 1850 and 1851, supplements were published covering later topics, made prominent in consequence of the California gold discoveries.

The writings of Mr. Du Bois were numerous, and continued up to the year of his death. His papers on numismatics were frequent and always attractive, his last appearance in print being in April of this year, in an article on the "Coinage of the Popes." To the "American Philosophical Society," of which he was elected a member in 1844, he made various communications on behalf of Mr. Eckfeldt and himself, mostly on topics suggested by experiences in the assay department. Among the most curious was one on "The Natural Dissemination of Gold," by which we were astonished to learn that this precious metal is found in appreciable quantity in the clays underlying our city.

In 1869 he wrote for the "Bankers' Magazine," "Propositions for a Revised System of Weights, and a Restoration of Silver Currency." The development of his views on these subjects is a model of clear exposition, and the conclusions reached were such as might be expected from a mind aiming to attain practical results rather than to impose visionary theories.

From the beginning he was highly esteemed at the Mint. It was his ambition to acquire a knowledge of every branch of the service, and with his capacity and opportunities this end was attained. He early became the trusted friend and counsellor of his colleagues, and was able to serve them in many ways, perhaps most of all with his ready pen. As time passed, and forty-eight years of experience was given to him, he was recognized by all as the Nestor of the Mint service. And here I pause to draw a lesson, from the example of Mr. Du Bois's life, as to the value of a properly organized civil service. In the department with which he was connected, political tests were never obtruded, and permanence of tenure followed on merit. On no other basis could his services have been claimed or retained. They would have been transferred to a private sphere, probably to his pecuniary gain, certainly to the public loss. He was very accessible, and ever ready to lend aid from the stores of his knowledge, but in particular did he delight to instruct and bring forward his younger friends.

Mr. Du Bois was able to fulfill his official duties until within a few months of his death. He was fully conscious of his approaching end, preserving his intelligence to the last, and the faith which had comforted him in this life supported him at its close.

The following minute was adopted at a meeting of the officers and employees after his decease:

"The remarkably close conformity of the United States coins to the standard assigned them by law, has been recognized by the highest Mint authorities of the world to be unsurpassed, if quite equalled, in its uniform exactness. The founding of such a reputation and its continuance during the last half-century, are largely due to the joint labors of the late Jacob R. Eckfeldt and William E. Du Bois."

MELTERS AND REFINERS.

JOSEPH CLOUD, appointed January, 1797; served until January, 1836 (39 years).

FRANKLIN PEALE, appointed January 5, 1836.

JONAS R. McCLINTOCK, appointed February 19, 1840.

RICHARD S. McCULLOH, appointed in April, 1846; served until April 1, 1849.

JAMES CURTIS BOOTH, Melter and Refiner, was born in Philadelphia in 1810, educated in the same place, and graduated in the University of Pennsylvania 1829. After study and field practice in the Rensselaer School, at Troy, N. Y., in 1831–32, under the late Professor A. Eaton, Mr. Booth studied Practical Chemistry in Germany, in 1833–34–35, in the laboratories of Professors F. Wohler and G. Magnus, and in visiting accessible manufacturing establishments in Germany and England having relation to chemistry. The late Prof. J. F. Frazer and Mr Booth were the two Assistants on the Geological Survey of Pennsylvania in its first year, 1836. Mr. Booth next had charge of the Geological Survey of Delaware in 1837–38 (being often assisted by Prof. Frazer), and published his report on the survey in 1839–40.

Mr. Booth, observing the great deficiency in the knowledge of Applied Chemistry in his native place, opened a laboratory for teaching the same, by chemical analysis and by operating, in 1836, and the same laboratory has been continued successfully to the present time by Dr. T. H. Garrett and Mr. A. Blair.

With the same object in view, Mr. Booth lectured at the Franklin Institute for nine successive winters, giving three full courses of lectures, each of three winters' duration (1836–1845).

Prior to 1850 Mr. Booth published the Encyclopædia of Chemistry, being the author of the majority of the articles contained in it, with valuable contributions by Prof. R. S. McCulloch and others. It was a valuable adjunct to the study of chemistry for many years.

The Director and officers of the Mint unsuccessfully solicited the appointment of Mr. Booth as Melter and Refiner of the Mint in 1838–40, but in 1849 Mr. Booth obtained, through his friend, Mr. Meredith, the appointment, over the signature of President Z. Taylor, and has continued in the same position from that date to 1887, a period of more than thirty-six years. He resigned his office at the close of the year 1887

Dr. David K. Tuttle, of the Carson City Mint, appointed Melter and Refiner January 10, 1888.

Nathaniel B. Boyd, Assistant Melter and Refiner, was born in Philadelphia, January, 1832. Twenty years later, he was graduated with honors at Burlington College. After leaving College he studied law, and was admitted to the Philadelphia Bar in 1854. In 1869 he accepted an appointment in the National Mint, tendered him by Director Pollock. In 1873 he was appointed Assistant Melter and Refiner, a position which he still occupies (1885).

THE MINT ENGRAVERS.

(Extract from Patterson Du Bois' Biographical Sketch of "Our Mint Engravers.")

Whatever may be said concerning the peculiar responsibilities of the officers of the Mint, who are occupied with the various operations of turning bullion into coin, it must be conceded that none of them occupies a position so dubious and, in some ways, so uneviable as the Engraver. In the general transactions of the Mint, he is the most retired—the most obscure—of its officers; yet his card is in every one's pocket.

As to the types of coinage, the standards are as numerous as the eyes that water for them, and there is no piece but may be said to be outside of *somebody's* tolerance. No other artist undergoes such an ordeal, for those who do not admire this painting or that statue are not compelled to hug and hoard it, much less to toil for its possession. The engraver who can, from his retired window, see the critical millions clutching for his little *relievos*, is in some sort a hero *ex-officio*, and it has been well suggested that we look briefly upon the uneventful lives of this worthy line of officers.

I. Robert Scot received his appointment as the first Engraver of the Mint, November 23, 1793. Information is wanting as to his nativity, but at the time of his appointment he seems to have been turning the down-hill of life. He is remembered as rather under size, and as an honorable and agreeable gentleman.

According to Loubat, Joseph Wright was "appointed first a draughtsman and die-sinker to the United States Mint, and made the dies of a medal, the bust on the obverse of which was considered to be the best medallic profile likeness of Washington.* He also made the medal voted by Congress to Major Lee." Wright died in 1793.

II. William Kneass, second of the line, was born in Lancaster, Pa., September, 1781, and was appointed Engraver January 29, 1824. Mr. Kneass had been chiefly a plate engraver for book-work. There were some changes in the coinage during his term, notably in 1834 and 1838, for gold, and 1836, 1837, 1838, and 1840, for silver. But some of this work was done by Gobrecht as assistant. Kneass appears upon a pattern half dollar of 1838; but the silver dollar of 1836, as well as a pattern half of 1838, were the work of his assistant. Prior to his appointment he had an engraving office on Fourth above Chestnut street, Philadelphia, which was a well-known rendezvous for the leading wits and men of culture, for which Philadelphia was then eminent.

Mr. Kneass died in office, August 27, 1840. A good engraving of him hangs in the Assayer's Office, inscribed "to

---

* The Phototype of Washington's Profile likeness in the bound edition of this book, is from this Medal, known as the Houdon Medal.

his friend Adam Eckfeldt, Chief Coiner,"—who had been chiefly instrumental in securing his appointment.

III. Christian Gobrecht was appointed December 21, 1840, to fill the vacancy made by the death of Kneass. He was born in Hanover, York Co., Pa., December 23, 1785. In 1811 he went to Philadelphia, and became an engraver of bank notes, seals, calico printers' rolls, bookbinders' dies, etc. In 1836 he received an appointment as assistant to Mr. Kneass at the Mint, in which capacity he executed some important work. Among other similar performances he was highly commended for his Franklin Institute Medal.

Christian Gobrecht continued in office until his death, July 23, 1844.

IV. James B. Longacre was born August 11, 1794, in Delaware Co., Pa. He served an apprenticeship as a line engraver with George Murray, Philadelphia, and did some high class plate-work before he was free, in 1819. He was one of the originators of the *National Portrait Gallery of Distinguished Americans*, the first volume of which appeared in 1834. Longacre drew from life and engraved many of the portraits entire.

Like his predecessors, he died in office—January 1, 1869. During his term Mr. Longacre was variously assisted by P. F. Cross, William Barber, Anthony C. Paquet, and William H Key. Cross was born in Sheffield, England, served several years in the Mint here, and died in 1856. He engraved the obverse of the Ingraham medal. Paquet was born in Hamburg, 1814, emigrated 1848, served as assistant 1857 to 1864, died, 1882. He engraved the medals of Grant, Johnson, Buchanan, Everett, and the Life Saving Medals, with some others. Key is a native of Brooklyn, was appointed an assistant, 1864, and is still in the service. He executed the Kane Expedition and Archbishop Wood Medals. The changes and additions during the Longacre term were numerous and important, both as to alloys and denominations. The pattern pieces also record various experiments in the art of coining.

V. William Barber, fifth Engraver of the Mint, was born in London, May 2, 1807. He learned his profession from his father, John Barber, and was employed on silver-plate work, after his emigration to this country.

He resided in Boston ten years, and was variously employed in his line of work. His skill in this way came to the knowledge of Mr. Longacre, then Engraver of the Mint, and he secured his services as an assistant in 1865.

In January, 1869, upon the death of Mr. Longacre, he was appointed as his successor, and continued in that position for the remainder of his life. His death, which resulted from severe chills, brought on by bathing at the seashore, occurred in Philadelphia, August 31, 1879.

Besides much original work on pattern coins, he also produced over forty medals, public and private. The work on all of them was creditable, but we may specify those of Agassiz, Rittenhouse, and Henry, as very superior specimens of art. Mr. Barber was assisted by Mr. William H. Key, Mr. Charles E. Barber, and Mr. George T. Morgan.

VI. Charles E. Barber, sixth Engraver, is a son of the preceding, and was born in London in 1840. He was appointed an assistant in 1869, and became the official head by promotion in 1880, to fill the vacancy caused by his father's death. The appointment was not unmerited. One of Mr. Barber's latest cards to the public is the new five-cent piece—a successful venture in very low relief. But his handiwork is more or less visible in all the principal medals executed since 1869. Since his appointment as Chief Engraver, the work of his department has been enormously increased by the number of medal dies demanded for the War Department and from other Government sources. Mr. Barber's best work is seen in the medals of Presidents Garfield, Arthur, Indian Peace, Army Marksmanship, and Great Seal. He is particularly happy in "catching a likeness." The head of Superintendent Snowden is a rare specimen of medallic portraiture.*

Messrs. Key and Morgan are the Engraver's assistants. The former has already received notice; the latter, Mr. George T. Morgan, was born in Birmingham, England, in 1845; he studied at the Art School there, and won a National Scholarship at the South Kensington, where he was a student two years. He is best known to the country by the so-called "Bland dollar," which is his design and execution.

We have reason to congratulate both the Government and the people that the engraving service is well and judiciously furnished.

BENJAMIN RUSH,

An eminent physician and philanthropist, was born near Philadelphia, December 24, 1745; he graduated from Princeton College in 1760; he afterwards studied medicine in Edinburgh,

---

* Mr. Barber has lately completed a large and very fine medallic likeness of President Cleveland.

London, and Paris; returning to this country, he was elected
Professor of Chemistry in the Medical College of Philadelphia
in 1769.   In 1776 he was elected to the Continental Congress,
and was one of the signers of the Declaration of Independence in the same year; he was afterwards appointed Surgeon-
General of Revolutionary Army, and voted for the adoption
of the Constitution of the United States in 1787.   Dr. Rush
was a popular lecturer, and eminently qualified as a teacher
of medicine.   When the yellow fever scourged the City, and
the public buildings were closed in 1799 and 1800, he was
very successful in his treatment of the victims of that epidemic.   It is said that he visited and prescribed for one
hundred patients in a single day.   He was treasurer of the
first United States Mint during the last fourteen years of his
life.   Dr. Rush died in Philadelphia in April, 1813.   Among
his nine children was Richard Rush, the statesman.

Note.—Dr. Rush was the author of the first pamphlet on temperance published in
this country, showing the injurious effects of alcoholic drinks on the human system,
and is justly regarded as the father of the temperance movement, the Centennial of
which has lately been celebrated throughout the United States. September, 1885.

CASHIER.

MARK H. COBB, the Cashier of the Mint from 1871 until the
present time (1885), was born in Colebrook, Connecticut, in
1828.   In 1861, Hon. Simon Cameron, then Secretary of War,
appointed him Chief Clerk in the War Department, he having
previously been his private secretary.   After Mr. Cameron's
resignation as Secretary, Mr. Cobb, at the solicitation of the
late Col. John W. Forney, accepted the position of Enrolling
Clerk of the United States Senate in 1862.   In 1871 he was
appointed to the responsible position of Cashier in the United
States Mint.

ALBION COX, first assayer of the Mint was appointed April
4, 1794.   His commission, signed by Washington, until
recently, hung upon the walls of the assay office.   But little is
known of Mr. Cox, save that he was an Englishman by birth,
and a good officer, as appears from the following report to the
Secretary of the Treasury made by Director Boudinot, under
date, December 3, 1795.   He says: "The sudden and un-
expected death of the assayer, Mr. Albion Cox, on Fryday
last by an apoplectic fit, deprived the Mint of an intelligent
officer, essentially necessary to the future progress in the coinage of the precious metals.   Until this officer is replaced, the
business at the Mint must be confined to striking cents only."

He therefore held office about a year and eight months.

Joseph Richardson, second assayer, was appointed December 12, 1795. He belonged to an old Quaker family distinguished for ability and character. Mr. Richardson fulfilled the duties of his office with credit and honor. He died in March, 1831. A water color portrait of him, dressed in plain Quaker garb, hangs in the assayers' room. He held office over thirty-five years.

John Richardson, son of the preceding, was appointed assayer March 31, 1831. Finding the office not congenial with his tastes, and so subjecting him to undue responsibilities, he resigned April, 1832, holding office only a little over a year.

CURATOR.

R. A. McCLURE, a gentleman skilled in the science of numismatics, was appointed Assistant Curator of the Coin Cabinet in 1868, and, upon the death of the Assayer and Chief Curator in 1881, the responsibilities of the Curatorship fell upon Mr. McClure.

STANDARD WEIGHTS.

The earliest series of standard weights now known, are two sets discovered by Mr. Layard in the ruins of Nineveh. They are now in the British Museum. William the Conqueror decreed the continuance, as the legal standard, of the pound in use by the Saxons. This and other standards of weight and measure were removed by the King from the City of Winchester to the Exchequer at Westminster, and placed in a consecrated building in charge of his chamberlains. The place of deposit is said to have been the crypt chapel of Edward the Confessor, in Westminster Abbey. In 1866 the office of Exchequer was abolished, and the Standards Department of the Board of Trade was established in London, assuming charge of the standards—an arrangement still in force.

The old Saxon pound was the earliest standard of England. It was identical in weight with the old apothecaries' pound of Germany, and equal to 5,400 of our later Troy grains. The pound sterling was determined from this weight in silver. Henry III., in 1266, decreed the following standards: The sterling, or penny, to weigh equal to thirty-two wheat corns, taken from the middle of the ear; twenty pence, one ounce; twelve ounces, one pound; eight pounds, one gallon of wine, which is the eighth part of a quarter. The idea of the grain was borrowed by the English from the French, and the Black Prince brought back with him from France the pound Troye, which was derived from the commercial town of that name. The use of the Troy standard was adopted by the druggists and jewelers, on account of its convenient reduction into grains.

The pound avoirdupois, weighing 7,000 grains Troy, (Fr. *Avoir-du-poids*, "to have weight"), first appears in use during the reign of Edward III., and it, as well as the Troy pound, has been employed without change ever since. In the year 1834 the English standards of weight and measure, consisting of a yard and pound Troy of brass, were destroyed by fire at the burning of the Houses of Parliament. A few years later a commission of scientific men was appointed to determine upon the restoration of the standards. This resulted in a succession of difficult problems resultant upon the oxidation to a greater or less extent of duplicates of the standard still existing, as also of the variation of the cubic inch of water, as in use in different lands. A cubic inch of distilled water, weighed in air against brass weights, at a temperature of 62 degrees Fahr., the barometer being at 30 inches, had been determined by scientific men to be equal to 252.458 grains, of which the standard Troy pound contained 5,760.

As the unit of length was also lost, a series of experiments was made in the vibration of a pendulum in a vacuum, marking seconds of mean time in the latitude of London at the level of the sea. These deductions, however, failed to be satisfactory, and the commission was compelled to fall back upon the best preserved of the duplicate standards existent. The Imperial Standard Pound is declared to be the true weight of an avoirdupois pound in a vacuum. It is a curious fact that the Imperial standards of platinum (which metal is not subject to oxidation), although balancing brass weights in a vacuum, weigh in air more than one-half a grain heavier than the latter. This is due to their greater displacement of space.

The unit of weight in the United States is a Troy pound weight obtained from England, a duplicate of the original standard fixed by the commission of 1758, and reasserted by the commission of 1838. It is a bronze weight of 5,760 grains Troy. It is kept in a strong safe at the United States Mint, in Philadelphia. The President appoints an assay commission, whose members meet at Philadelphia annually, upon the second Wednesday in February, open the safe, and compare the copies, or the working weights, with the original upon the most delicately poised balances. Working standards of weights and measures are supplied by the Secretary of State to the State governments, which in turn supply them to the sealers of weights and measures of the various countries, who must compare with the State standard once a year.

All of the scales and delicate test instruments in use by the government, not only in Philadelphia Mint, but at the several branch mints, are manufactured in this country, and as examples of wonderful mechanical machines of minute accuracy they lead the world. Some of them are the work of Mr. Henry Troemner, of Philadelphia, to whom, it is proper to say, the writer is largely indebted for the facts given in this article. Mr. Troemner, in the capacity of government expert, makes frequent visits to the most distant points in the Union for the verification of national standards.

TROY STANDARD POUND WEIGHT.
Fac-simile, exact size.

The Treasury Department made an especial request of him to exhibit at the New Orleans Exposition, a line of his fine balances.

EXTRACT FROM CONSTITUTION OF THE UNITED STATES.

ARTICLE I., Sect. 8. The Congress shall have power . . . to coin money, regulate the value thereof and of foreign coins, and fix the standard of weights and measures, . . . to provide for the punishment of counterfeiting the securities and current coin of the United States.

ARTICLE I. Sect. 2. No State shall . . . coin money, emit bills of credit, make anything but gold and silver coin a tender in payment of debts, . . .

Coinage, fiscal year 1887.

Description.	Pieces.	Value.
Gold	3,724,720	$22,393,279 00
Silver	44,231,288	34,366,483 75
Minor Coins	50,166,509	943,650 65
Total	98,122,517	$57,703,413 40

Total number of Coinage Dies made during the year 1887.

Gold coinage	120
Silver coinage	359
Minor coinage	684
Proof coinage	27

Bullion for the Silver Dollar Coinage, 1887.

Mode of acquisition.	Standard ounces.	Cost.
Purchases, Treasury Department, Bureau of the Mint.	29,018,932.12	$25,624,487 37
Purchases by mint officers..........	282,626.95	249,150 73
Partings, bar charges and fractions................	131,783.20	114,982 36
Total delivered on purchases................	29,433,342.27	$25,988,620 46
Balance on hand July 1, 1886....	**3,258,495.66**	2,960,969 02
Available for coinage of silver dollars during the fiscal year 1887................	32,691,837.93	$28,949,589 48

Value of the Gold and Silver (not including re-deposits) received at the Mints and Assay Offices during the fiscal years 1880–1887.

Fiscal years.	Gold.	Silver.	Total.
1880................	$98,835,096	$34,640,522	$133,475,618
1881................	130,833,102	30,791,146	161,624,248
1882................	66,756,652	33,720,491	100,477,143
1883................	46,347,106	36,869,834	83,216,940
1884................	46,326,678	36,520,290	82,546,968
1885................	52,894,075	36,789,774	89,683,849
1886................	44,909,749	35,494,183	80,403,932
1887................	68,223,072	47,756,918	115,979,990

Silver Coins of the United States.

Denominations.	Coinage commenced.	Coinage ceased.	Amount coined to June 30, 1884.	Standard weight, grains.	Amount for which a legal tender.
Standard dollars........	1878	....	$175,355,829 00	412.5	Unlimited.
Trade dollars............	1873	1878	35,959,360 00	420.	Not a legal tender.
Dollars................	1793	1873	8,045,838 00	412.5	Unlimited.
Half dollars............	1793	....	122,765,735 00	192.9	Ten dollars.
Quarter dollars........	1796	....	38,495,918 75	96.45	Ten dollars.
Twenty cents........	1875	1878	271,000 00	77.16	Five dollars.
Dimes................	1796	....	18,293,172 50	38.58	Ten dollars.
Half dimes............	1793	1873	4,906,946 90	19.29	Five dollars.
Three cents............	1851	1873	1,281,850 20	11.52	Five dollars.

FAC SIMILE REPRODUCTIONS OF CONTINENTAL CURRENCY.

Trade-Dollars Coined, Exported, Imported, Melted, and Redeemed
(Act of March 3, 1887).

Coined:
```
    Mint at Philadelphia..............................................  $5,107,524
    Mint at San Francisco............................................  26,647,000
    Mint at Carson...................................................   4,211,400
                                                                       ------------  $35,965,924
Exported .................................................................  28,778,802
Imported .................................................................   1,706,020
                                                                       ------------
    Net export...........................................................               27,072,842
                                                                                        ----------
                                                                                        8,893,082
```

Melted:
```
                ( Previous to Redemption Act............  $915,346
    As  bullion.{ Excluded from redemption (mutilated
                (    pieces, etc.).........................    4,113
                                                                        919,459
                ( Mint at Philadelphia..........  3,427,369
    Redeemed.   { Mint at San Francisco......    764,263
                { Mint at New Orleans............      1,871
                ( Assay office at New York....  3,495,533
                                                  ----------
                    Total redeemed .......................  7,589,036
                                                                      -----------
                    Total melted...........................................  8,508,495
```

Not accounted for and not presented for redemption; employed in the arts;
specimen pieces in the hands of coin collectors, carried out by emigrants,
and in miscellaneous deposits of coin remelted at mints, etc.................... $284,587

GROSS PROFITS ON SILVER COINAGE IN 1887.

The seignorage or immediate gross profit on the coinage of
silver dollars—that is, the difference between the cost of the
bullion and the nominal value of the coins—during the fiscal
year 1887, was $7,923,558.61.

The seignorage on subsidiary coin manufactured during the
year was $31,704.94, of which $1,130.65 was gained from the
recoinage of old subsidiary coins in the Treasury.

The total seignorage on the silver coinage during the fiscal
year was $7,955,263.55.

As stated in last fiscal report, the balance of silver profits
remaining in the coinage mints on the 1st July, 1886,
amounted to $553,201.44.

Adding to this the seignorage of the year, the total gross
silver profits to be accounted for by the mints is $8,508,464.99.

Of this there was paid for expenses of distributing silver
coin $35,059.03, and reimbursed for wastage and loss on sale
of sweeps $20,294.88.

The seignorage on the coinage of silver at the mints of the
United States from July 1, 1878, to the close of the fiscal year
ended June 30, 1887, has amounted to $39,057,566.90.

Tabulated Statement of **Expenditures of** the Mint at **Philadelphia, for the**
Fiscal Year ended June 30, 1887.

Items.	Amount.	Items.	Amount.
Acids	$7,149 28	Metal work and castings	$1,607 61
Belting	315 07	Oil	1,047 12
Charcoal	1,873 42	Salt	117 56
Chemicals	832 58	Stationery, printing and binding	
Coal	16,332 20	ing	773 42
Copper	13,585 00	Sundries	6,230 61
Crucibles, covers, stirrers, and		Telegraphing	28 87
dippers	3,712 72	Washing	42 67
Dry goods	1,198 97	Wood	5,432 62
Fluxes	3,560 91	Zinc	935 57
Freight and drayage	252 12	Steam-power plant	11,464 27
Gas	4,098 78	Manufacture of 5-cent nickel	
Gloves and gauntlets	5,930 40	blanks	19,498 50
Hardware	957 01		
Ice	613 45	Total	117,332 84
Iron and steel	205 91	Salaries	40,665 69
Labor and repairs	3,417 82	Wages of workmen	426,593 93
Loss on sale of sweeps	1,301 15		
Lumber	2,109 74	Aggregate	584,597 46
Machinery and appliances	2,617 49		

Value of the Foreign **Gold Coins Deposited at the United States Assay**
Office at New York during **the Year ended June 30, 1887.**

Countries of Coinage.	Denominations of coin.	Total of each denomination of coin.	Total by countries of coinage.
Costa Rica	Mixed	257 56	$257 56
France	20 francs	1,219,351 92	1,219,351 92
Germany	20 marks	179,121 67	179,121 67
Great Britain	Sovereigns	1,018,036 21	1,018,036 21
Japan	Yens	18,608 37	18,608 37
Mexico	20 pesos	388,668 88	
"	10 pesos	1,341 64	
"	Doubloons	1,178 60	391,189 12
Russia	5 roubles	155,237 39	
"	Roubles	2,596 80	
"	½ imperials	577,223 34	735,057 53
Peru	20 soles	999 82	999 82
Spain	Doubloons	3,101,388 08	
"	Isabellines	98,151 58	
"	25 pesetas	957,276 17	
"	Mixed	179,863 62	4,336,679 45
U. S. Colombia	Cinco pesos	709 76	709 76
Total		$7,900,010 51	$7,900,010 51

The total value of both gold and **silver** deposited and purchased at the mints of the United States during the fiscal year 1887, not including redeposits, was $115,979,991.62, and including redeposits, $131,635,811.34.

The value of the gold and silver received at the mints and assay offices during the fiscal year 1887, was greater than any previous year since 1881.

IMPROVEMENTS MADE AT THE PHILADELPHIA MINT IN 1887, UNDER THE SUPERVISION OF HON. DANIEL M. FOX.

Impairment of the foundation of the old engine, together with the requirement of increased power, at the mint at Philadelphia led to a special appropriation by Act of Congress of $54,639.20, in accordance with specifications for the renewal of the steam motive plant and for its transfer from the centre of the building to space newly provided near the northern outer wall. The work, undertaken in July, was, by extraordinary exertions on the part of all engaged, completed early in September, with an interruption of less than two months to the regular course of complete operations. Two new 150-horse-power duplex steam-engines and one of 50-horse-power have been erected in the north basement, along with three tubular boilers, coal bunkers, etc.

By this important improvement in plant valuable space has been secured in the centre basement and ground floor for vaults and other necessities.

The number of assays made during the year was some 66,000, of which 48,000 were silver and 18,000 gold.

The melter and refiner of the mint operated upon a larger quantity of bullion than in any previous year in the history of the institution. The operations by this officer may be stated as follows :

	Ounces
Gold deposits	409,326
Silver deposits	44,239,331
Parted and refined	721,765

As this bullion is handled more than sixteen times in the processes of melting and preparation for coinage or for manufacture of fine bars, the combined operations represent a single handling of nearly 25,000 tons.

The operations of the coiner's department may be stated as follows :

	Ounces.
Gold	13,574
Silver	42,924,187
Minor coinage metal	5,588,807
Total	48,526,956

The total coinage was $23,277,600.80, the total number of pieces being 81,532,391.

In addition to the coinage executed during the year, gold and silver bars were manufactured as follows :

Gold	$58,188,953 66
Silver	6,481,611 25
Total	$64,670,564 91

Gold and Silver Bullion in the Mints and Assay Offices July 1, **1887**.

Metal.	Cost.
Gold...	$85,512,270
Silver...	10,455,650
Total...	$95,967,920

Total Metallic Stock **in the** United States July 1, 1887, **Coin and Bullion** included.

	Value.
Gold...	$654,520,335
Silver...	352,993,566
Total...	$1,007,513,901

At the beginning of the fiscal year 1887 there was on hand at the mints at Philadelphia, New Orleans and San Francisco, silver bullion purchased for the silver dollar coinage amounting to $2,960,969.02. There was delivered at the mints on purchases of all kinds during the year, as above, 29,433,342.27 standard ounces, at a cost of $25,988,620.46, making the total amount of silver available during the fiscal year for the silver dollar coinage 32,691,837.93 standard ounces, costing $28,949,589.48.

The price paid by this Bureau on November 1, 1887, for silver purchases for the silver dollar coinage was $0.9580.80 per ounce fine.

The production of silver, notwithstanding the large depreciation in the market value of that metal, has steadily increased from $115,000,000 in 1883 to $130,000,000 in 1886. The production of the world for the calendar years 1883, 1884, 1885 and 1886 is exhibited in the following table:

World's Production of Gold and Silver.

Calendar Years.	Gold.		Silver.	
	Kilograms.	Value.*	Kilograms.	Value.†
1883..	143,533	$95,392,000	2,769,197	$115,088,000
1884..	153,017	101,694,000	2,804,725	116,564,000
1885..	154,942	102,975,000	3,062,009	127,237,000
1886..	147,097	97,761,000	3,137,175	130,383,000

* Kilogram of gold valued at $664.60.   † Kilogram of silver valued at $41,56.

The United States still maintains first rank among the nations of the world as the largest producer of the precious metals, having produced during the calendar year 1886 gold and silver of the coining value of $86,000,000. Mexico retains second rank, with a production of $33,614,000, of which $33,000,000 was silver. Australia has a production of $27,647,000, of which $26,425,000 was gold. Russia is credited with a production of $21,046,000, of which $20,-518,000 was gold.

Circulation of Standard Silver Dollars at the end of each six months, from July 1, 1885, to July 1, 1887, and on October 1, 1887.

Period.	Total coinage.	In the Treasury. Held for payments of certificates outstanding.	Held in excess of certificates outstanding.	In circulation.
July 1, 1885	$203,884,381	$101,530,946	$63,882,166	$38,471,269
January 1, 1886	218,289,761	93,179,465	72,558,725	52,541,571
July 1, 1886	233,723,286	88,116,225	93,137,341	52,469,720
January 1, 1887	249,683,647	117,246,670	71,259,568	61,177,401
July 1, 1887	266,990,117	142,118,017	69,365,953	55,506,147
October 1, 1887	273,660,157	154,354,826	58,688,970	60,616,361

Appropriations for the support of Mints and Assay Offices for the fiscal year 1888.

Institutions.	Salaries.	Wages of workmen.	Contingent expenses.	Repairs of buildings.	Total.
Coinage mints.					
Philadelphia	$41,550	$293,000	$100,000		$434,550
San Francisco	41,900	170,000	40,000		251,900
Carson	29,550	60,000	25,000		114,550
New Orleans	31,950	74,000	35,000		140,950
Assay offices.					
New York	39,250	25,000	10,000		74,250
Denver	10,950	14,000	6,000	$2,000	32,950
Helena	7,700	12,000	6,000		25,700
Boisé City	3,000		5,000	1,000	9,000
Charlotte	2,750		2,000		4,750
Saint Louis	3,500		2,400		5,900
Total	$212,100	$648,000	$231,400	$3,000	$1,094,500

Comparison of expenditures, years 1886 and 1887.

Appropriations.	1886.	1887.
Salaries	$189,331 48	$192,907 13
Wages of workmen	593,865 07	601,787 25
Contingent expenses	164,183 47	*193,704 93
Standard silver dollar	119,976 00	200,189 02
Total	$1,067,356 02	$1,188,588 33

* Includes $11,464.27 expended from appropriation for renewal of steam-power plant at Philadelphia.

Production in round numbers of precious metals in United States for 1886.

State or Territory.	Gold.	Silver.	Total.
Alaska	$446,000	$2,000	$448,000
Arizona	1,110,000	3,400,000	4,510,000
California	14,725,000	1,400,000	16,125,000
Colorado	4,450,000	16,000,000	20,450,000
Dakota	2,700,000	425,000	3,125,000
Georgia	152,500	1,000	153,500
Idaho	1,800,000	3,600,000	5,400,000
Montana	4,425,000	12,400,000	16,825,000
Nevada	3,090,000	5,000,000	8,090,000
New Mexico	400,000	2,300,000	2,700,000
North Carolina	175,000	3,000	178,000
Oregon	990,000	5,000	995,000
South Carolina	37,500	500	38,000
Utah	216,000	6,500,000	6,716,000
Washington	147,000	80,000	227,000
Texas		200,000	200,000
Alabama, Tennessee, Virginia, Vermont, Michigan, and Wyoming	5,000	5,000	10,000
Total	$34,869,000	$51,321,500	$86,190,500

Production of the United States from 1880 to 1886.

Calendar Years.	Gold.	Silver.	Total.
1880	$36,000,000	$39,200,000	$75,200,000
1881	34,700,000	43,000,000	77,700,000
1882	32,500,000	46,800,000	79,300,000
1883	30,000,000	46,200,000	76,200,000
1884	30,800,000	48,800,000	79,600,000
1885	31,800,000	51,600,000	83,400,000
1886	35,000,000	51,000,000	86,000,000

Gold and silver product in the United States and amount coined in 1886.

GOLD.

Value of the product of the mines, 1886		$98,000,000
Colnage executed in 1886	$92,650,000	
Recoinage	9,600,000	
Net coinage 1886		83,050,000
Leaving new gold for employment in the arts		$14,950,000

SILVER.

Value of the product of the mines, 1886		$130,000,000
Coinage executed in 1886	$124,670,000	
Recoinage	13,950,000	
Net coinage 1886		110,720,000
Leaving new silver for employment in the arts		$19,280,000

Minor Coins Shipped to the Different States and Territories from the Mint
at Philadelphia during the Fiscal Year 1887.

State or Territory.	1-cent bronze.	5-cent nickel.	State or Territory	1-cent bronze.	5-cent nickel.
Alabama	$25.00	$5,375.00	Missouri	$7,650.00	$49,490.00
Arkansas	20.00	890.00	New York	128,125.00	73,870.00
Arizona	20.00		North Carolina	1,035.00	1,290.00
California	1,215.00	11,585.00	New Jersey	12,965.00	11,835.00
Colorado	105.00	6,090.00	New Hampshire	800.00	2,500.00
Connecticut	6,230.00	6,910.00	New Mexico		400.00
Delaware	385.00	950.00	Nebraska	2,710.00	14,865.00
District of Columbia	200.00	300.00	Ohio	29,015.00	34,990.00
Dakota	1,500.00	3,646.00	Oregon	20.00	3,510.00
Florida	190.00	840.00	Pennsylvania	25,509.00	45,045.00
Georgia	490.00	3,020.00	Rhode Island	6,95;.00	3,100.00
Indiana	10,669.37	18,710.00	South Carolina	800.00	2,865.00
Iowa	8,330.00	11,970.00	Texas	150.00	7,320.00
Illinois	51,831.00	68,355.00	Tennessee	1,280 00	15,820.00
Idaho		80.00	Utah		1,320.00
Kentucky	1,775.00	12,850.00	Virginia	3,080.00	5,540.00
Kansas	4,440.00	8,720.00	Vermont	1,370.00	900.00
Louisiana	400.00	6,510.00	West Virginia	1,225.00	2,380.00
Michigan	17,840.00	11,786.00	Wisconsin	7,230.00	10,755.00
Massachusetts	38,815.00	39,210.00	Washington Terri-		
Minnesota	10,405.00	13,615.00	tory		500.00
Maine	1,325.00	1,215.00	Wyoming		260.00
Mississippi	25.00	250.00			
Montana		2,020.00	Total	$400,510.37	$544,686.00
Maryland	14,270.00	22,070.00			

Minor Coins Struck and Remelted from the Organization of the Mint, and
the Amount Outstanding June 30, 1887.

Denomination.	Coined.	Remelted.	Outstanding. June 30, 1887.
Copper cents	$1,562,887.44	$372,741.70	$1,190,145.74
Copper half cents	*39,926.11		
Copper nickel cents	2,007,720.09	735,516.39	1,272,103.70
Bronze cents	4,319,275.48	24,517.11	4,294,738.37
Bronze 2-cent pieces	912,028.00	292,128.08	619,801.92
Nickel 3-cent pieces	903,705.00	175,541.44	728,163.86
Nickel 5-cent pieces	8,691,671.75	61,934.00	8,629,737.75
Total	$18,437,205.78	$1,662,478.63	$16,734,801.04 *

On the 30th June, 1886, the amount of minor coin in the
Treasury was $377,814. Of this amount over $160,000
proved to be in 3-cent nickel pieces, for which there was no
demand, and over $60,000 in uncurrent minor coins of former
issues was transferred for recoinage, confined to 1-cent bronze
and 5-cent nickel pieces. The demand for 1-cent bronze and
5-cent nickel pieces, at first sudden, has since been urgent and
continuous; at times largely beyond the ability of the mint to
promptly meet.

Operations Fiscal Year, 1887.

Bars manufactured:
Gold.. $58,188,953 66
Silver.. 6,481,611 25

Total 64,670,564 91

Coinage executed:
Gold.. $22,393,279 00
Silver.. 34,366,483 75
Minor... 943,650 65

Total 57,703,413 40

Refinery earnings.. $143,258 52

SUMMARY OF THE OPERATIONS OF THE MINTS AND ASSAY OFFICES.

The value of the gold and silver deposited at the mints and assay offices of the United States during the fiscal year 1887 was $131,635,811.34. This aggregate, however, but partially measures the successive operations upon the bullion represented by this value. For example, it may be interesting to show the operations by the melters and refiners of the four mints and of the assay office at New York, as measured by the value of the bullion successively operated upon. These may be stated as follows:

Bullion Operated upon by the Melters and Refiners, 1887.

Metal.	Standard ounces.	Value.
Gold	5,919,878	$110,137,265
Silver	70,764,794	82,344,487
Total value		$192,481,752

The operations of the coinage departments of the mints were as follows

Operations of Coinage Departments, 1887.

Metal.	Standard ounces.	Value.
Gold	2,632,005	$48,967,440
Silver	61,896,692	72,025,241
Total value		$120,992,681

The 1-cent and 2-cent bronze pieces were recoined into 1-cent bronze pieces, and the copper nickel 1-cent, and the 3-cent and 5-cent nickel pieces were used in the coinage of new 5-cent nickel pieces.

Form and Location of the Moneys of the United States and the Bullion awaiting Coinage in the Mints July 1, 1887.

[Exclusive of Minor Coin and Minor-Coinage Metal.]

	In Treasury.	In National Banks.*	In other Banks and General Circulation.	Total.
METALLIC.				
Gold bullion	$85,512,270			$85,512,270
Silver bullion	4,091,414			4,091,414
Silver bullion (melted trade dollars)	6,364,236			6,364,236
Gold coin	192,368,915	†298,137,439	$278,501,711	569,008,065
Silver dollars	211,483,970	6,343,213	49,162,934	266,990,117
Subsidiary silver coin	26,977,493	2,813,138	45,757,168	75,547,799
Total	$526,798,298	$307,293,790	$373,421,613	$1,907,513,901
REPRESENTATIVE.				
Legal-tender notes	‡$28,783,796	$74,477,342	$243,419,878	$346,681,016
Old demand notes			57,130	57,130
Certificates of deposit	310,000	7,810,000	960,000	9,080,000
Gold certificates	30,261,380	54,274,940	36,950,497	121,486,817
Silver certificates	3,425,133	3,535,479	138,582,538	145,543,150
National bank notes	197,046	22,962,737	256,058,065	279,217,788
Fractional paper currency	2,366	564,266	6,380,332	6,946,964
Total	$62,979,721	$163,624,764	$682,468,380	$909,012,865

* The statement of the amounts in National Banks is of date August 1.
‡ Includes $24,044,000 Clearing-house gold certificates.
† Includes $8,770,000 held for the redemption of certificates of deposit for legal-tender notes under Act June 8, 1872.

Gold and **Silver Coin** in the United States November 1, 1887.

Date.	Gold Coin.	Silver Coin			Total Gold and Silver Coin.
		Full Legal Tender.	Subsidiary.	Total Silver.	
Last official statement July 1, 1887	$569,008,065	$266,990,117	$75,547,799	$342,537,916	$911,545,981
Gain subsequent to above statement (estimate)	5,919,808	10,120,040	210,387	10,330,427	16,250,235
Estimate for November 1, 1887	$574,927,873	$277,110,157	$75,758,186	$352,868,343	$927,796,216

Estimate of Coin Circulation July 1, 1887.

Items.	Gold.	Silver.	Total.
Estimated circulation July 1, 1886	$548,320,031	$308,784,223	$857,104,254
Coinage for fiscal year 1887	22,593,279	34,166,483	56,759,762
Net imports	2,311,739	409,151	2,720,890
Total	$573,025,049	343,359,857	$916,584,906
Less deposits of United States coin	516,984	821,941	1,338,925
Used in the arts	3,500,000	200,000	3,700,000
Total	4,016,984	1,021,941	5,038,925
Estimate circulation July 1, 1887	$569,008,065	$342,537,916	$911,545,981

Table showing the Total Paper and Specie Circulation in each of the Principal Countries of the World, and the Amount of Specie in Bank and National Treasuries, and the Amount of Active Circulation.

(Officially Reported in 1884.)

Countries.	Population.	Total metallic and paper circulation.	Amount of specie in national treasuries and banks	Active circulation.	Per capita of active circulation
United States.............	50,155,783	$1,745,926,755	$534,033,074	$1,211,893,681	$24 16
Great Britain and Ireland....................	35,246,562	876,318,139	154,182,691	722,135,448	20 49
Dominion of Canada, including Manitoba and Newfoundland...	4,506,563	59,596,084	9,111,148	50,484,936	11 22
British India.............	252,541,210	1,099,383,126	78,358,000	1,021,925,126	4 05
Ceylon.....................	2,758,166	2,335,300	1,273,800	1,061,500	38
Australia, Tasmania, and New Zealand...	2,798,898	96,010,722	48,737,837	47,272,885	16 90
Cape of Good Hope....	780,757	38,078,000	8,092,000	29,986,000	38 40
France.....................	37,321,186	1,990,961,912	402,939,754	1,588,022,158	42 55
Algiers....................	2,867,626	27,567,000	5,564,476	22,002,524	7 67
Guadeloupe..............	185,460	1,627,750	564,935	1,062,815	5 73
Belgium...................	5,536,654	186,326,515	17,991,450	168,335,065	30 40
Switzerland..............	2,846,102	53,180,731	11,609,618	41,571,113	14 60
Italy.......................	28,452,639	533,548,521	69,357,358	464,191,163	16 31
Greece....................	1,979,423	29,143,000	1,800,000	27,343,000	13 81
Spain......................	16,625,860	270,812,446	27,223,950	243,588,481	14 65
Cuba.......................	1,394,516	73,043,543	14,181,243	58,862,300	42 21
Luzon......................	4,450,191	4,198,000	3,765,677	432,323	10
Portugal, including Azores and Madeira	4,550,699	46,367,680	11,718,874	34,648,806	7 61
Germany	45,234,061	825,473,023	181,706,674	643,766,349	14 23
Austria-Hungary........	35,839,428	431,646,314	98,131,401	333,514,913	9 31
Sweden and Norway...	6,479,168	43,058,443	12,740,975	30,317,468	4 68
Danish Kingdom........	2,096,400	39,228,000	14,070,000	25,158,000	12 00
Netherlands	4,061,580	163,847,949	55,114,112	108,733,837	26 77
Russia.....................	98,323,000	646,431,794	124,008,153	522,423,641	5 31
Turkey.....................	24,987,000	83,315,976	14,520,000	68,795,976	2 75
Roumania.................	5,376,000	27,372,383	3,995,298	23,377,085	4 35
Mexico....................	9,957,279	52,048,529	1,763,008	50,285,521	5 26
Central America.........	2,891,600	4,701,861	....	4,701,861	1 62
Argentine Republic....	2,540,000	71,371,850	14,196,461	57,175,389	22 51
Colombia..................	3,000,000	5,097,830	200,000	4,897,830	1 63
Brazil......................	11,108,291	139,871,255	....	139,871,255	12 59
Peru	3,050,900	14,980,820	1,882,018	13,098,802	4 29
Venezuela	2,075,245	2,682,700	....	2,682,700	1 00
Chili	2,420,500	32,555,341	2,398,000	30,157,341	12 45
Bolivia....................	2,325,000	6,908,533	443,597	6,464,936	2 78
Uruguay	438,245	11,587,000	4,601,000	6,986,000	15 94
Hayti ...	572,000	4,780,000	....	4,780,000	8 35
Japan......................	36,700,110	248,744,805	28,486,973	220,257,832	6 00
Hawaiian Islands........	80,895	1,834,900	808,200	1,026,700	15 35
	9,991,964,524	1,959,571,764	8,032,392,760		

WORLD'S COINAGE.

Calander years.	Gold.	Silver.
1884..	$99,432,795	$95,832,084
1885..	94,728,008	105,105,299
1886..	92,653,400	124,676,678

The value of the United States gold coin deposited for re-coinage, principally by the Treasurer of the United States, was $516,984.63, against $393,545.28 in the preceding year.

In addition to the gold bullion both of domestic and foreign production, and the foreign and domestic gold coin deposited, old material in the form of jewelry, bars, old plate, etc., was received containing gold of the value of $2,265,219.85.

The marked increase in the deposits of gold was at the assay office at New York, the value of the foreign gold bullion and coin deposited at that institution during the year being $30,621,006.95, exclusive of fine bars of its own manufacture, of the value of $7,933,743.98, imported and re-deposited.

The value of the foreign gold bullion deposited was $22,571,328.70, against $4,317,068.27 in 1886.

The value of the foreign gold coin received and melted was $9,896,512.28, against $5,673,565.04 in the year preceding.

The value of the total deposits of gold during the fiscal year 1887, including all re-deposits as above cited, was $83,416,779.40, against $49,606,534.65 in 1886, an excess in the year 1887 of $33,810,244.75.

The value of silver bullion of foreign extraction deposited at the mints during the year 1887 was $1,457,406.01.

The value of foreign silver coin deposited during the year was $350,598.86, against $812,664.50 in the preceding year.

The value of the United States silver coin deposited (calcu-lated at the coining rate in silver dollars), not including trade-dollars, was $768,739.32, most of which consisted of worn and uncurrent silver coins transferred from the Treasury of the United States for recoinage.

Trade-dollars were received mostly by transfer from the Treasury of the United States and melted. The bullion con-tained 5,837,791.87 standard ounces, of the coinage value in standard silver dollars of $6,793,066.89.

EARNINGS AND EXPENDITURES OF THE MINTS AND ASSAY OFFICES.

The total earnings amounted to $8,842,819.70, and the total expenditures and losses of all kinds to $1,437,442.95. The profits from operations on bullion during the past year amounted to the large sum of $7,405,386.75.

A large portion of these earnings consisted of seignorage or profits on the manufacture of silver and minor coins.

Highest and lowest prices of Gold in New York. Each month in 1862–1878.

Month.	1862. H.	1862. L.	1863. H.	1863. L.	1864. H.	1864. L.	1865. H.	1865. L.	1866. H.	1866. L.	1867. H.	1867. L.
January	103¾	101¾	160¾	133⅝	159⅝	151½	234⅜	197¼	144¼	136¾	137⅞	132½
February	104⅝	102⅛	172½	152½	161	157⅛	216⅝	196⅝	140⅝	135¾	140⅝	135½
March	102⅜	101⅛	171¾	139	169¾	159	201	148¼	136½	124⅞	140⅝	133⅝
April	102⅛	101½	157⅞	145½	184¾	166¼	154⅛	143½	129½	125¼	141⅝	132⅝
May	104⅜	102⅛	154¾	143⅝	190	168	145⅛	128½	141⅛	125⅛	138⅞	135
June	109⅞	103½	148⅝	140½	250	193	147⅝	135¼	167¾	137½	138⅜	136⅝
July	120⅜	108¾	145	123¼	285	222	146⅜	138¾	155¾	147	140⅝	138
August	116¼	112½	129¾	122½	261¾	231½	145½	140¼	152⅛	146¼	142⅛	139⅞
September	124	116⅛	143⅜	126⅝	254½	191	145	142⅝	147⅛	143½	146⅝	141
October	133½	122	156¾	140⅝	227¾	189	149	144½	154⅝	145½	145⅝	140¼
November	133¼	129	154	143	260	210	148¾	145½	148⅝	137½	141½	138½
December	134	128⅛	152¾	148½	243	212¾	148½	144½	141¼	131¼	137⅞	133
Year	134	101⅛	172½	122⅛	285	151½	234⅜	128½	167¾	125¼	146⅝	132⅛

Month.	1868. H.	1868. L.	1869. H.	1869. L.	1870. H.	1870. L.	1871. H.	1871. L.	1872. H.	1872. L.	1873. H.	1873. L.
January	142¼	133¼	136⅝	134⅝	123¼	119⅝	111⅛	110⅛	110⅝	108¼	114¼	111⅝
February	144	139¾	136¼	130⅞	121½	115½	112¼	110¾	111	109½	115⅛	112⅝
March	141⅛	137⅞	132½	130⅝	116⅝	110¼	111⅝	110⅛	110⅝	109¾	118⅛	114⅝
April	140⅝	137¾	134⅝	131⅜	115⅝	111½	111¾	110⅛	113⅛	109⅝	119⅛	116¾
May	140⅛	139⅛	144¾	134½	115¼	113¾	112¾	111	114⅜	112½	118⅝	116⅝
June	141¼	139⅝	139⅝	136½	114¾	110⅞	113⅛	111¾	114¾	113	118¼	115
July	145¼	143⅛	137¾	134¼	122¼	111½	113¾	111¾	115¼	113⅛	116⅝	115
August	150	143½	136½	131⅝	122	114¼	113⅝	111⅝	115⅝	112½	116¼	114⅝
September	145½	141½	162½	129¾	116¾	112¼	115⅝	112⅝	115½	112⅝	116¼	110⅞
October	140½	133¾	132	128½	113¾	111⅛	115	111½	115¼	112¼	111¼	107¾
November	137	132	128⅝	121½	113¼	110	112⅝	110⅝	114½	111⅛	110¼	106⅛
December	136¾	134⅝	124	119½	111⅞	110⅝	110¼	108⅝	113½	111⅝	112⅝	108⅝
Year	150	132	162½	119½	123¼	110	115⅝	108⅝	115⅝	108¼	119	106⅛

Month.	1874. H.	1874. L.	1875. H.	1875. L.	1876. H.	1876. L.	1877. H.	1877. L.	1878. H.	1878. L.
January	112⅛	110⅛	113¾	111¾	113¼	112⅞	107⅛	105¼	102⅞	101¼
February	113	111⅛	115⅝	113¼	114⅛	112¾	106⅛	104⅝	102⅝	101½
March	113⅞	111¼	117	114⅝	115	113¾	105⅜	104½	102	100¾
April	114⅜	111¾	115½	114	113⅞	112½	107⅞	104¼	101¼	100½
May	113⅛	111⅛	116¾	115	113¼	112¼	107⅜	106¼	101¼	100⅝
June	112¼	110½	117½	116¾	113	111⅞	106⅜	104¾	101	100⅝
July	110⅜	109	117¾	111⅛	112⅝	111⅜	106½	103¼	100¾	100⅜
August	110¼	109¼	114¾	112⅝	112½	109¾	105½	103⅞	100¾	100½
September	110¼	109⅜	117¾	113¾	110⅜	109¼	104	102⅞	100½	100⅜
October	110⅝	109¾	117⅝	114⅛	113¼	108⅞	103⅝	102½	100⅝	100⅛
November	112⅜	110	116⅝	114½	110⅛	108⅛	103⅝	102½	100½	100⅛
December	112⅜	110½	115¼	112⅝	109	107	103⅝	102½	100½	100
Year	114⅜	109	117⅝	111¾	115	107	107⅞	102½	102⅞	100

NOTE.—Specie payment resumed January 1, 1879, after a suspension of nearly 18 years

Latest official estimate of the values of foreign coins in the United States, January, 1887.

Country.	Standard.	Monetary Unit.	Standard.	Value in U. S. Money.	Standard Coin.
Argentine Republic	Double	Peso	Gold and silver	96.5	Ar. b, 1, ½ and 1 peso, ½ argentine.
Austria	S. silver	Florin	Silver	35.9	
Belgium	Double	Franc	Gold and silver	19.3	5, 10 and 20 francs.
Bolivia	S. silver	Boliviano	Silver	72.7	Boliviano.
Brazil	S. gold	Milreis of 1000 reis	Gold	54.6	
British Possessions in N. A.		Dollar	Gold	$1 00	
Chili	Double	Peso	Gold and silver	91.2	Condor, doubloon and escudo.
Cuba	Double	Peso	Gold and silver	93.2	1⁄16, ¼, ½ and 1 doubloon.
Denmark	S. silver	Crown	Gold	26.8	10 and 20 crowns.
Ecuador	S. silver	Peso	Silver	72.7	Peso.
Egypt	S. gold	Piaster	Gold	04.943	5, 10, 25, 50 and 100 piasters.
France	Double	Franc	Gold and silver	19.3	5, 10 and 20 francs.
German Empire	S. gold	Mark	Gold	23.8	5, 10 and 20 marks.
Great Britain	S. gold	Pound sterling	Gold	4 86.6½	½ sovereign and sovereign.
Greece	Double	Drachma	Gold and silver	19.3	5, 10, 20, 50 and 100 drachmas.
Hayti	Double	Gourde	Gold and silver	96.5	1, 2, 5 and 10 gourdes.
India	S. silver	Rupee of 16 annas	Silver	34.6	
Italy	Double	Lira	Gold and silver	19.3	**5, 10, 20, 50 and 100 lire.**
Japan	Double	Yen	Silver	78.4	1, 2, 5, 10 and 20 yen, gold and silver yen.
Liberia	S. gold	Dollar	Gold	1 00	
Mexico	S. silver	Dollar	Silver	07.9	Peso or **dollar, 5,** 10, 25 and 50 centavo.
Netherlands	Double	Florin	Gold and silver	40.2	
Norway	S. gold	Crown	Gold	26.8	10 and 20 **crowns.**
Peru	S. silver	Sol	Silver	72.7	Sol.
Portugal	S. gold	Milreis of 1000 reis	Gold	1 08	2, 5 and 10 milreis.
Russia	S. silver	Rouble of 100 copecks	Silver	53.2	¼, ½ and 1 rouble.
Spain	Double	Peseta of 100 centimes	Gold and silver	19.3	5, 10, 20, 50 and 100 pesetas.
Sweden	S. gold	Crown	Gold	26.8	10 and 20 crowns.
Switzerland	Double	Franc	Gold and silver	19.3	5, 10 and 20 francs.
Tripoli	S. silver	Mahbub of 20 piasters	Silver	63.6	
Turkey	S. gold	Piaster	Gold	04.4	25, 50, 100, 250, **500 piasters.**
United States of Colombia	S. silver	Peso	Silver	72.7	Peso.
Venezuela	Double	Bolivar	Gold and silver	19.3	5, 10, 20, 50 and 100 bolivar.

NOTE.—The "standard" of a given country is indicated as follows, namely: *Double*, where its standard silver coins are unlimited legal tender, the same as its gold coins; *S. gold* or *S. silver*, as its standard coins of one or the other metal are unlimited legal tender. The par of exchange of the monetary unit of a country with a single gold, or a double, standard is fixed at the value of the gold unit as compared with the United States gold unit. In the case of a country with a single silver standard, the par of exchange is computed at the mean price of silver in the London market for a period commencing October 1 and ending December 26, 1886, as per daily cable dispatches to the Bureau of the Mint.

TREASURY DEPARTMENT.

WASHINGTON, D. C., JANUARY 1, 1887.

VALUES OF FOREIGN COINS.

In accordance with the provisions of section 3564 of the Revised Statutes of the United States, the value of the standard coins of the various nations of the world were estimated by the Mint Bureau and proclaimed by the Department on January 1, 1887.

These estimates, to be followed at the custom-houses of the United States on and after January 1, 1887, in determining the values of invoices expressed in terms of foreign units of account, are shown in the following table (see opposite page):

The average price of silver in London for the period embraced between October 1 and December 26, 1886, was 45.862 pence per ounce, British standard, equivalent at the par of exchange to $1.00535 per ounce fine.

The corresponding value of silver for the three months ending December 24, 1885, was $1.038141 per ounce fine, a decline of $0.03279, a little over three cents a fine ounce.

The depression in the price of silver occasioned a change in the estimated values given the following coins:

Changes in Values of Foreign Coins from 1886 to 1887.

Coins.	Value, Jan. 1, 1886.	Value, Jan. 1, 1887.
Florin of Austria	$0.371	$0.359
Boliviano of Bolivia	.751	.727
Sucre of Ecuador	.751	.727
Rupee of India	.357	.345
Yen of Japan	.810	.784
Dollar of Mexico	.816	.790
Sol of Peru	.751	.727
Rouble of Russia	.601	.582
Mahbub of Tripoli	.677	.656
Peso of United States of Colombia	.751	.727

The monetary unit of Egypt has been nominally changed from the piaster to the pound containing one hundred piasters.

The monetary unit of Ecuador also has been nominally changed from the peso to the sucre, but with no change as to weight or fineness.

In regard to Japan, in the table for 1887 the values of the gold and silver yen were estimated separately, for the reason that while by law the standard of Japan is gold, silver is practically the standard of value, and invoices of merchandise from Japan are generally in terms of the silver yen.

Aggregate Issues of Paper Money in War times.

The following table exhibits the amount per capita issued of the Continental money, the French assignats, the Confederate currency, and the legal-tender greenbacks and National bank notes of the United States.

	Population.		
Continental money.	3,000,000 in 1780.		$119 84
French assignats.....	26,500,000 (France in 1790)		343 98
Confederate curr'cy	9,103,332 (11 Confederate States, 1860)		71 89
Greenbacks and national bank notes.	31,443,321 (United States in 1860)	$750,829,228	23 87

Refining (by acids), fiscal year 1887.

Mint or Assay Office.	Gross ounces.	Gold.		Silver.		Total value.
		Standard ounces.	Value.	Standard ounces.	Value.	
Philadelphia............	721,765	196,539	$3,554,912	553,487	$643,999	$4,188,911
San Francisco............	1,506,217	365,970	6,808,744	1,248,071	1,452,366	8,261,044
Carson	45,447	3,606	67,088	45,665	53,137	120,225
New Orleans.............	15,544	4,840	90,046	11,167	12,994	103,040
New York.................	3,822,148	764,676	14,226,530	3,005,812	3,497,672	17,724,202
Total................	6,111,121	1,329,631	$24,737,320	4,864,152	$5,660,102	$30,397,422

Value in United States Money, of One Ounce Troy of Gold, at different Degrees of Fineness.

500 Fine.....$10.33.6	630 Fine.....$13.02.3	760 Fine.....$15.71.1	890 Fine.....$18.39.8
510 " 10.54.3	640 " .....13.23.	770 " 15.91.7	900 " 18.60.5
520 " 10.74.9	650 " 13.43.7	780 " 16.12.4	910 " 18.81.1
530 " 10.95.6	660 " 13.64.3	790 " 16.33.1	920 " 19.01.8
540 " 11.16.3	670 " .....13.85.	800 " 16.53.8	930 " 19.22.5
550 " 11.36.9	680 " 14.05.7	810 " 16.74.4	940 " 19.43.1
560 " 11.57.6	690 " 14.26.3	820 " 16.95.1	950 " 19.63.8
570 " 11.78.3	700 " .....14.47.	830 " 17.15.8	960 " 19.84.5
580 " .....11.99.	710 " 14.67.7	840 " 17.36.4	970 " 20.05.2
590 " 12.19.6	720 " 14.88.4	850 " 17.57.1	980 " 20.25.8
600 " 12.40.3	730 " 15.09.4	860 " 17.77.8	990 " 20.46.5
610 " .....12.61.	740 " 15.28.7	870 " 17.98.4	1000 " 20.67.2
620 " 12.81.7	750 " 15.50.4	880 " 18.19.1	

N. B.—When there is an intermediate degree of fineness, a short calculation is necessary. For every one-thousandth, add 2.07 cents per ounce for gold. Thus, one ounce of gold at 992 fine—$20.50.6

Comparison of Expressing the Fineness of Gold in Thousandths, and in Carats.[*]

500 Fine 12.00 Carats	630 Fine 15.04 Carats	760 Fine 18.08 Carats	890 Fine 21.11 Carats
510 " 12.08 "	640 " 15.11 "	770 " 18.15 "	900 " 21.19 "
520 " 12.15 "	650 " 15.19 "	780 " 18.23 "	910 " 21.27 "
530 " 12.23 "	660 " 15.27 "	790 " 18.31 "	920 " 22.02 "
540 " 12.31 "	670 " 16.03 "	800 " 19.07 "	930 " 22.10 "
550 " 13.07 "	680 " 16.10 "	810 " 19.14 "	940 " 22.18 "
560 " 13.14 "	690 " 16.18 "	820 " 19.22 "	950 " 22.25 "
570 " 13.22 "	700 " 16.25 "	830 " 19.29 "	960 " 23.01 "
580 " 13.29 "	710 " 17.01 "	840 " 20.05 "	970 " 23.09 "
590 " 14.05 "	720 " 17.09 "	850 " 20.13 "	980 " 23.17 "
600 " 14.13 "	730 " 17.17 "	860 " 20.20 "	990 " 23.24 "
610 " 14.20 "	710 " 17.24 "	870 " 20.28 "	1000 " 24.00 "
620 " 14.28 "	750 " 16.60 "	880 " 21.04 "	

* The Carat is sub-divided into thirty-two parts.

U. S. Mint Test for Gold and Silver.

The following is a test for determining whether coin is good or bad. Use the liquids as near the edge of suspected coin as possible, as that is the part most worn. A drop of the preparation will have no effect on genuine coin, while it can be plainly seen on the counterfeit. Coins should be scraped slightly before using:

TEST FOR GOLD.	TEST FOR SILVER.
Strong Nitric Acid (36°), 39 parts.	24 grains Nite of Silver.
Muriatic Acid, 1 part.	30 drops Nitric Acid.
Water, 20 parts.	1 ounce Water.

The above tests should be taken in conjunction with *Diameter, Thickness,* and *Weight* the tests used at the Mint.

GLOSSARY.

Terms used in treating of Bullion, Mints, Coinage, and Money.

ASSAYING.—Chemical analysis of metals or ores. This term is employed in reference to mints and coinage, refers particularly to the process for determining the component parts and relative proportions of a mixed alloy of gold and silver, or the various alloys used for the manufacture of minor coins.

REFINING.—Extract of base from precious metals; usually performed by the aid of heat and oxidizing fluxes.

PARTING.—The separation of gold and silver when the two metals compose an alloy, either native or artificial, for the purpose of obtaining the metals, respectively, in the form of fine bars. This is accomplished, first, by dissolving the silver with acids and subsequently precipitating; or, second, by converting silver into chloride by heat and chlorine gas, and then reducing the chloride to a metallic state.

ALLOYING.—Compounding two or more metals together in suitable or legal proportions for coinage. Gold and silver are alloyed with copper for standard coins, and alloys are variously made of nickel and copper, or of copper, tin, and zinc for minor coins.

FINE BARS.—Gold and silver bars resulting from the operations of parting and refining. Bars containing 99 per cent. of pure metal are generally considered as fine bars.

UNPARTED BULLION.—Gold containing silver or silver containing gold which has not been subjected to the parting operation.

AMALGAM.—Gold and silver extracted from ores or other substances by the use of mercury and left in a porous or spongy condition, when the mercury is removed by distillation.

FINENESS.—A term indicating the proportion of pure metal contained in a piece of gold or silver. Fineness is expressed in thousandths; that is, pure metal is 1000. United States coin is $\frac{900}{1000}$ fine, or decimally .900 fine. Fineness is estimated by jewelers and workers in the precious metals by "carats," pure metal being 24 carats. Thus 22 carats, the British standard for gold coins, is $\frac{22}{24}$, or decimally, 916⅔ fine.

DEPOSIT—MELTING.—The operation of melting a deposit of gold or silver at the Mint to secure a homogeneity of metals, preliminary to taking a sample for assaying.

REMEDY OF THE MINT.—The legal variation allowed from the fineness and weight prescribed by law for the coins.

TRIAL OF THE PYX.—The annual test made by special commissioners of the fineness and weight of coins reserved from each delivery of coin by the coiner to the superintendent. These coins are known as Pyx coins, because kept in a pyx or chest.

REFRACTORY BULLION.—Gold or silver bullion which contains a small percentage of lead, tin, or antimony, and which is therefore too hard or brittle to roll, cut, or stamp with facility.

WASTAGE.—The amount of gold and silver lost in the processes which these metals undergo preparatory to striking the coins. This "wastage" by law must not exceed a certain percentage of the gross amount of metals worked.

SWEEPINGS.—The ashes, fluxes, crucibles, sweepings, and all other refuse materials from rooms in which the metals are worked, containing a small amount of gold and silver.

STANDARD.—The weight and fineness fixed by law for the coins; hence the term "standard weight" or "standard fineness."

BASE BULLION.—Gold or silver bullion not fit for coinage purposes, by reason of the presence of base metals, until refined.

MINT MARK.—The letter or mark on the coin, designating the mint at which it was struck; as "S" for San Francisco, "C C" for Carson City, "O" for New Orleans.*

MONEY OF ACCOUNT.—The ideal unit, or money term, in which accounts are stated or transactions made, as the *pound sterling* of Great Britain, the *dollar* of the United States, the *franc* of France, and the *reichsmark* of the German Empire.

COINS OF STANDARD VALUE.—In modern times a government first establishes a money of account or ideal unit, and then fixes by law the quantity of gold or silver which shall, in the form of a coin with unlimited legal-tender power, represent that ideal unit. Such coins, with their multiples and divisions, are termed "coins of standard value" or "standard coins."

SUBSIDIARY COINS.—In the United States silver coins of less denomination than the dollar, which have a nominal value exceeding their intrinsic or bullion value, and limited as legal tender to sums not exceeding five dollars.

MINOR COINS.—Coins of small denominations used for change, and struck from other metals than gold or silver.

MINT PRICES OF GOLD AND SILVER (COINING VALUE).—The rate per standard ounce at which the mint converts bullion into legal-tender coins. The coining rate of an ounce of standard gold bullion, *i. e.*, bullion $\frac{900}{1000}$ fine in the United States is $18.604 +. The coining rate of the silver dollar of 412½ grains, discontinued by law April 1, 1873, was 1.16\frac{1}{4}$ per standard ounce.

THE BASIS OF THE MONEY SYSTEM of all civilized nations is gold or silver, or both, in a ratio fixed by law. The relative valuation of the two metals in the coins of nations using the double standard, is about one of gold to *fifteen and a half of silver*.

Partial List of Medals in Copper-Bronzed, also, in Gold and Silver, which may be obtained at the Mint.

ARMY.	Size.	Price.
Washington before Boston	42	$2 50
Colonel William Washington, for Cowpens	28	1 50
Major-General Harrison, for the Thames	40	1 50
Major-General Scott, for Chippewa and Niagara	40	1 50
Major-General Gaines, for Fort Erie	40	1 50
Major-General Porter, for Chippewa, Niagara, and Erie	40	1 50
Major-General Macomb, Battle of Plattsburgh	40	1 50
Major-General Jackson, Battle of New Orleans	40	1 50
Major-General Taylor, Palo Alto	40	1 50

* The coins struck at the parent mint in Philadelphia bear no mint mark.

Major-General Taylor, for Monterey	40	$1 50
Major-General Taylor, for Buena Vista	56	3 00
Major-General Scott, for Battles in Mexico	56	3 00
Major-General Grant	64	8 00
Colonel Lee, "Light-Horse Harry"	29	1 50
Count DeFleury, for Stony Point	15	2 25

NAVY.

John Paul Jones, for Serapis	36	2 00
Captain Hull, for Capture of Guerriere	40	1 50
Captain Jacob Jones, for Capture of the Frolic	40	1 50
Captain Decatur, for Capture of the Macedonian	40	1 50
Captain Bainbridge, for Capture of the Java	40	1 50
Captain Lawrence, for Capture of the Peacock	40	1 50
Captain Burrows, for Capture of the Boxer	40	1 50
Captain Perry, for Capture of British Fleet on Lake Erie	40	1 50
Captain Elliott, for Capture of British Fleet on Lake Erie	40	1 50
Captain Warrington, for Capture of the Epervier	40	1 50
Captain Blakely, for Capture of the Reindeer	40	1 50
Captain MacDonough, for Capture of the British Fleet on Lake Champlain	40	1 50
Captain Henley, Capture of British Fleet on Lake Champlain	40	1 50
Lieut. Cassin, Capture of British Fleet on Lake Champlain	40	1 50
Captain Biddle, for Capture of the Penguin	40	1 50
Captain Stewart, for Capture of the Cyane and Levant	40	1 50
Captain Edw. Preble before Tripoli	40	1 50

PRESIDENTIAL.

John Adams	32	1 50
Thomas Jefferson	47	2 50
James Madison	40	1 50
James Monroe	40	1 50
John Q. Adams	40	1 50
Andrew Jackson	40	1 50
Martin Van Buren	40	1 50
John Tyler	40	1 50
James K. Polk	40	1 50
Zachary Taylor	40	1 50
Millard Fillmore	40	1 50
Franklin Pierce	40	1 50
James Buchanan	48	2 00
Abraham Lincoln	48	2 00
Andrew Johnson	48	2 00
Ulysses S. Grant	48	2 00
Rutherford B. Hayes	48	2 00
James A. Garfield	48	2 00
Chester A. Arthur	48	2 00

SUB-NATIONAL MEDALS.

Captain Perry (State of Pennsylvania), for Capture of the British Fleet on Lake Erie	40	1 50
Pennsylvania Volunteers, Action on Lake Erie	40	1 50
Major-General Scott (Commonwealth of Virginia)	56	3 00

MISCELLANEOUS AMERICAN.

Professor Agassiz Medal	30	1 50
Colonel Armstrong, for Destruction of the Indian Village of Kittanning	27	1 00
Captains Creighton, Low, and Stouffer, Wreck of Steamer San Francisco	47	2 00

Captains Creighton, Low, and Stouffer, Wreck of Steamer
    San Francisco, by Congress.. 50 $3 00
Cornelius Vanderbilt, by Congress........ 48   2 50
First Steam Coinage................... 16   25
Commodore M. C. Perry, from Merchants of Boston.......... 40   2 00
Pacific Railroad Medal... 29   1 25
Emancipation Proclamation Medal................................. 29   1 00
Cyrus W. Field, Atlantic Cable Medal............................. 64   8 00
Dr. Joseph Pancoast.. 48   3 00
Grant Indian Peace Medal... 40   3 00
Garfield Indian Peace Medal...........................(oblong)   2 00
Arthur Indian Peace Medal............................ "   2 00
"Let Us Have Peace".. 29   1 25
Metis (Shipwreck) Medal.. 42   1 50
John Horn (Life Saving) Medal...................................... 30   1 00
U. S. Diplomatic Medal, July 4, 1776............................ 45   2 00
Valley Forge Centennial.. 25   50
Great Seal Medal.. 39   1 50

DIRECTORS OF THE MINT.

David Rittenhouse.. 28   1 25
Robert M. Patterson........... 42   1 50
James Ross Snowden... 50   2 50
James Pollock.. 29   1 25
H. R. Linderman.. 50   2 00
James P. Kimball..

SUPERINTENDENTS.

A. Loudon Snowden... 50   2 00
Daniel M. Fox..

FINE GOLD MEDALS.
(See Rule 3.)

Time Increases His Fame.. 16   12 00
James A. Garfield.. 16   9 00
Commencement of Cabinet.. 12   6 25
Washington and Jackson... 10   4 50
Lincoln and Garfield... 10   4 50

FINE SILVER MEDALS.
(See Rule 3.)

Cabinet Medal.. 37   6 00
Presidency Relinquished.. 25   3 00
Allegiance Medal... 18   1 00
Time Increases His Fame....." 16   75
James A. Garfield.. 16   60
Pennsylvania Bi-Centennial... 16   50
Commencement of Cabinet.. 12   35
Washington and Jackson... 10   25
Washington and Lincoln... 10   25
Washington and Grant... 10   25
Washington Wreath.. 10   25
Lincoln and Grant.. 10   25
Lincoln Broken Column.. 10   25
Lincoln and Garfield... 10   25
Valley Forge Centennial.. 25   1 50

The diameter of the medals is expressed by numbers, each of which
indicates the sixteenth of an inch.

Medals struck to order in gold, silver, **or** bronze, from dies of public
institutions.

MEDALS AND CABINET COINS.

MINT OF THE UNITED STATES.

Philadelphia, January, **1888**.

Regulations.

1. The price of Medals, Proof Coins, Pattern Pieces, &c., shall be **fixed** by the Superintendent of the Mint, with the approval of the Director.

2. No Coin or Pattern Piece shall be struck after the year of its date, nor in any other metal or alloy than that in which the Coin was issued or intended to be issued, except experimental pieces in Copper or other soft metal to prove the dies, under the direction of the Superintendent The dies shall be defaced at the end of each year, and such impressions as the Engraver may find necessary to take while preparing the dies shall be destroyed in the presence of the Superintendent when the dies are finished.

3. When a Pattern Piece is adopted and used in the regular coinage in the same year it shall then be issued as a proof, at a price near its current value; or if it comes out early in the year, it will be placed in the regular **Proof Set.** The Superintendent will furnish, without charge, on application therefor, a Pattern Piece to any incorporated Numismatic Society in the United States. In such cases, if the pattern is in Gold or Silver, the value of the metal will be required.

4. The price of the regular Proof Set of Gold Coins will be Forty-three Dollars; the Proof Set of Silver and Minor Coins, Three Dollars. Single Gold Pieces, in proof, are sold at Twenty-five Cents each above their intrinsic value. Silver Sets are not separated. Proof sets are furnished of the current year only. The Mint has no Coins or Sets of back dates for sale.

5. The Coins of the United States are:—

GOLD.	SILVER.	COPPER-NICKEL.
Double-Eagle,	Dollar,	Five Cents.
Eagle,	Half-Dollar,	Three Cents.
Half-Eagle,	Quarter-Dollar,	
Three-Dollar,	Dime.	**BRONZE.**
Quarter-Eagle,		One Cent.
Dollar.		

The coinage of the Silver Dollar of 412½ grains, the Five and Three-Cent Silver Pieces and Bronze Two-Cent Pieces was discontinued in 1873, but the Silver Dollar was restored by the Act of February 28, 1878.

All orders must be sent to Superintendent of the Mint at Philadelphia.

DANIEL M. FOX,
Superintendent.

PORTRAIT OF WASHINGTON.

The frontispiece in the bound volume of this book, is an exact reproduction, by the Gutekunst phototype process, of the obverse of the Washington medal executed by Charles C. Wright, about the year 1850, and particularly described on page 34 of the "Medallic Portraits of Washington," by W. S. Baker, lately published (the price of which is five dollars). The bust was modeled by Wright, after the original by the celebrated French sculptor, Jean Antoine Houdon, executed from a cast taken from the face of Washington at Mount Vernon, in October, 1785, and is considered be good judges to be the best medallic portrait of Washington yet produced. An impression of the medal is in the Washington Cabinet of the Mint; the reverse presents an excellent copy of Trumbull's well known picture of the Declaration of Independence.

JANUARY 1888.

COIN (APPROXIMATE) PRICE CURRENT.

Prepared by Mason & Co., Coin Dealers, 175 Washington St., Boston. Mass.

GOLD COLONIAL COINS.

	FINE.	GOOD.
1785, Justice-eye, "Immune Columbia"	$600 00	$500 00
1787, Sun-eagle, "Nova Eboraca"	300 00	150 00

SILVER COLONIALS.

	FINE	GOOD
1652, N. E. XII, New-England shilling	$35 00	$25 00
1652, " VI, " sixpence	40 00	20 00
1652, " III, " threepence	100 00	40 00
1659, Pinetree XII, "Masathusets" shilling	45 00	30 00
1652, " " "Massachusets" "	10 00	5 00
1652, " Smaller and thicker "	8 00	3 00
1652, " XII, "Masatusets" variety shilling	25 00	15 00
1652, " VI, "Masachusets" sixpence	15 00	5 00
1652, " III, " threepence	15 00	5 00
1652, " II, " twopence	15 00	5 00
1652, Oaktree XII, " shilling	5 00	3 00
1652, " VI, " sixpence	6 00	4 00
1652, " III, " threepence	8 00	4 00
1662, " II, · " twopence	8 00	4 00
1662, " I, " penny	30 00	10 00
1659, head, shield, Lord Baltimore shilling	15 00	10 00
1659, " " " sixpence	20 00	10 00
1659, " " " fourpence	20 00	10 00
1760, Charles III. rose, Florida half dollar	30 00	20 00
1773, George III. shield, Virginia shilling	20 00	15 00
1783, U. S. 1000-eye, "Nova Constellatio"	200 00	100 00
1783, " 500-eye, "	150 00	75 00
1785, " Justice-eye, "Nova Constellatio" quarter dollar	75 00	40 00
1783, hands clasped, Annapolis shilling	15 00	5 00
1783, " " sixpence	15 00	8 00
1783, " " threepence	15 00	8 00
1790, head "Standish Barry" "	25 00	10 00
1796, female head, "Castorland" half dollar	2 00	1 50

TIN COLONIAL.

	FINE	GOOD
1690, horseman-shields, James II. tin piece	$3 00	$1 50
1776, Sun-dial, "Continental Currency"	15 00	5 00

COLONIAL COPPER COINS.

	FINE	GOOD
1616, hog-ship, "Summer Islands" shilling		$300 00
1616, " " " sixpence		400 00
1694, Elephant, "God preserve Carolina," half dollar	$40 00	20 00
" "God preserve New England"	150 00	50 00
" "God preserve London"	2 50	1 50
1721, 2 L's, "Col's Francoises," Louisiana	2 50	1 00
1722, 2 L's, " " "	2 50	1 00

	FINE.	GOOD.
1667, L's, "Col's Francoises," stamped R. F., Louisiana ha'penny...	$2 00	$1 00
1767, L's, "Col's Francoises," without R. F., Louisiana ha'penny...	4 00	1 50
1766, head ship, no stamps, Pitt halfpenny...	2 50	1 50
1773, George III. shield, Virginia halfpenny...	1 00	25
1773, " " smaller size, Virginia halfpenny,	75	25
U. S. A., 13 bars, Bar cent...	3 50	2 00
1722, George I. rose, "Rosa Americana" penny...	4 00	1 50
1722, " " " " halfpenny...	2 50	1 00
1722, " " " " farthing...	3 00	1 50
1722, " " " " farthing...	4 00	2 00
1723, " " not crowned, "Rosa Americana farthing...	15 00	5 00
George I. rose, "Rosa sine spina," halfpenny...	30 00	15 00
1723, George I. crowned rose, "Rosa Americana," penny,	4 00	2 00
1723, George I. crowned rose, "Rosa Americana," halfpenny...	2 50	1 50
1724, George I. crowned rose, "Rosa Americana," halfpenny...	15 00	10 00
1723, George I. crowned rose, "Rosa Americana," farthing,	2 50	1 50
1723, George I. crowned rose, "Rosa Americana," halfpenny...	5 00	3 00
1733, George II. crowned rose, "Rosa Americana" penny,	30 00	20 00
1737, Three hammers, "Connecticut" cent...	40 00	20 00
1737, "I am good copper," cent...	40 00	20 00
1739, " " " Granby cent...	40 00	20 00
1737, "Connecticut," Granby cent...	40 00	20 00
1737, Axe, "I cut my way through," Granby cent...	40 00	20 00
No date, axe, "I cut my way through," Granby cent...	40 00	20 00
1778, Head Indian, "Non dependens," cent...	25 00	15 00
1783, U. S. eye, "Nova Constellatio," cent...	1 00	40
1783, " " " "	1 00	40
1785, U. S. eye, "Nova Constellatio," cent...	1 00	30
1783, Liberty caged, "Georgius Triumpho," cent...	3 00	1 25
1787, Indian stars, "Inimica Tyrannis," cent...	40 00	20 00
1785, " " in circle, "Inimica Tyrannis," cent...	40 00	20 00
Scroll-triangle, Kentucky cent, plain edge...	3 50	2 00
" lettered edge, Kentucky cent...	3 50	2 00
1796, Britania-children, British settlements...	25 00	15 00
1787, Indian-eagle, Massachusetts cent...	1 00	40
1787, " " half-cent...	3 00	1 25
1788, " " cent...	1 00	50
1788, " " half-cent...	3 00	1 25
1787, Sun-dial links, "We are one," Franklin cent...	50	25

NEW YORK CENTS.

	FINE.	GOOD.
1786, Head, Justice, "Non vi virtute vici,"...	$75 00	$40 00
1787, Indian-eagle, "Neo Eboracus,"...	50 00	30 00
1787, " arms of New York, "Excelsior,"...	40 00	20 00
1787, George Clinton arms of New York, "Excelsior,"...	50 00	25 00
1786, Eagle, arms of New York, "Excelsior,"...	60 00	30 00
1787, " " " " ...	60 00	30 00
1787, Justice-eagle, "Immunis Columbia,"...	8 00	4 00
1787, Head, Liberty to right, "Nova Eborac,"...	2 00	50
1787, Head, Liberty to left, "Nova Eborac,"...	2 00	75

Vermont Cents.

	FINE.	GOOD.
1785, Head Justice, "Immune Columbia"	$15 00	$10 00
1785, Justice-eye, "Immune Columbia"	25 00	15 00
1785, Sun-eye, "Vermontis Respublica"	3 00	1 00
1785, " "Vermontes-Res-Publica"	5 00	2 00
1786, " "Vermontensium Respublica"	2 50	1 00
1786, Head, Britannia "Vermon Auctori"	60	30
1787, " " " "	50	25
1788, " " " "	75	30
1786, Baby head, Britannia "Vermon Auctori"	1 50	50
1787, Head, Britannia "Vermon," "Et lib Inde"	1 00	50
1787, " " " "Britannia,"	1 00	40
1787, " " George III., "rex Inde et lib"	2 00	1 00

New Jersey Cents.

	FINE.	GOOD.
1786, Horse head, shield, "Nova Cæsarea"	$1 00	$0 30
1786, Horse head, shield (date under beam), "Nova Cæsarea"	100 00	75 00
1787, Horse head, shield, large size, "Nova Cæsarea"	60	25
1787, " " " smaller, "Nova Cæsarea"	30	10
1787, " " " "E pluribs," "Nova Cæsarea"	2 00	1 00
1788, " " " "Nova Cæsarea"	50	20
1788, " " " "Fox type," "Nova Cæsarea"	1 50	40
1788, Horse head to left, shield, "Nova Cæsarea"	4 00	1 00
1787, Justice-shield, "Immunis Columbia"	25 00	15 00

Connecticut Cents.

	FINE.	GOOD.
1787, Head to right, Britannia "Auctori Connec"	$0 25	$0 10
1785-6-8, Head to right, Britannia "Auctori Connec"	50	20
1785, (Negro head) Britannia "Auctori Connec"	1 00	50
1785, (Laughing head) Britannia "Auctori Connec"	1 50	75
1785, Head to left, Britannia "Auctori Connec"	50	20
1786-7-8, Head to left, Britannia "Auctori Connec"	50	25
1786-7, " " " "Et lib Inde Connec"	1 00	50
1787-8, " " " "Auctori Connec"	1 00	1 30

There are many more minor types of the Connecticut and New Jersey 5 cents to 25 cents, etc.

Silver Dollars.

	FINE.	GOOD.		FINE.	GOOD.
1794, flowing hair	$125 50	$50 00	1836, name in field	$40 00	$23 00
1795, " "	3 00	1 50	1836, flying eagle	10 00	6 00
1795, fillet head	3 50	1 50	1838, " "	50.00	25 00
1796	4 00	2 00	1839, " "	30 00	20 00
1797, 6 stars facing	5 00	2 50	1840, Liberty seated	2 25	1 60
1797, 7 "	4 00	2 50	1841	2 00	1 60
1798, 13 " small eagle	6 00	4 00	1842	2 00	1 60
1798, 15 " " "	12 00	8 00	1843	2 25	1 60
1798, 13 " large eagle	2 50	2 00	1844	2 00	1 00
1799, 5 " facing	7 00	5 00	1845	2 50	1 00
1799, 6 " "	2 00	1 60	1846	2 00	1 00
1800, spread eagle	3 00	1 50	1847	1 75	1 00
1801	5 00	2 00	1848	3 00	1 25
1802	4 00	1 50	1849	1 75	1 00
1803	3 00	2 00	1850	2 00	1 10
1804	1000 00	500 00	1851	40 00	30 00

	FINE.	GOOD.		FINE.	GOOD.
1852	$50 00	$30 00	1867	$1 80	$1 50
1853	2 00	1 50	1868	2 00	1 70
1854	8 00	6 00	1869	1 50	1 45
1855	6 00	4 00	1870	1 50	1 40
1856	2 50	1 75	1871	1 50	1 40
1857	4 00	2 00	1872	1 30	1 25
1858	40 00	30 00	1873	2 00	1 60
1859	1 50	1 40	1873, trade dollar	2 00	1 50
1860	1 80	1 50	1874, " "	1 75	1 40
1861	1 80	1 50	1875, " "	1 50	1 40
1862	1 80	1 50	1876, " "	1 20	1 15
1863	1 80	1 50	1877, " "	1 20	1 10
1864	1 80	1 50	1878, " "	1 20	1 15
1865	1 80	1 50	1879 to 1884, proof	2 00	1 75
1866	2 00	1 60			

HALF DOLLARS.

	FINE.	GOOD.		FINE.	GOOD.
1794, flowing hair	$8 00	$5 00	1807	$1 50	$1 25
1795, " "	2 50	1 50	1807, head to left	2 00	1 50
1796, 15 stars	75 00	50 00	1808	2 00	1 00
1796, 16 "	100 00	60 00	1809	1 00	75
1797, 15 "	75 00	40 00	1810	1 00	75
1801, fillet head	8 00	5 00	1811	1 25	75
1802	10 00	8 00	1812	1 00	75
1803	3 00	1 50	1813	1 00	75
1805	3 00	1 50	1814	1 00	75
1806	1 50	1 25	1815	8 00	5 00

Half dollars from 1817 to 1885, inclusive (excepting 1851 and 1852, worth from $2.50 to $5.00), from 75c. to $1.00.

QUARTER DOLLARS.

	FINE.	GOOD.		FINE.	GOOD.
1796, fillet head	$8 00	$4 00	1820	$1 00	$0 75
1804	7 00	3 00	1821	1 00	75
1805	3 00	1 50	1822	2 00	1 00
1806	2 00	1 00	1823	75 00	30 00
1807	2 50	1 25	1824	2 00	1 00
1815, head to left	2 00	50	1825	1 00	75
1818	1 00	75	1827	100 00	50
1819	1 50	1 00			

Quarter dollars, from 1827 to 1885, inclusive (excepting that of 1853, *without* arrow heads, worth from $6.00 to $10.00), worth 30c. to 50c.

TWENTY-CENT PIECES.

	FINE.	GOOD.		FINE.	GOOD.
1875, Liberty seated	$0 40	$0 30	1877, Liberty seated	$5 00	$4 00
1876, " "	60	50	1878, " "	5 00	4 00

DIMES.

	FINE.	GOOD.		FINE.	GOOD.
1796, fillet head	$4 00	$2 00	1803	$4 00	$2 50
1797, 13 stars	6 00	3 00	1804	12 00	10 00
1797, 16 "	8 00	4 00	1805	1 50	75
1798, fillet head	6 00	3 00	1807	2 00	1 00
1800	8 00	5 00	1809, head to left	3 00	2 00
1801	6 00	4 50	1811	3 00	2 00
1802	10 00	6 00			

Dimes, from 1811 to 1885, inclusive (excepting that of 1846, worth $1 00 to $2.50), from 20c. to 35c.

HALF DIMES.

	FINE.	GOOD.		FINE.	GOOD.
1794, flowing hair...	$6 00	$4 00	1800, fillet head......	$2 00	$1 50
1795, " "	2 00	1 00	1801	5 00	3 00
1796, 15 stars........	6 00	4 00	1802	125 00	80 00
1797, 15 "	5 00	3 00	1803	5 00	3 00
1797, 16 "	4 00	2 00	1805	15 00	5 00

Half dimes, from **1805** to **1873**, inclusive (**excepting 1846**, worth from $1.00 to $2.50), from **10 to 30 cents.**

SILVER THREE-CENT PIECES.

From **1851** to **1872, inclusive, worth from 5 to 50** cents, according to condition.

1873.. $2 00 $1 50

NICKEL FIVE-CENT PIECES.

	PROOFS.	FINE.		PROOFS.	FINE.
1866	$0 15	$0 10	1873	$0 15	$0 10
1867, with rays........	2 50	50	1874	15	10
1867, without rays.....	15	10	1875	20	15
1868	15	10	1876	15	10
1869	15	10	1877	2 00	1 00
1870	15	10	1878	40	25
1871	15	10	1879	12	10
1872	15	10			

NICKEL THREE-CENT PIECES.

	PROOFS.	FINE.		PROOFS.	FINE.
1865	$0 15	$0 08	1873	$0 15	$0 08
1866	15	8	1874	15	8
1867	15	8	1875	20	15
1868	15	8	1876	10	8
1869	15	8	1877	2 00	1 00
1870	15	8	1878	25	20
1871	15	8	1879 to 1888, proofs...	25	5
1872	15	8			

TWO-CENT PIECES.

	PROOFS.	FINE.		PROOFS.	FINE.
1864	$0 40	$0 10	1869	$0 40	$0 08
1865	40	10	1870	40	8
1866	40	10	1871	25	15
1867	40	10	1872	50	40
1868	40	10	1873	1 25	75

COPPER CENTS.

	*FINE.	GOOD.		FINE.	GOOD.
1793, chain America	$20 00	$10 00	1795, **liberty, thin die,**	$1 50	$0 50
1793, " "	10 00	6 00	1796, " " "	2 00	75
1793, wreath..........	8 00	5 00	1796, fillet head.........	2 00	1 00
1793, lettered edge...	9 00	6 00	1797	1 50	40
1793, liberty cap......	25 00	8 00	1798	1 00	10
1794, " "	1 50	75	1799	35 00	15 00
1795, " **lettered**			1800	1 00	50
edge............	4 50	1 50	1801	1 00	50

	FINE.	GOOD.		FINE.	GOOD.
1802	$0 50	$0 25	1806	$1 25	$0 75
1803	50	20	1807	1 10	40
1804	10 50	6 00	1808, head to left	2 00	75
1805	1 50	50	1809	4 00	1 50

From 1810 to 1857, inclusive, worth from 2c. to $3, according to condition.

NICKEL AND BRONZE CENTS.

	FINE.	GOOD.		FINE.	GOOD.
1856, eagle nickel	$5 00	$3 50	1868	$0 05	$0 01
1857	50	1	1869	5	1
1858	50	1	1870	5	1
1859, Indian head	50	1	1871	5	1
1860	25	1	1872	5	1
1861	25	1	1873	5	1
1862	25	1	1874	5	1
1863	25	1	1875	5	1
1864	25	1	1876	5	1
1864, bronze	10	1	1877	50	5
1865	10	1	1878	5	1
1866	10	1	1879 to 1887	5	1
1867	10	1			

HALF CENTS.

	FINE.	GOOD.		FINE.	GOOD.
1793, liberty cap	$5 00	$2 50	1831 (proof)	$12 00	......
1794, " "	2 50	1 50	1832	20	$0 15
1795, " lettered			1833	20	10
edge	3 00	1 50	1834	20	10
1795, liberty, thin die	2 00	1 00	1835	20	10
1796, " cap	40 00	20 00	1836 (proof)	12 00	......
1797, " "	2 00	1 00	1840 "	8 00	......
1797, " lettered			1841 "	8 00	......
edge	5 00	3 00	1842 "	15 00	......
1800, fillet head	1 00	50	1843 "	10 00	......
1802	5 00	3 00	1844 "	10 00	......
1803	50	25	1845 "	10 00	......
1804	25	10	1846 "	10 00	......
1805	50	25	1847 "	10 00	......
1806	50	25	1848 "	8 00	......
1807	50	25	1849 " small date	8 00	......
1808	50	25	1849, large date	40	25
1809, head to left	25	15	1850	30	20
1810	2 50	1 00	1851	25	10
1811	3 00	1 50	1852 (proof)	10 00	......
1825	40	20	1853	15	10
1826	25	15	1854	25	15
1828, 12 stars	40	20	1855	25	15
1828, 13 "	20	10	1856	20	15
1829	30	20	1857	30	25

GOLD DOUBLE EAGLES.

	FINE.	GOOD.		FINE.	GOOD.
1849	$1000 00	......	1853	$21 00	$20 00
1850, head to left	25 00	$20 00	1854	21 00	20 00
1851	25 00	20 00	1855-79, consecutive	21 00	20 00
1852	25 00	20 00			

GOLD EAGLES.

	FINE.	GOOD.		FINE.	GOOD.
1795, head to left	$15 00	$13 00	1801	$14 00	$13 00
1796, 16 stars	20 00	15 00	1803	15 00	13 00
1797, 16 spread eagle	15 00	13 00	1804	15 00	13 00
1798, 13 stars	16 00	14 00	1838, head to left	15 00	13 00
1799, 13 spread eagle	14 00	12 00	1839	15 00	12 00
1800	14 00	13 00	1840-68, only proofs worth premium		

GOLD HALF EAGLES.

	FINE.	GOOD.		FINE.	GOOD
1795, head to right	$10 00	$8 00	1809	$8 00	$7 00
1796, 16 stars	15 00	10 00	1810	8 00	7 00
1797, 16 spread eagle	12 00	10 00	1811	8 00	7 00
1798, 13 stars, "	8 00	7 00	1812	8 00	7 00
1799, " "	10 00	8 00	1813	8 00	7 00
1800	10 00	8 00	1814	8 00	7 00
1801	30 00	20 00	1815	100 00	50 00
1802	10 00	8 00	1818	8 00	7 00
1803	8 00	7 00	1819	8 00	7 00
1804	8 00	7 00	1820	8 00	7 00
1805	8 00	7 00	1821	8 00	7 00
1806	8 00	7 00	1822	8 00	7 00
1807	8 00	7 00	1823-54, consecutive	6 00	5 75
1808, head to left	8 00	7 00	1855-79, only proofs worth premium.		

GOLD THREE DOLLARS.

	FINE.	GOOD.		FINE.	GOOD.
1854, head to left	$4 00	$3 75	1857-87, consecutive	$3 25	$3 00
1855	3 75	3 50	1875	40 00	25 00
1856	4 00	3 75			

· GOLD QUARTER EAGLES.

	FINE.	GOOD.		FINE.	GOOD.
1796, without stars	$8 00	$6 00	1821	$5 00	$4 00
1796, 16 stars	10 00	6 00	1824	5 00	4 00
1797, 16 "	7 00	5 00	1825	5 00	4 00
1798, 13 "	5 00	4 00	1826	8 00	6 00
1802	6 00	5 00	1827-49, consecutive	4 00	3 50
1804	5 00	4 00	1850	3 25	3 00
1805	5 00	4 00	1851	3 25	3 00
1806	5 00	4 00	1852	3 25	3 00
1807	5 00	4 00	1853-87, consecutive	3 00	2 50
1808, head to left	5 00	4 00			

. GOLD DOLLARS

	FINE.	GOOD.		FINE.	GOOD
1848, head to left	$1 50	$1 30	1852	$1 40	$1 25
1850	1 50	1 30	1853-87, consecutive	1 40	1 25
1851	1 40	1 25			

CALIFORNIA GOLD.

$50 1851, octagon and round	$65 00	Half doll., octagon, diff. dates	$0 55
$20 (Territorial), varieties	30 00	" " circular "	55
Eagle, " "	15 00	Quar. " " "	35
Half eagle, " "	10 00	" " octagon,	35
Quarter " " "	5 00	Bechtler dollar (N. Carolina)	1 50
Dollar (California), octagon	1 25	Bechtler ¼ eagle "	3 50
Dollar (California), circular	1 25		

NOTE.—Persons who wish to buy or sell rare coins, or to ascertain their present value are recommended to write to Mason & Co., coin dealers, 175 Washington street, Boston, Mass.—EDITOR MINT BOOK.

PHILADELPHIA MINT.

As there are many places of interest in "Penn's Favorite City," the publisher of this work would respectfully suggest that visitors, who have the leisure, should see some of the well-known institutions of "The City of Brotherly Love." Among the rare places of interest, after the United States Mint, is 1st.—THE NEW PUBLIC BUILDINGS (in same square), known as the NEW CITY HALL, the Largest and Finest in the World, surpassing even the Capitol at Washington. 2d.—FAIRMOUNT PARK, the largest and most beautiful public pleasure ground in the United States, embracing nearly three thousand acres, on both sides of the Schuylkill River, from Fairmount Water Works to Indian Rock, on the romantic Wissahickon. 3d.—GIRARD COLLEGE, where eleven hundred and fifty Orphan Boys are maintained, clothed and educated through the bountiful munificence of Philadelphia's great benefactor, STEPHEN GIRARD. 4th.—WANAMAKER'S GREAT STORE, East of and almost adjoining the Mint. This immense establishment (the largest of the kind in the World) has grown to such vast proportions during the past decade that we feel compelled to give it a brief notice, as it has become one of the features of our city, and an object of interest to our visitors. The building itself is unique; it occupies an entire square, viz:—from Thirteenth to Juniper and from Market to Chestnut Streets—entrance on each of the four streets. The flooring space occupied in the interior, including first floor, basement and galleries, embraces more than twelve acres, and all this immense space is occupied with such goods as everybody, at some time in life, feels the necessity of purchasing. The general arrangement and classification of goods from all nations (there being over fifty separate and distinct departments), suggests a reproduction of the Main Building of our late great Centennial Exposition, with the Department of Public Comfort added. One of the great features of this Mammoth Bazaar is that visitors are made to feel at home, every provision being made for their convenience. There are commodious Retiring and Reading Rooms on either floor. One's Satchel and Parcels are checked without cost, and no one is importuned to purchase. Visitors will find it hard to resist the Tempting Offers and Low Prices marked on the goods. 5th.—INDEPENDENCE HALL, (The Nation's Birth-place) Chestnut Street between Fifth and Sixth Streets; National Museum, in same building, containing many interesting relics of the Revolution and of Washington's Camp Life; The Old Liberty Bell hanging in the hallway leading to Independence Square, where the Declaration of Independence was read to the people, July 4th, 1776. 6th.—ACADEMY OF FINE ARTS, Broad Street (west side) between Arch and Race Streets, should be visited by all lovers of the Fine Arts. 7th.—The NEW MASONIC TEMPLE, Northeast corner Broad and Filbert Streets. Visiting days every Thursday. 8th.—The NEW POST OFFICE and U. S. COURT BUILDING. This is one of the finest buildings of the kind in the country, and well worthy of a visit; also, the NEW "RECORD" BUILDING, adjoining. 9th.—The BURIAL PLACES OF BENJAMIN and DEBORA FRANKLIN can be seen at South-east corner Fifth and Arch Streets. 10th.—There are other notable places of interest in the City of "Brotherly Love," among which may be mentioned CARPENTERS' HALL, UNION LEAGUE, DEAF AND DUMB AND BLIND ASYLUMS, LAUREL HILL CEMETERY, PENNSYLVANIA AND WILL'S HOSPITALS, and the hundred and one other benevolent institutions for which Philadelphia is justly celebrated.

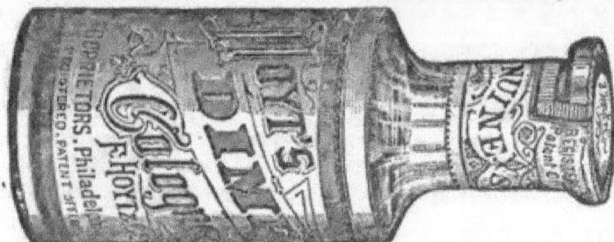

www.ingramcontent.com/pod-product-compliance
Lightning Source LLC
Chambersburg PA
CBHW030313270326
41926CB00010B/1351